GERMANY AT THE POLLS

The Bundestag Election of 1976

Edited by Karl H. Cerny

American Enterprise Institute for Public Policy Research
Washington, D.C.

Library of Congress Cataloging in Publication Data

Main entry under title:
Germany at the polls.

  (AEI studies ; 208)
  Includes index.
  1.   Germany (Federal Republic, 1949-   )
Bundestag—Elections—Addresses, essays, lectures.
2.   Elections—Germany, West—Addresses, essays,
lectures.   I.   Cerny, Karl H.   II.   Series:
American Enterprise Institute for Public Policy
Research.   AEI studies ; 208.
JN3971.A95G48   329'.023'43087   78-15362
ISBN 0-8447-3310-5

AEI Studies 208

Printed in the United States of America

CONTENTS

PREFACE

Karl H. Cerny

Germany at the Polls: The Bundestag Election of 1976 is another in the series of studies of national elections in selected democratic countries sponsored and published by the American Enterprise Institute for Public Policy Research. The first volumes covered important elections held in 1974: the two parliamentary elections in Britain, the Canadian general election, the French presidential election, and the House of Councillors election in Japan. In addition, a volume appeared that discussed the parliamentary elections in Denmark, Norway, and Sweden in 1973, 1975, and 1976. Other important elections in 1975 covered in At the Polls books include the national elections in Australia and the referendum on British entry into the Common Market. For 1976, the series includes not only the present volume but also a study of the Italian parliamentary elections; for 1977, studies of the Indian, Irish, Israeli, Greek, Australian, and Spanish elections; and for 1978, studies of the French parliamentary election and the Colombian presidential election.

The selection of topics for the seven German and three U.S. contributors to the present volume was guided to a large extent by the format of earlier AEI election studies. Gerhard Loewenberg analyzes the development of the German party system in the post–World War II period and calls attention to the important changes that have occurred since the time of the Weimar Republic. David Conradt describes the institutional framework of the German electoral system, sketches the major outlines of the 1976 election campaign, and examines the outcome for the parties and for the West German political system. There follow four chapters on the major German parties: Kurt Sontheimer and Heino Kaack deal with the Social Democratic party (SPD) and its ally, the Free Democratic party (FDP); Werner Kaltefleiter and

Paul Noack with the Christian Democratic Union (CDU) and its Bavarian branch, the Christian Social Union (CSU). The volume concludes with three somewhat more specialized contributions: Klaus Schönbach and Rudolf Wildenmann test the impact of the four nationwide "prestige" newspapers of the German Federal Republic on public opinion formation during the election campaign; Max Kaase traces the development of public opinion polling in West Germany in the post–World War II period and analyzes survey findings important for the 1976 campaign; and in an appendix Richard Scammon presents useful detailed statistics on recent German parliamentary elections.

The national election of October 3, 1976, was the eighth since the establishment of the Federal Republic of Germany in 1949. The eligible electorate totaled 41.6 million voters. They were being asked to choose 496 members from among 3,244 candidates for the Bundestag, the major legislative organ of the German Parliament. (Berlin, because of its special occupation status, sends 22 additional nonvoting members to the Bundestag.) As in other parliamentary systems, the outcome of a Bundestag election helps determine the choice of the German chancellor and his cabinet. Although there is a second chamber of the German Parliament, the Bundesrat, it is not directly elected by the German voters but rather is composed of cabinet members (or their delegates) of the ten state governments. (Once again, Berlin sends nonvoting members as a city-state.) The partisan make-up of the Bundesrat does not affect the composition of the German cabinet. Because of its absolute as well as suspensive veto power, however, the Bundesrat can affect the outcome of the legislative process.

The immediate background to the 1976 Bundestag election campaign was dominated by two features. For one thing, the election was perceived to be a real contest. Neither side had an overwhelming advantage. If anything, the opposition parties, the CDU/CSU, appeared to have an edge over the government parties, the SPD and FDP, because of their success in a series of recent state elections. Specifically, in the state assembly elections held between 1974 and 1976, the CDU/CSU had received a composite 51.4 percent of the votes. Granted that state elections are no certain guide for national elections, the fact remains that the CDU/CSU demonstrated—and public opinion polls confirmed— that they had as great a potential for winning an absolute majority of the votes as the SPD-FDP, which had received 54.2 percent in the 1972 national election.

The second marked feature of the immediate background to the 1976 campaign was the disunity within and among the two sets of coalition partners. In the case of the government coalition parties, the

SPD was torn by an internal ideological dispute that is described in Sontheimer's chapter. Moreover, in 1974 a spy scandal triggered a change in the top leadership of the party when Willy Brandt resigned and Helmut Schmidt took over the chancellorship. The FDP, the SPD's coalition partner, had its own internal problems. The weakest of the four important parties in West Germany, the FDP is caught between the SPD on the one hand and the CDU/CSU on the other. Now the coalition partner of the SPD, but once the partner of the CDU/CSU, the FDP struggles to maintain a sense of identity among its electorate, very few of whom consider themselves stable party adherents. The search for identity leads to divided counsels within the party leadership; some stress the need to come out in open support of continued coalition with the SPD, while others urge the need to remain available for possible coalition with the CDU/CSU. Hans-Dietrich Genscher, the new leader of the FDP after Walter Scheel resigned in 1974 to become president of the Federal Republic, had to mediate between these conflicting points of view at the very time that public opinion polls indicated the overwhelming preference of FDP supporters for continuing the coalition with the SPD.

Disunity within the opposition camp was above all highlighted by the quarrel between the CDU and CSU, more specifically between Helmut Kohl, the new and more liberal leader of the CDU, and Franz Josef Strauss, the long-time conservative leader of the CSU. As Kaltefleiter and Noack make quite clear, Strauss refused to accept the 1973 decision of the CDU to replace Rainer Barzel with Kohl and to present him as the joint CDU/CSU candidate for chancellor. The result was a never-ending series of maneuvers inspired by Strauss both to postpone CDU/CSU cooperation and to foment opposition to Kohl's leadership within the ranks of the CDU. The maneuvers persisted right into the first half of 1976. Kaltefleiter argues that they prevented the CDU/CSU from fielding an attractively new leadership team to counter the new Schmidt-Genscher team representing the government coalition parties.

To a U.S. observer, the spectacle of party disunity may hardly seem to warrant the emphasis given to it in the German context. It should be remembered, however, that political parties in Germany are expected to be, and in practice really are, far more cohesive organizations both electorally and legislatively than they are in the United States. Disunity can immediately threaten the tenure of a chancellor and make a shambles of his legislative program. Given German expectations, party disunity can also have a seriously adverse impact on voter preferences—especially when traditional voter allegiances are beginning, as Loewenberg and Conradt note, to dissolve. In 1976, when the coalition parties of both the government and the opposition were seriously divided, neither side could gain a commanding advantage from its opponent's internal difficulties. Here was still another reason why the 1976 campaign could shape up to be a genuine contest.

As far as the campaign itself is concerned, the authors of this volume raise a number of points that deserve special mention. To begin with, all of them agree that the campaign was devoid of major issues. Compared with the campaign of 1972, which was dominated by the sharp confrontation between the SPD-FDP and CDU/CSU over *Ostpolitik* policy, the 1976 campaign was a rather dull affair. The marathon television debate between the leaders of the four parties came at the end of the campaign and apparently had little impact on the election outcome. In any case it focused attention on the personalities of the leaders, where the major interest of the campaign had been all along. And at this level of competition, Helmut Schmidt, the incumbent chancellor, had a clear edge. The CDU/CSU, meanwhile, had the better campaign organization and mobilized its supporters earlier.

As Kaltefleiter notes, one of the reasons that the campaign avoided substantive issues was that it got sidetracked by the controversial slogan of the CDU/CSU: originally, "Freedom or Socialism," then "freedom instead of socialism." Championed in its original form by Strauss and reluctantly accepted in its modified form by Kohl, the slogan had a mixed impact on the election outcome. All the authors of this volume agree that the slogan was thoroughly misleading, insofar as it suggested that the entire SPD was opposed to freedom. The authors do not entirely agree, however, about the impact of the slogan on the final outcome of the election. Sontheimer thinks that the slogan was much more effective than the SPD's initial slogan, "Model Germany." Noack attempts to show how the slogan helped the CSU exploit the political mood of the Bavarian electorate. Kaase, while granting that the emotions of party leaders were "aroused" by the slogan, questions whether it influenced the net strength of the political parties. On the other hand, Conradt and Kaltefleiter point to the problems that the slogan caused for the CDU especially in the northern and western industrialized sections of Germany where the contrast between the "hard" tone of the slogan and the "soft" folksy tone of Kohl as party leader proved to be counterproductive.

On balance, it would seem that while the slogan may have helped to mobilize CDU/CSU supporters in the south of Germany, it helped even more to mobilize SPD activists to bring out the traditional socialist vote in central and northern Germany at the expense of possible electoral gains for the CDU. A key test area may well have been the Ruhr, a traditional SPD stronghold, where Kurt Biedenkopf, then general secretary of the CDU, mounted a determined electoral challenge. The results, despite the first CDU gains since 1957, proved disappointing; the Ruhr remained an SPD stronghold. In the end, it was not only the CDU that was adversely affected by the slogan; the FDP was too. Insofar as the slogan helped polarize the election campaign between the SPD and the CDU/CSU, the FDP lost its appeal as an alternative to voters who decided they had best rally behind one or the other of the main contestants.

The authors' treatment of the role of the media in the election campaign raises some interesting questions. As Conradt points out in his chapter, the CDU in part organized its 1976 campaign on the thesis advanced by Elisabeth Noelle-Neumann, a leading German pollster, that media coverage of party campaigning can help create a misleading "climate of opinion" capable of influencing voters who are only marginally interested in politics to support the party that appears to be in the lead. In 1972, for example, early media visibility for SPD-FDP campaign activities fostered the impression that the government coalition parties were ahead. Supporters of the CDU/CSU opposition, caught in a "spiral of silence," held back from expressing their full support. Under these circumstances undecided voters tended to support the apparently winning side and helped swell the winning margin of the government coalition parties well beyond what had actually been the case during the campaign. In this fashion, Noelle-Neumann sought to explain the unexpectedly large victory of the SPD-FDP coalition in the 1972 election.

Campaign managers for the CDU took the cue in 1976 and sought to make the party more "visible" in the media by such means as membership drives and early nationwide advertising. By all accounts the CDU was successful; it got off to a good start and had public momentum going for it. Yet, as the campaign moved through September, the public no longer anticipated a CDU/CSU victory. Had the media once again helped create a misleading climate of opinion? Schönbach and Wildenmann face this question head on and come to the conclusion, based on their content analysis of the four national quality newspapers, that in 1976 the media reflected the interests and issue orientations of the electorate more consistently than did the political parties. Far from manipulating public opinion, the media faithfully articulated the public mood.

The Schönbach-Wildenmann chapter will probably add fuel to the controversy over the role of the media in German public affairs.

In this connection, attention should be called to one of the conclusions of the Kaase chapter. As his analysis demonstrates, the media have come to play the major role in presenting the findings of public opinion polling to the wider German public. In doing so, they assure diversity of information and supervision and control over the manipulation of polling data by self-interested politicians. The temptation is great, therefore, to view the media as the most appropriate institutions for the performance of these vital political functions. Yet Kaase warns against confusing political control by the media with control by parliaments and political parties. The media can never be an adequate substitute for these properly functioning democratic political institutions. If the media have come to play such an important role in German public affairs, this is in part the consequence of badly functioning parties and parliaments.

For a U.S. audience, the financing of the 1976 German campaign points up some interesting lessons. The brief references of several authors in this volume to the sums of money that were involved in the campaign make it quite clear that in Germany precise information about campaign financing is just as difficult to obtain as it is in most other functioning democracies. In Germany parties are partially reimbursed for their campaign costs out of the public treasury. Yet it is interesting to note that public financing is not combined with legal limits on the campaign expenditures of the parties. The result is that, as far as the major parties are concerned, there were ample funds and they were freely spent. The spd could supplement its public funds with membership dues and the cdu/csu could rely on contributions, especially from industry. It was the weakest of the main parties, the fdp, that struggled with a shortage of funds. The reduced size of its electorate gave it a restricted claim on the public treasury and limited access to donations. Not surprisingly, as Kaack notes in his chapter, plans to reorganize and revitalize the fdp soon ran up against very definite financial constraints. Yet ironically, fringe parties received encouragement from public financing. Under German law in 1976, any party that received more than 0.5 percent of the popular vote received 3.5 marks per voter. The result was that although only four parties (the spd, the fdp, the cdu, and the csu) won seats in the Bundestag, sixteen parties actually entered the campaign and helped swell the number of candidates over the three thousand mark.

With respect to the outcome of the 1976 parliamentary election, these chapters illustrate how different time perspectives lead to different emphases in conclusions. Thus, if the outcome of the 1976 election is compared with the immediate past—the election outcomes of

1969 and 1972—then the title of Kaltefleiter's chapter on the CDU ("Winning without Victory") captures the key conclusion. The SPD and FDP had been able to form a winning coalition in 1969 by a narrow margin. In 1972 they had expanded that margin, the SPD actually becoming the largest party in terms of votes and seats for the first time since the establishment of the Federal Republic. In 1976, however, the tide was reversed. Although the SPD-FDP coalition "won," it did so by a margin of only 1.9 percentage points and ten parliamentary seats. In the process the SPD lost its position as leading party to the CDU/CSU. In fact, with 48.6 percent of the popular vote, the CDU/CSU made a better showing than it had in any election except 1957, when it received 50.2 percent of the popular vote, the first and only time any German party has secured an absolute majority of the vote since World War II. According to Strauss, the CSU leader, the CDU/CSU should have won an absolute majority in 1976. The near victory of the CDU/CSU and Strauss's dissatisfaction with Kohl's leadership help explain the disruptive tactics of the CSU since the election.

As Conradt attempts to demonstrate, the CDU/CSU owed its 1976 comeback chiefly to its ability on the one hand to mobilize its traditional Catholic and rural electoral support and on the other to recapture a part of the white-collar and civil-servant vote it had lost in the 1969 and 1972 elections. These social groups have had the least stable attachments to political parties in the postwar period. And in 1976, despite its comeback, the CDU/CSU still had only a minority position among them. In Kaltefleiter's words, the CDU needs a "northern" strategy. With due allowance for certain exceptions, the regional distribution of the vote in the 1976 election is striking. Roughly speaking, the CDU did least well in the northern part of the country, moderately well in the center, and best of all in the south. In this respect, it is interesting to note that the northern part of the country has fewer Catholics, traditional CDU supporters, and relatively fewer trade unionists, who traditionally support the SPD. In short, it is electorally the most unstable area of the country, containing the lowest number of committed party voters—and thus the area that can hold the key to electoral success. The SPD's better showing in the north, when added to its traditional trade union support, provided the necessary margin for a narrow victory.

The discussion of the 1976 election outcome has centered thus far on comparisons with the immediately preceding elections. If the base for comparison, however, is the entire post–World War II period, some rather different conclusions are emphasized by the authors of this volume. In this wider perspective, the key theme is the increasing competitiveness of the German party system. Until 1969, the dominant political force in the Federal Republic was the cdu/csu. In the 1950s and 1960s commentators spoke of the "one-and-a-half" party system, in which the cdu/csu played the dominant role (usually in coalition with the fdp) and the spd played a decidedly subordinate role. The 1969 election marked a watershed. By forming a coalition, the spd and the fdp forced the cdu/csu into the role of an opposition for the first time. The subsequent massive victory of the coalition in 1972 seemed to foreshadow a period of long-term spd electoral dominance. In fact, some commentators speculated whether the spd was launching an era of socialist dominance akin to the long era of Social Democratic dominance in the Scandinavian countries of Denmark, Norway, and Sweden.

The 1976 election outcome indicated that the spd was not to become the dominant German political party for the coming decade(s). The spd-fdp and cdu/csu coalitions were much more evenly balanced. The fact of spd-fdp victory—even if narrow—should not divert attention from the scope of the spd-fdp's decline in electoral support between 1972 and 1976. The proportional representation system of distributing seats in the Bundestag tends to play down the scope of shifts in voting behavior. However, one significant measure of the spd's decline in 1976 is its performance in the single-member-constituency elections, documented in the appendix prepared by Scammon. The spd's percentage share of the vote declined in every single one of the 248 single-member constituencies of the country. To pinpoint the conclusion in another way, in 1972 the spd won 152 single-member seats and the cdu/csu, 96. In 1976, the ratio was dramatically reversed: the cdu/csu won 135 seats; the spd, 108. The outcome for the fdp was equally disappointing. As in earlier elections, the party failed to win any single-member constituencies. Yet it was an open secret that fdp leaders had expected the party-list vote to reach "double figures"—10 percent or more. Their high hopes made the fdp's drop from 8.4 percent to 7.9 percent a bitter blow.

The increasing competitiveness of the German party system leads to a third and final perspective in terms of which the authors of this volume assess the outcome of the 1976 election. Unlike the fragmented multiparty system of the Weimar Republic, the party system of the Federal Republic has permitted one or another coalition to receive a majority of the seats in the Bundestag and thereby has assured that the government would have a reasonably stable base from which to formulate and implement policy. German voters could effectively decide whether Schmidt would remain chancellor or be replaced by Kohl.

The 1976 election was not the first to offer this power of decision to the German electorate. It did, however, reconfirm the power. And it did so under conditions of economic uncertainty and considerable unemployment. In Weimar days, the threat of extremist voting would have been very real. Yet in 1976, only 0.9 percent of the German electorate voted for extremist solutions. Equally important, 90.7 percent of the eligible electorate turned out to vote. When 91.1 percent did so in 1972, commentators attributed the high level of participation to excitement over the controversial *Ostpolitik* policy. But in 1976 there was no comparable policy issue, and still the overwhelming majority of the citizenry participated.

In short, the 1976 election demonstrated that West Germans are continuing the process of establishing a stable functioning democratic political order in the Federal Republic of Germany. In the light of Germany's history of political instability, not to mention the dictatorial model of the neighboring German Democratic Republic, the record of the 1976 election is most encouraging.

GERMANY
AT THE
POLLS

DENMARK

BALTIC SEA

NORTH SEA

Kiel ●
SCHLESWIG-HOLSTEIN

HAMBURG ●

● BREMEN

LOWER SAXONY

NETHERLANDS

Hanover ●

Berlin
(under special four-power status)

GERMAN

DEMOCRATIC

REPUBLIC

FEDERAL

NORTH RHINE-WESTPHALIA

Kassel ●

REPUBLIC

● Düsseldorf

OF

Cologne ●

BONN ✱

GERMANY

HESSE

BELGIUM

Frankfurt ●
Wiesbaden ●

Mainz ●

RHINELAND-PALATINATE

● Nuremberg

CZECHOSLOVAKIA

LUXEMBOURG

SAAR

● Saarbrücken

BAVARIA

● Karlsruhe

● Stuttgart

FRANCE

BADEN-WURTTEMBERG

● Munich

SWITZERLAND

AUSTRIA

POLAND

● State Capitals   ✱ Federal Capitals

0   50   100 miles

1

The Development of the German Party System

Gerhard Loewenberg

Introduction

The German voters chose between two alternative governments in the election of October 3, 1976. At its preelection conference in May, the Free Democratic party (FDP) had committed itself to continuing its coalition with the Social Democratic party (SPD) if the two groups jointly received a parliamentary majority.[1] The voters assumed that the Christian Democratic Union and the Christian Social Union would continue to work as a single parliamentary party (CDU/CSU) and that they would form the government if they received a parliamentary majority. Each of these alternative governments had designated its candidate for the chancellorship well before the election. The voters knew that an SPD-FDP coalition would continue to be led by the incumbent chancellor, Helmut Schmidt, and that a CDU/CSU government would be led by its nominee for the nation's highest office, Helmut Kohl.

British and American voters take such clear alternatives for granted. But until quite recently, German voters were only able to affect the relative strengths of the parties in Parliament. The large number of parties represented in that body made necessary a long and arcane bargaining process among the party leaders after each election to determine which parties would govern. That process sometimes had to be repeated during the parliamentary term if the existing coalition broke up. The voters were powerless spectators of this parliamentary game. Some of their measurable distrust of the parliamentary system was due to the failure of the party system to link the choice of government directly enough with the voters' choice.

All this had changed by the 1970s, as a result of one of the most

---

[1] *Frankfurter Allgemeine Zeitung*, June 1, 1976.

remarkable transformations in the history of modern political party systems. It was a transformation which contradicted the general conclusion reached by Seymour M. Lipset and Stein Rokkan that "the party systems of the 1960s reflect . . . the cleavage structures of the 1920s." Having examined the development of European party systems in the nineteenth and twentieth centuries, Lipset and Rokkan asserted that party systems established "during the final phase of suffrage extension" had an inertia which left them unaffected by subsequent changes in the socioeconomic substructure of politics or by changes in the political culture.[2]

From the perspective of the 1960s, when Lipset and Rokkan were writing, this appeared to have been the experience of much of the Western world. The party systems of Scandinavia, Western and Southern Europe, and the nations of the old British Commonwealth seemed to be frozen in their molds, apparently insensitive to social and economic changes in their environments. In the face of this general experience, it is unlikely that the undeniable socioeconomic and political-cultural changes that occurred in postwar Germany could have produced the transformation of the German party system by themselves. To explain that transformation, Lipset and Rokkan's theory of the origin of party systems suggests the need to identify changes in the German political structure similar in importance to the extension of the suffrage which originally shaped European party alignments. The profound alterations in the constitutional order which occurred in Germany between 1930 and 1933, and again between 1945 and 1949, would seem to constitute such structural changes. Specifically, the destruction of the prewar parties by the Hitler dictatorship and the impact of military government on the recreation of political parties and the rules of party competition after 1945 were changes of this kind. The argument I will advance is that these events created conditions that made the new German party system after the Second World War far more responsive to the changed socioeconomic setting of politics and to the changed political culture than an established party system would have been.

I will consider in turn the effects of the Nazi regime and the Allied military government on German political parties, the subsequent influence of the postwar social and economic structure, and the general orientations of the public toward politics in the postwar period. What needs explanation is the sharp reduction in the number of political parties competing for the voters' favor, the even

---

[2] Seymour M. Lipset and Stein Rokkan, *Party Systems and Voter Alignments: Cross National Perspectives* (New York: Free Press, 1967), pp. 50 and 51.

greater reduction in the number of political parties represented in Parliament, and the narrowing of party differences between the time of the Weimar Republic and the Federal Republic of Germany. These changes transformed a system with an extreme multiplicity of parties into one that provides voters with a two-coalition, if not a two-party, choice.[3] Nothing in the previous development of the German party system suggested that such a transformation would occur. To demonstrate that fact, let us briefly consider the continuities exhibited by the German party system during the first three decades of the twentieth century and compare that pattern with the party system that emerged after the war.

Continuity and Discontinuity in the German Party System

Until the election of 1930, the German party system had shown considerable continuity, even between the Imperial and the Weimar regimes. On the left a powerful Social Democratic party, the amalgamation of a Marxist and a workers' party, had been receiving between 30 and 35 percent of the vote since the turn of the century; after the First World War a Communist party competed with it for working-class votes, obtaining around one-third of the left-wing vote. Two types of parties divided the vote in the center of the political spectrum: a Catholic party, appealing across social class lines to the Catholic religious minority in the nation, and two competing liberal parties, appealing to the more or less conservative economic interests of the German middle classes. The Catholic Center party won between 15 and 20 percent of the vote in the first decade of the century, between 10 and 15 percent during the third decade. The combined vote of the liberal parties declined gradually, from over 20 percent in the first decade of the century to less than 15 percent in the late 1920s. The two types of center parties—Catholic and liberal—were therefore losing support while the right wing gained. Nationalistic and antidemocratic parties, which had gathered less than 15 percent of the vote at the start of the twentieth century, were

---

[3] Giovanni Sartori regards what he calls a system of "moderate pluralism" as fundamentally different from a system of "extreme pluralism." He writes: "The formula of moderate pluralism is not alternative government but governing in coalition within the perspective of alternative coalitions. . . . Aside from this major difference . . . the mechanics of moderate pluralism tends to resemble . . . the mechanics of two-partism." *Parties and Party Systems: A Framework for Analysis* (London: Cambridge University Press, 1976), p. 178. In the following pages I have drawn on material I first presented in "The Remaking of the German Party System; Political and Socio-economic Factors," *Polity*, vol. 1 (1968), pp. 86–113.

winning 25 percent in the 1920s, though their strength fluctuated somewhat in inverse relation to gains and losses on the left. Generally seven principal parties divided 85 to 90 percent of the vote among themselves: two left-wing parties, a Catholic party, two liberal parties, and two right-wing parties. An equal number of regional and special-interest parties—together receiving only 10 to 15 percent of the vote—added to the fragmentation of the party system (see Figure 1-1).

All of the parties were faithfully represented in Parliament. During the Empire, the electoral system provided for single-member constituencies with a second-ballot runoff, which favored parties that could bargain with each other between ballots. During the Weimar Republic, a pure system of proportional representation gave any party capable of winning as few as 30,000 votes nationally its proportionate share of parliamentary seats. Both systems preserved the extreme fragmentation of the German electorate.

This fragmentation appeared to reflect Germany's underlying socioeconomic structure, for it survived the period of rapid industrialization between the founding of the nation in 1871 and the outbreak of the First World War and continued through the Weimar Republic. The standard interpretation is that the party system represented a divided society in which preindustrial class privileges and subnational patriotisms persisted in the face of industrialization and national unification. Socioeconomic changes prior to 1933 generated new divisions in society, capable of sustaining new parties, without replacing the old ones, thereby preserving the conditions for an extreme party pluralism.

But the traditional German party system, which sixty years of socioeconomic changes had not substantially altered, was wiped out in the first months of 1933 by the Nazi dictatorship. Within half a year of coming to power, the government led by Hitler outlawed all party organizations except the Nazis. Some parties, including the Catholic Center party, disbanded before the final decree.[4] The Communists and the Social Democrats went into exile or underground, to reappear in 1945. But no other parties survived the Hitler regime, and even these two parties on the left suffered grievous losses through the persecution and murder of their leaders, the confiscation of their assets, and twelve years of official propaganda against their views.

The Allied military government eliminated the remaining party organization in 1945 with an edict prohibiting all political activities

---

[4] Erich Matthias and Rudolf Morsey, *Das Ende der Parteien 1933* [The end of the parties, 1933] (Düsseldorf: Droste Verlag, 1960), passim.

FIGURE 1-1
MAIN COMPONENTS OF THE GERMAN PARTY SYSTEM, 1903–1928

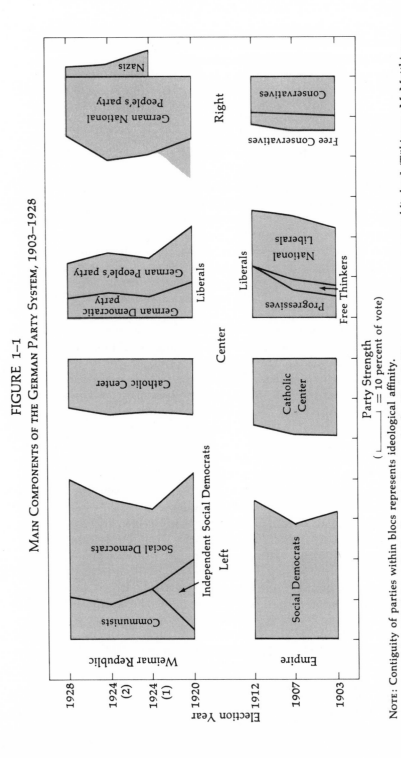

NOTE: Contiguity of parties within blocs represents ideological affinity.

SOURCE: Ernst Rudolf Huber, ed., *Quellen zum Staatsrecht der Neuzeit* [Sources on contemporary public law] (Tübingen: M. Matthiesen & Co., 1951), vol. 2, pp. 652–55.

including, of course, those of the Nazi party.[5] When the occupation regime began to license new political parties (only a few months after the prohibition was imposed), many observers anticipated a revival of the traditional German party system. But it soon became apparent that the Nazi regime and the war had destroyed not only most of the old party organizations, but their socioeconomic foundations as well. Furthermore, the manner in which the military government permitted the formation of political parties had the effect of changing some of the rules of party competition. The German party system that evolved under Allied auspices between 1945 and 1949 was therefore significantly different from what had gone before.

The difference becomes apparent from a comparison between the results of the last democratic election before the depression in 1928 and the first national election in the Federal Republic of Germany in 1949. The extreme left and the extreme right attracted far less support in 1949 than they had twenty-one years earlier, a single new liberal party obtained nearly the same support as its two predecessors had received, the Social Democratic party slightly improved its fortunes, and a new interdenominational Christian party received 45 percent more votes than had its Catholic antecedent (see Table 1-1).

Fourteen parties competed in 1949 as compared to forty-one parties in the earlier election. Above all, the three largest parties won over four-fifths of the seats in the first postwar German Parliament, while they had won fewer than three-fifths of the seats in 1928. The process of consolidation, which transformed a system of extreme party pluralism into a system of alternative coalition governments, was already visible, although a set of small political parties remained for the time being to obscure the general outline of change. With each succeeding election between 1949 and 1961, the number of parties winning seats in Parliament and the number of parties presenting candidates declined. Beginning with the election of 1961, only three parties were represented in Parliament: the Social Democratic party, direct descendant of the German Workingman's Association founded nearly a century earlier; the Free Democratic party, heir to the German liberal tradition; and the Christian Democratic Union allied with the Christian Social Union, interdenominational successors to the Catholic Center party. By the 1970s these three parties were obtaining over 99 percent of the votes of the German electorate, making all other parties trivial (see Table 1-2).

---

[5] Joint Chiefs of Staff Directive No. 1067 (April 1945), reprinted in Beate Ruhm von Oppen, *Documents on Germany under Occupation* (Oxford: Oxford University Press, 1955), p. 19.

TABLE 1-1

Results of the Parliamentary Elections of 1928 and 1949

(in percentages of valid votes)

Political Tendency and Party	Germany, 1928	West Germany, 1928[a]	West Germany, 1949
Extreme right			
National Socialist party (NSDAP)	2.6	3.3	
German Right party (DRP)			1.8
German National People's party (DNVP)	14.2	9.8	
Regional			
Economic Reconstruction (WAV)			2.9
German (Hannoverian) party (DP)	0.6	1.2	4.0
Bavarian (People's) party (BP)	3.1	5.6	4.2
Christian Social Union (CSU)			5.8
Christian center			
Center party (Z)	12.1	17.6	3.1
Christian Democratic Union (CDU)			25.2
Liberal middle class			
German People's party (DVP)	8.7	8.7	
German Democratic party (DDP)	4.9	4.7	
Free Democratic party (FDP)			11.9
Socialist			
Social Democratic party (SPD)	29.8	26.8	29.2
Extreme left			
Communist party (KPD)	10.6	8.6	5.7
Others	13.4	13.7	6.2

[a] For the sake of comparability, 1928 voting figures are presented in this column for the electoral districts that together make up roughly what became the Federal Republic of Germany, namely, Weimar districts 13 through 27 and 31 through 34.

SOURCE: Calculated from *Statistisches Jahrbuch für das Deutsche Reich 1928* [Statistical yearbook for Germany, 1928] (Berlin: Verlag von Reimar Hobbing, 1928), pp. 580–81; and from Bernhard Vogel et al., *Wahlen in Deutschland* [Elections in Germany] (Berlin: de Gruyter, 1971), p. 306.

TABLE 1-2

CONSOLIDATION IN THE GERMAN PARTY SYSTEM, 1928–1976

Indicator	1928	1949	1953	1957	1961	1965	1969	1972	1976
Number of parties presenting candidates	41	14	15	14	8	10	11	7	15
Number of parties gaining parliamentary seats	15	11	6	4	3	3	3	3	3
Percentage of votes won by three largest parties[a]	56.1	72.1	83.5	89.7	94.3	96.4	94.5	99.1	99.1
Percentage of seats won by three largest parties	58.7	80.1	91.0	96.6	100.0	100.0	100.0	100.0	100.0

[a] Except for 1949, when the figures refer to votes cast for individual candidates only, all other figures refer to votes cast for party lists. The CDU/CSU is counted as one party.

SOURCE: For the election of 1928, *Statistisches Jahrbuch, 1928*, pp. 580–81. For the elections of 1949–1957, Dolf Sternberger, et al., *Wahlen und Wähler in Westdeutschland* [Elections and voters in West Germany] (Villingen: Ring Verlag, 1960), pp. 321–23. For the elections of 1961–1976, *Amtliches Handbuch des deutschen Bundestages* [Official handbook of the German Bundestag] (Darmstadt: Neue Darmstädter Verlagsanstalt), appropriate years.

The Impact of Nazism and Military Government

Twelve years of Nazi dictatorship destroyed more than the German party system. They radically altered the social structure which that party system had reflected. In Ralf Dahrendorf's interpretation, the Nazi regime was the unwitting agent of a social revolution that destroyed the traditional German pattern of authority and of social hierarchy as well as the privileges of a long-established ruling class.[6] Among the casualties of a brutal totalitarian regime were such bases of the old political parties as the great landed estates of Eastern Prussia, the principal economic interest groups, regional political authorities, and at least some part of the industrial cartels. Defeat in war had led to the partitioning of the country; the territory of what became the Federal Republic was just half the size of the prewar Reich. Furthermore, its boundaries cut across the old state boundaries, notably carving up Prussia, and its population was more Catholic and more urban than that of Weimar Germany had been. It is highly improbable that the prewar party system would have reappeared in a political community so different from its prewar counterpart, even if the Allied military government had not intervened.

Leadership Recruitment. The intervention of the Allied occupation authorities was far-reaching. The military government in the three Western zones of occupation abandoned its initial policy of prohibiting indigenous German political life as soon as it became apparent that the Soviet authorities were attempting to create a Communist Germany in their zone. In the summer of 1945 the Western Allies began to recruit German administrative personnel to run essential governmental services at the local level. Many of those who were recruited went on to prominent political careers, favored by this early patronage and by the opportunity to exert influence in a highly fluid political situation. The recruitment policies that the Allies followed thereby affected the composition of the new German political leadership. The military commanders sought to exclude known Nazis and to favor political leaders who had had experience in local government before the war. Thus, men like Konrad Adenauer returned to mayoral positions they had held in the Weimar Republic. In Catholic regions, the military authorities trusted the advice of church leaders, facilitating the return of old Center party politicians to local offices. In the British zone of occupation, labor union leaders were fre-

---

[6] Ralf Dahrendorf, *Society and Democracy in Germany* (New York: Doubleday, 1967), pp. 387–88.

quently consulted, a policy that favored Social Democrats. Often having little to go on, the military government also sought talent among those with administrative experience outside of party politics and among intellectuals, bringing into government service men like Ludwig Erhard and Carlo Schmid.

The earliest postwar German political leaders chosen in this way included both old-time leaders of the Center and Social Democratic parties of the Weimar Republic and newcomers to politics. The Allies did not favor any particular political point of view. But in their eagerness to find responsible Germans to whom they could turn over administrative duties, they in effect favored the reestablishment of political leaders from the strongest of the democratic parties of the Weimar Republic and the entry into political life of intellectuals and other professionals who had not previously had political experience.[7]

Party Reorganization. Improvisation also played a part in the reestablishment of political party organizations, again to the advantage of some of the survivors of the old order. As long as there was a ban on party formation, during the summer of 1945, genuinely new political parties could not get started. However, informal communication among surviving leaders of the largest of the Weimar parties enabled them to recover some semblance of organization. The Social Democrats, best preserved of the old parties, showed the earliest signs of life, under the leadership of Kurt Schumacher who had survived the Nazi regime in a concentration camp.[8] In several cities Catholic Center party politicians met with Catholic intellectuals, with Catholic and Protestant clergy newly accustomed to cooperating with each other after the hardships imposed by Nazi hostility to organized religion, and with political conservatives who were embarrassed by their parties' compromises with the Nazis. Out of such meetings came rapid and widespread agreement to build a new interdenominational center party, with the churches and the old Center party lending organizational aid.[9] Communist party leaders were also actively reestablishing contact among themselves, as were politicians who had

---

[7] Lutz Niethammer, "Amerikanische Besatzung und bayerische Politik (1945)" [American occupation and Bavarian politics], *Vierteljahreshefte für Zeitgeschichte,* vol. 15 (1967), pp. 164–65, 173, 179–80; Harold Zink, *The United States in Germany, 1944–55* (Princeton: Princeton University Press, 1957), pp. 170–75; F. Roy Willis, *The French in Germany, 1945–1949* (Stanford, Calif.: Stanford University Press, 1962), pp. 185–90.

[8] Lewis Edinger, *Kurt Schumacher: A Study in Personality and Political Behavior* (Stanford, Calif.: Stanford University Press, 1965), p. 71.

[9] Arnold J. Heidenheimer, *Adenauer and the CDU* (The Hague: Nijhoff, 1960), chap. 2.

belonged to the principal liberal parties of the Weimar Republic. When the Allied military government suddenly ended the ban on political parties in August 1945,[10] this informal organizing activity gave the Social Democrats, the Christian Democrats, and the liberals a head start they never lost. It also gave the Communist party early advantages which, however, it could not maintain.

The Allies attempted to control the reorganization of parties by imposing a licensing requirement. This had the principal effect of precluding the formation of a new Nazi party and of imposing procedural obstacles which were most readily overcome by the four groups that had been engaging in informal organization during the summer. While the licensing policies differed somewhat in the different zones of occupation, applicants were generally screened for the sources of their funds, the degree of internal democracy suggested by their statutes, and the political backgrounds of their leaders. Minor regional parties could not obtain licenses in the French zone of occupation. In all zones, parties specifically appealing to refugees and expellees from the East were disallowed. The Allied military governments feared the revanchism such parties might exhibit and were anxious to assimilate the newcomers into West German society.[11]

Because of variations in policy among the three zones of occupation and because of the red tape involved in the screening process, only the four parties that had benefited from the summer of informal organization among previously existing groups were able to compete in the first local elections held during 1946, and only these four were able to present candidates in all of the states for the first national elections three years later. These parties played the dominant role in the constituent assemblies that were appointed or elected in 1946 and 1947 to draft state constitutions.

---

[10] On August 2, 1945, the four Allied powers, meeting in Potsdam, agreed that "all democratic political parties . . . shall be allowed and encouraged throughout Germany." Report on the Tripartite Conference of Berlin (Potsdam), reprinted in von Oppen, Documents, p. 44.

[11] Richard M. Scammon, "Political Parties," in Governing Postwar Germany, ed. Edward H. Litchfield (Ithaca: Cornell University Press, 1953), pp. 475–80; Seymour R. Bolten, "Military Government and the German Political Parties," Annals of the American Academy of Political and Social Science, vol. 267 (January 1950), p. 55; Willis, The French in Germany, pp. 190–96; Raymond Ebsworth, Restoring Democracy in Germany: the British Contribution (London: Stevens, 1960), chap. 2; James K. Pollock and James H. Meisel, Germany under Occupation: Illustrative Materials and Documents (Ann Arbor, Mich.: George Wahr, 1947), p. 144; Ossip K. Flechtheim, Dokumente zur parteipolitischen Entwicklung in Deutschland seit 1945 [Documents on the development of political parties in Germany since 1945] (Berlin: Wendler, 1962), vol. 1, pp. 33, 38, and 51.

The New Electoral Law. In the long run the most important advantage enjoyed by these early starters in the postwar party system was the influence they were able to exert on the formulation of the new electoral system. Most of the state constituent assemblies opted for proportional representation, the system in effect in the Weimar Republic and the safest system for parties uncertain of their electoral strength.[12] But the experience of party fragmentation under pure proportional representation in the Weimar Republic persuaded most politicians to favor a restriction that would deny parliamentary representation to parties receiving less than 5 (or, in some states, 10) percent of the votes. This restriction, written into most of the state constitutions, was obviously in the interest of the four parties already sitting in the assemblies, since it placed an obstacle in the path of new parties. By inserting the restriction into the constitutions, their framers precluded future challenge by the courts. During the Weimar Republic, the Supreme Court had declared minimum-vote requirements in several states unconstitutional as violating the equal protection of the law.[13]

A minimum-vote requirement also found its way into the first national electoral law. This was a direct consequence of the intervention of the Allied military government in the work of the Parliamentary Council, the body that drafted the Grundgesetz, or Basic Law, as the constitution is called, during the winter of 1948–1949. By a narrow margin, the Main Committee of the Parliamentary Council had defeated a constitutional provision that would have explicitly permitted a minimum-vote clause in the electoral law. The vote was eleven to ten, with the representatives of four small parties and some Social Democrats on the prevailing side. The argument was that such minimum-vote requirements were inconsistent with the equality of the vote.[14] Accordingly, the first electoral law, enacted by

---

[12] In the British zone of occupation, the military government favored a system of single-member constituencies with plurality voting. As a result, a compromise system was adopted there, partly proportional, partly single-member district. This eventually became the model for the federal system. However, in the federal system the distribution of seats among the parties is proportional to their overall votes, although half of the members are elected in single-member districts. Ebsworth, *Restoring Democracy*, chap. 3.

[13] Friedrich Karl Fromme, *Von der Weimarer Verfassung zum Bonner Grundgesetz* [From the Weimar constitution to the Bonn Basic Law] (Tübingen: Mohr, 1960), pp. 159–60.

[14] *Parlamentarischer Rat, Verhandlungen des Hauptausschusses* [Parliamentary Council, deliberations of the Main Committee], 48th session, February 9, 1949, pp. 629–31; *Jahrbuch des öffentlichen Rechts* [Yearbook of constitutional law], vol. 1 (1951), pp. 202–5, 351–53.

the Parliamentary Council, contained no such clause. However, the military governors, the chief executives of the Allied military governments of Germany, had reservations about other aspects of the law. Since the Parliamentary Council had adjourned immediately after enacting the law, the military governors addressed their objections to the ministers-president, the civilian chief executives of the German states, who were the only German political authorities in office pending the first federal election. Having expressed their specific reservations, the military governors added, knowingly, that they were "prepared to consider such [other] modifications of the law as may be proposed by the Ministers-President. . . ."

The military governors had reason to believe that the ministers-president, all of whom belonged to the three largest parties and most of whom were accustomed to minimum-vote clauses in their own states, would favor such a clause in the federal law. Indeed, within two days the ministers-president responded with several recommendations to modify the proportional elements of the law, among them a proposal that required parties to obtain at least 5 percent of the vote in a state (or a plurality in at least one constituency) to obtain a share in that state's proportional representation in Parliament. The military governors approved these proposals the same day they were made and authorized the ministers-president to promulgate the revised law. When some political parties advanced sharp criticism of this change in the law, the ministers-president hesitated about their right to alter the work of the Parliamentary Council. Thereupon the military governors took responsibility for the result "in virtue of our supreme authority."[15]

Thus, the minimum-vote clause that governed the first national election had a profound effect on the fortunes of the parties. It prevented three of the fourteen parties that had nominated candidates from obtaining any parliamentary representation. The incorporation in the law of the formula of the "highest average" for assigning each successive seat slightly underrepresented some of the other small parties; the formula of the "highest remainder" in the electoral law of the Weimar Republic had favored these. The seats denied to the smaller parties were distributed among the larger, which were consequently

---

[15] The exchange of correspondence between the military governors and the ministers-president is contained in *Documents on the Creation of the German Federal Constitution*, Civil Administration Division, Office of Military Government for Germany (U.S.), September 1, 1949, pp. 148–52. See also John Ford Golay, *The Founding of the Federal Republic of Germany* (Chicago: University of Chicago Press, 1958), chap. 4, esp. pp. 145–47.

DEVELOPMENT OF THE GERMAN PARTY SYSTEM

overrepresented. Their share of parliamentary seats was eight percentage points greater than their share of the popular vote. Before the
next election, the leaders of the governing coalition put through a
strengthened 5 percent clause, and they strengthened it again three
years later. Now parties had to obtain at least 5 percent of the *national*
vote (or pluralities in *three* constituencies) in order to obtain any
parliamentary representation. Nine of the fifteen parties competing in
the second national elections failed to get parliamentary seats, and
ten out of fourteen failed in the third elections. Beginning with the
election of 1961, only three parties have managed to obtain the legal
minimum. Several of the unsuccessful parties made vain attempts to
merge their strengths. In 1969 an extreme right-wing party, the National Democrats, failed to gain parliamentary representation by just
seven-tenths of one percentage point. Increasingly, small parties were
discouraged from seriously competing, although a variety of tiny
factions, especially on the left, continued to nominate candidates in
order to voice their views (see Table 1-2).

The new electoral system, therefore, placed special obstacles in
the way of party fragmentation. An index of fractionalization which
takes account of both the number and the relative sizes of the parties
shows a sharp decline in fragmentation from 1949 onwards and a
marked contrast between the fragmentation characterizing the German party system before 1930 and after 1949 (see Figure 1-2).[16]
Furthermore, a comparison between the fragmentation of the popular
vote and the fragmentation of parliamentary seats shows that votes
and seats were similarly fragmented under the pure system of proportional representation used in the Weimar Republic. However,
after 1949, parliamentary fragmentation was distinctly lower than

---

[16] The index was developed by Douglas Rae. See *The Political Consequences of
Electoral Laws*, rev. ed. (New Haven: Yale University Press, 1971), p. 56. It is
calculated according to the following formula:

$$F_e = 1 - \left(\sum_{i=1}^{n} T_i^2 \right)$$

where F = index of fractionalization (of votes or seats), and

T = any party's decimal share of the vote (or of parliamentary seats).

The index was applied to the German party system by Frank Dishaw, "Bemerk-
ungen zur Konkurrenz im deutschen Parteiensystem 1871–1969" [Comments on
competition in the German party system, 1871–1969], in *Sozialwissenschaftliches
Jahrbuch für Politik* [Social scientific yearbook for politics], vol. 2 (Munich:
Günter Olzog, 1971), pp. 61–71.

FIGURE 1-2

ELECTORAL AND PARLIAMENTARY FRAGMENTATION IN GERMANY, 1903–1976

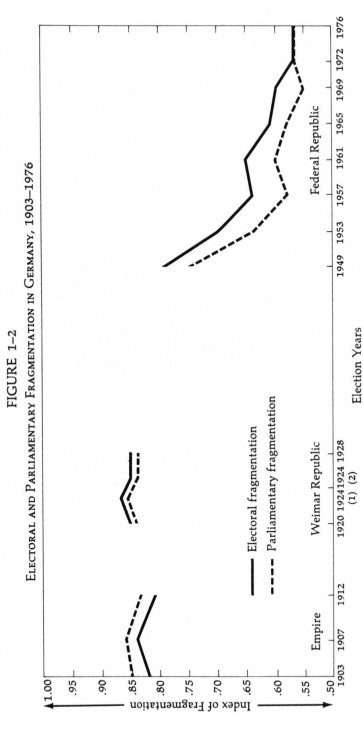

SOURCE: Official election returns given in Huber, *Quellen zum Staatsrecht der Neuzeit*, pp. 652–55; Sternberger, *Wahlen und Wähler*, pp. 321–23; and *Amtliches Handbuch des deutschen Bundestages*, appropriate years.

NOTE: For an explanation of the index of fragmentation, see footnote 16.

electoral fragmentation.[17] This is a measure of the extent to which the new electoral law limited the proliferation of parties in Parliament. By the 1970s this had correspondingly limited the electoral appeal of the small parties. Those that failed to win seats in 1972 and 1976 together won less than 1 percent of the popular vote.

In 1952 the Federal Constitutional Court declared minimum-vote clauses to be consistent with the equal protection of the law. Exhibiting a sophistication that the Supreme Court of the Weimar Republic had lacked, the court declared that the equal protection of the law required that every vote be counted equally, not that every ballot have equal effect on the distribution of seats among the parties. After all, the court argued, in the systems of plurality voting in single-member constituencies, which were accepted in the oldest democracies, it was taken for granted that votes cast for losing candidates were wasted, in the sense of not affecting the outcome. A system of proportional representation that allotted no representation to parties receiving less than 5 percent of the votes violated the equality of the ballot only in this sense.[18]

The Allied military government, as we have seen, facilitated the entry of particular individuals into postwar German political life. Inadvertently it favored four political parties; deliberately it barred others for several important years and prevented a system of pure proportional representation from determining the distribution of seats in the first postwar national Parliament. Military government also had one indirect, though profound, effect on the postwar party system. In producing the originally unintended division of occupied Germany into a Soviet-dominated Eastern zone and three eventually merged Western zones, it enabled the Soviet military government to force the consolidation of all of the political parties in its zone under the control of the Communist party. As a result, in the Western

---

[17] During the Empire, the fragmentation of seats was actually higher than the fragmentation of votes, partly because of the failure to redistrict the constituencies.This silently gerrymandered the system against parties receiving most of their votes in the growing and increasingly underrepresented urban areas, notably the Social Democrats. It was also the result of differences in the parties' ability to bargain with each other between the first and second ballots. Bargaining enabled the "bourgeois" parties to consolidate their strength; it left the Social Democrats isolated. The combined effects of the silent gerrymander and the inability to bargain left the Social Democrats underrepresented in Parliament and all other parties, even the smallest among them, overrepresented. This made the fragmentation in Parliament worse than it was in the electorate. As a measure of the disparity between votes and seats, the Social Democrats received 29 percent of the votes but only 11 percent of the seats in the election of 1907.

[18] Federal Constitutional Court, *Entscheidungen* [Decisions], 1952, p. 208ff., esp. pp. 241–60.

zones the Communist party was associated in the public mind with a foreign occupying power, a disability that crippled its electoral appeal from the start.

The destruction of the old German party system and its social basis between 1933 and 1945 and the channeling of indigenous German political forces by the Allied military government, therefore, broke the inertia by which most party systems maintain the principal characteristics acquired in their early development. This created the conditions that permitted a changed German social structure and a changed set of public orientations toward politics to reshape the German party system. The successive results of the first postwar elections at the state level and the eight national elections which have followed depict the resulting transformation (see Table 1-3). Let us now examine the social, economic, and attitudinal changes that shaped this transformation.

Socioeconomic Determinants of the Postwar Party System

German industrial production regained its prewar levels remarkably fast after 1946, thanks to American aid, a steady supply of labor from refugees and expellees coming from the Eastern territories, and a high rate of taxation which kept consumer demand low and promoted capital investment. By 1950 the gross national product per capita had returned to its 1936 level. From that point, the German economy grew at an average annual rate of nearly 7 percent per capita during the next decade. The gross domestic product per capita in Germany was equal to that of Great Britain and France by 1960. Thereafter the rate of growth continued at a reduced but steady 4 percent annually, so that in the mid-1970s Germany's economic output per capita was close to the U.S. level.[19] This impressive economic expansion brought with it a profound change in the composition of the German labor force. The proportion of the work force employed in agriculture declined by two-thirds in the generation after 1950, while the proportion employed in service trades increased 50 percent. In 1974 nearly half of the entire work force was employed in the tertiary sector; only 7 percent was employed in agriculture.

From a sociological point of view, the most profound consequence was a doubling of the proportion of salaried employees in the labor

---

[19] Agency for International Development, Statistics and Reports Division, Office of Financial Management, Bureau for Program and Management Services, "Gross National Product: Growth Rates and Trend Data," May 1, 1974, p. 15; United Nations, *Statistical Yearbook, 1974* (New York: 1975), pp. 651–52.

TABLE 1-3

BUNDESTAG ELECTION RESULTS, 1946–1976

Party	1946–47[a]	1949	1953	1957	1961	1965	1969	1972	1976
Christian Democratic Union/ Christian Social Union									
% of valid vote	38.5	31.0	45.2	50.2	45.3	47.6	46.1	44.9	48.6
Seats		139	244	270	242	245	242	225	244
Social Democratic party									
% of valid vote	35.7	29.2	28.8	31.8	36.3	39.3	42.7	45.8	42.6
Seats		131	151	169	190	202	224	230	213
Free Democratic party									
% of valid vote	8.2	11.9	9.5	7.7	12.7	9.5	5.8	8.4	7.9
Seats		52	48	41	67	49	30	41	39
German party[b]									
% of valid vote	2.6	4.0	3.2	3.4	2.8				
Seats		17	15	17	0				
Bavarian party									
% of valid vote		4.2	1.7						
Seats		17	0						
All-German Bloc (expellees)									
% of valid vote			5.9	4.6					
Seats			27	0					

Radical left[c]									
% of valid vote	9.3	5.7	2.2	1.0	1.9	1.3	0.6	0.3	0.3
Seats		15	0	0	0	0	0	0	0
Radical right[d]									
% of valid vote	0.4	1.8	1.1	1.3	0.8	2.0	4.3	0.6	0.3
Seats		5	0	0	0	0	0	0	0
Other parties and independents									
% of valid vote	5.3	12.2	2.4	1.3	0.2	0.3	0.5	0.1	0.3
Seats		26	2	0	0	0	0	0	0

[a] First state constituent-assembly or legislature elections.

[b] Merged with All-German Bloc in 1961; previously this party had stand-down agreements with the CDU to enable it to win single-member constituencies.

[c] Communist party in 1949, 1953, 1972, and 1976; German Peace Union in 1961 and 1965; Action for Democratic Progress in 1969.

[d] German Right party in 1949; German Reich party in 1953–1961; National Democratic party in 1965, 1969, 1972, and 1976.

SOURCE: Vogel et al., *Wahlen in Deutschland*, pp. 306–8; *Amtliches Handbuch des Deutschen Bundestages*, 1972, p. 2; 1976, p. 2.

TABLE 1-4

OCCUPATIONAL COMPOSITION OF THE GERMAN LABOR FORCE, 1882–1974
(in percentages of labor force)

Occupational Category	1882	1925	1950	1974
Self-employed	25.6	15.9	14.5	9.1
Participating family members	10.0	16.9	13.8	5.3
Salaried employees	7.0	17.0	20.6	40.9
Workers	57.4	50.2	51.0	44.8

SOURCE: *Statistisches Jahrbuch für die Bundesrepublik Deutschland, 1971* [Statistical yearbook for the Federal Republic of Germany, 1971] (Stuttgart: Verlag W. Kohlhammer, 1971), p. 121; *Statistisches Jahrbuch, 1975*, p. 149.

force within a single generation. In the middle of the Weimar Republic salaried employees constituted just over one-sixth of the labor force; in 1974 they constituted over two-fifths (see Table 1-4). These salaried employees were characteristically better educated and more mobile than the members of the traditional working class, with whom they shared only the status of being employees. In their social and political outlook, they constituted a new middle class that comprised almost as large a proportion of those gainfully employed as did the working class. No political party could take their support for granted. None of the old political ideologies attracted their loyalty. Like a newly enfranchised sector of the population in the days of the expansion of the suffrage, they constituted an electorate that was newly available for political mobilization.[20]

In the Weimar Republic voting had followed social class lines. Voters had perceived the parties as belonging to one of three social-cultural blocs: Marxist working class, Catholic middle class, and Protestant middle class. Members of the electorate had exhibited lasting commitments to one of these blocs and had made their commitments on the basis of their social-cultural class identification. From election to election, they might have switched among the parties within each bloc, but very little switching between blocs had occurred.

---

[20] Kendall L. Baker, Russell J. Dalton, and Kai Hildebrandt, *Political Affiliations: Transition in the Bases of German Partisanship* (Ann Arbor: Center for Political Studies, Institute for Social Research, University of Michigan, 1975), esp. pp. 9–16; Franz Urban Pappi, "Parteiensystem und Sozialstruktur in der Bundesrepublik" [Party system and social structure in the Federal Republic], *Politische Vierteljahresschrift*, vol. 14 (1973), pp. 191–213.

Even the collapse of the conservative and liberal parties between 1928 and 1933 and the explosive growth of the Nazi party, with all its cataclysmic consequences, had been the result of a redistribution of party strength within the Protestant middle-class bloc.[21]

For that part of the population belonging to the traditional working class and the traditional middle class or identifying with traditional Catholicism, voting continued to follow social class lines in the Federal Republic. However, this was not true of the growing proportion of the population comprising the new salaried middle class. Finding in their occupational and social status no clear source of partisan loyalties, the members of this class evaluated the parties in terms of their competence to deal with such issues as educational opportunity, economic planning, and foreign policy to which this section of the population was especially sensitive.[22]

The existence of a large number of voters who did not react to parties in traditional social class terms posed a serious challenge to the three established parties. These voters constituted 40 percent of the electorate by the 1970s. They were the key to electoral victory in a three-party system, for the criterion of victory was no longer the ability to obtain the support of a fourth or a third of the electorate, as it had been in the multiparty system of the Empire and the Weimar Republic, but the ability to obtain the support of half of the electorate, either alone or with a single coalition partner.

The Christian Democratic Union was the first of the postwar parties to appeal to the new middle classes. In doing so it did not lose the support of its traditional Catholic constituency among former Center party voters or the support of its Protestant constituency among voters for the old middle-class parties.[23] As a new party, a union of Catholics and Protestants, unburdened by ideological commitments, it was well placed to attract voters across class lines. Its status as a governing party during the 1950s further helped to keep the CDU a pragmatic, voter-oriented party. It was far more difficult for the Social Democrats to add to their traditional working-class constituency. Inclined toward ideological commitments, run by an entrenched organizational elite, led at first by a man whose political vision had been shaped by the political experience of the Weimar Republic and the Nazi concentration camps, this oldest of German

---

[21] W. Phillips Shively, "Voting Stability and the Nature of Party Attachments in the Weimar Republic," *American Political Science Review*, vol. 66 (1972), pp. 1203–25, esp. pp. 1220–23.

[22] Baker, Dalton, and Hildebrandt, "Political Affiliations," pp. 12–13, 22–23.

[23] Juan J. Linz, "Cleavage and Consensus in West German Politics: The Early Fifties," in Lipset and Rokkan, *Party Systems*, esp. pp. 287–304.

parties seemed condemned to remain a working-class movement, incapable of becoming a majority governing party. However, by the end of the first decade of the Federal Republic, a new set of leaders saw correctly that the criteria for success had changed and that a substantial section of the electorate was susceptible to new appeals. In 1959 the SDP adopted a new party program and began to emphasize personality and leadership. Finally, their participation in the "Grand Coalition" between 1966 and 1969 demonstrated that the Social Democrats were a responsible governing party and had succeeded in broadening their appeal to attract the new middle class.[24] The Free Democrats underwent their own reorientation in the late 1960s, acquiring a new, less conservative constituency.[25]

Thus the changing social composition of the electorate brought with it a substantial redefinition of party appeals and an attempt on the part of all three established parties to add to the support of a traditional class constituency the support of some portion of the new middle class. The Social Democrats' success in winning support in this part of the electorate brought about the transfer of power from a CDU-led to an SPD-led coalition in 1969, a critical election which documented the existence of new voting patterns and of alternative governing coalitions.

By the late 1960s, the parties' records, in government or opposition, were more important to many voters than the parties' traditional social class identifications. Also important were the parties' candidates for the chancellorship. The elections of 1969 and 1972 turned on the voters' evaluations of the candidates for chancellor and of the government's performance.[26] In the voters' mind, the Free Democrats were associated after 1969 with the Social Democrats, with whom they had governed. No longer could the third party defer its choice of coalition partner until after the election, as it had done in the

---

[24] David P. Conradt, *The West German Party System: An Ecological Analysis of Social Structure and Voting Behavior, 1961–1969*, Sage Professional Papers in Comparative Politics no. 28 (Beverly Hills: Sage Publications, 1972), esp. pp. 19–27.

[25] H. D. Klingemann and F. U. Pappi, "Die Wählerbewegungen bei der Bundestagswahl am 28. September 1969 [Voting behavior in the parliamentary election of September 28, 1969], *Politische Vierteljahresschrift*, vol. 11 (1970), pp. 111–38, esp. p. 126.

[26] Max Kaase, "Determinanten des Wahlverhaltens bei der Bundestagswahl 1969" [Determinants of voting choice in the parliamentary election of 1969], *Politische Vierteljahresschrift*, vol. 11 (1970), pp. 46–110, esp. pp. 60–72. Max Kaase, "Die Bundestagswahl 1972: Probleme und Analysen" [The parliamentary election 1972: problems and analyses], *Politische Vierteljahresschrift*, vol. 14 (1973), pp. 145–70.

1960s.[27] Voters so clearly expected to be able to choose between alternative governing coalitions that the Free Democrats feared they would suffer serious losses if they were unwilling to commit themselves to one side or the other. It would also have been extraordinarily risky for the Free Democrats to switch sides, since their voting constituency clearly favored a socialist-liberal coalition. This was an indication of the bipolarity that had developed in the German party system.

The common focus of the three parliamentary parties on the new middle class, and the two-sidedness of the party system left some potential for the rise of extremist parties at times of crisis. This became apparent between 1966 and 1969, when the first recession in Germany's postwar history coincided with the success of a hypernationalist party in a series of state elections. Concurrently, student unrest manifested itself in the appearance of several extreme leftist movements. For different reasons, neither extreme succeeded in obtaining parliamentary representation in the election of 1969. The appeal of the right-wing National Democratic party was chiefly in small towns among older people of low educational attainment and with traditional middle-class occupations.[28] The Christian Democrats were able to compete effectively with the National Democrats for the favor of this disaffected constituency. The extreme left appealed to young university students, who caused the Social Democratic party considerable embarrassment in party meetings but who were unable to mobilize any significant number of voters. In short, both the Christian Democrats and the Social Democrats demonstrated the ability to contain threats of being outflanked. This was further evidence that both parties had the remarkable ability to amalgamate the interests of the social-status groups traditionally associated with them and the interests of a new middle class produced by the economic development of the previous twenty-five years.

Political Attitudes toward the Party System

The system of political parties that developed in postwar Germany was in many respects the product of historical events from which the contemporary German voter feels disassociated and of disruptive

---

[27] For a detailed analysis of the decision of the FDP to enter a coalition with the SPD after the election of 1969, see Klaus Bohnsack, "Bildung von Regierungskoalitionen, dargestellt am Beispiel der Koalitionsentscheidung der F.D.P. von 1969" [The formation of governing coalitions, illustrated by the FDP's coalition decision of 1969], *Zeitschrift für Parlamentsfragen*, vol. 7 (1976), pp. 400–25.

[28] Hans D. Klingemann and Franz U. Pappi, *Politischer Radikalismus* [Political radicalism] (Munich: Oldenbourg, 1972), esp. chap. 4, 6.

social changes he does not control. It was conceivable that voters would regard such a party system with indifference or hostility, that the system would lack support in the political culture. In fact, the principal institutions of government were established in the Federal Republic of Germany while the country was still under Allied military occupation: the constitutional convention was an unelected body that received little public notice. While the new institutions, like the parties, bore some similarity to their Imperial and Weimar predecessors, they were also significantly different. Although unfamiliar and remote at the beginning, these political institutions, including the system of political parties, soon received general public support. Three principal factors generated this support: the success of the policies adopted through the new institutions, the absence of alternatives, and the low demands made by these institutions on the political energies of the mass public.

At the beginning of the 1950s, over half of the German population thought an elected parliament an unnecessary institution; nearly as many were unwilling to say that they favored the existence of more than one political party. But support for the principal institutions of democratic participation grew rapidly, first among those sections of the population most satisfied with the policies of the government and, by the end of the decade, even among those who identified with the opposition. By the beginning of the 1960s, two-thirds of the population expressed a commitment to Parliament and three-quarters favored a competitive party system.[29] In a survey in the early 1970s, nearly 90 percent of the population supported the party system.[30] A commitment to the new system of government had developed that was independent of satisfaction with its policies.

Paralleling this positive orientation to the new regime was the virtual disappearance of support for its predecessors. Throughout the Weimar Republic, substantial sections of the population had continued to regard the Empire that had preceded it as a preferable regime. But in the postwar period, the Empire was only a distant memory, the Hitler regime had been discredited at least by its failure

---

[29] G. R. Boynton and Gerhard Loewenberg, "The Development of Public Support for Parliament in Germany, 1951–59," *British Journal of Political Science*, vol. 3 (1973), pp. 169–89; Boynton and Loewenberg, "The Development of Public Support for Party Competition in Postwar Germany," paper delivered at the annual meeting of the Midwest Political Science Association, Chicago, Illinois, May 4, 1973.

[30] Elisabeth Noelle and Erich Peter Neumann, *Jahrbuch der öffentlichen Meinung, 1968 bis 1973* [Yearbook of public opinion, 1968 to 1973] (Allensbach: Verlag für Demoskopie, 1974), p. 222.

in war, and the Weimar Republic had no adherents. Few people could see any alternatives to the new institutions. It is true that in 1950 nearly half the population continued to hold favorable views of Hitler ("if the war had not taken place") and one-third thought the restoration of the monarchy would be a good idea. But these residual attachments to past regimes weakened rapidly during the 1950s. The sections of the population that were prospering under the new system were the first to lose interest in its predecessors, and by the 1960s no significant sections of the population yearned for a restoration. Since public support for political institutions depends at least in part on public perceptions of the alternatives, the fading of the alternatives helped to stabilize the existing system.[31]

The development of general public support for the institutions of democracy affected the party system in two important respects. First, parties opposed to the regime found it impossible to obtain even the minimum number of votes they needed to gain parliamentary representation; thus the number of parties and the range of party alternatives were reduced. Second, positive attitudes toward the institution of Parliament and toward the competitive party system enabled the parties to establish themselves securely in German public life with public financing and legal privileges. They could not be easily challenged by mass movements or other forms of unconventional political participation. A law on political parties enacted in 1967 attempted to ensure that parties would have democratic internal organizations, recognized them as official institutions of government, required disclosure of their contributors and their internal accounts, and provided them with federal subsidies reaching DM150 million ($60 million*) for each election.[32]

The electorate accepted this legal establishment of the parties. Although the public opposed government subsidies for the parties, three-fifths of the nation's economic and political leaders were prepared to condone the idea.[33] The public's general willingness to have political parties endowed with legal privileges did not arise from the

[31] G. R. Boynton and Gerhard Loewenberg, "The Decay of Support for Monarchy and the Hitler Regime in the Federal Republic of Germany," *British Journal of Political Science*, vol. 4 (1974), pp. 453–88.

* Editor's note: Throughout this volume, approximate dollar equivalents for sums in deutsche marks are based on the exchange rate at the time of the election— approximately DM2.5 to the dollar.

[32] Ulrich Dübber, *Geld und Politik: die Finanzwirtschaft der Parteien* [Money and politics: the financing of the parties] (Freudenstadt: Lutzeyer, 1970), pp. 101–35.

[33] Uwe Schleth, *Parteifinanzen* [Party finance] (Meisenheim: Anton Hain, 1973), pp. 252–55, 261–62.

approval of specific privileges but rather from a generally positive attitude toward the party system. This permitted political leaders the discretion to work out the details.

In any case, public involvement in party activity was shallow. While 15 percent of the voters belonged to political parties during the early years of the Weimar Republic[34] and a much higher proportion belonged to the Nazi party later on, party membership after 1945 remained below 5 percent of the electorate.[35] Till they were publicly subsidized, the parties were chronically short of funds. The legal establishment of the parties therefore enabled them to maintain themselves without depending on active public involvement.

The public's attachment to the parties expressed itself not only in the acceptance of a legally established competitive party system, but also in the willingness of 90 percent of the eligible voters to participate in elections and to choose among the three established parties. Yet these were both expressions of the voters' general commitment to the party *system* rather than their particular commitment to a party. As we have seen, a growing proportion of the population belonging to a new middle class chose freely among the parties on the basis of its evaluations of their competence at any given moment, uncommitted to any of them by traditional ties of class or status.

In the early 1970s for the first time, some persuasive evidence appeared that a majority of the voters were developing psychological attachments to particular parties comparable to the party identifications that exist in Scandinavia, Great Britain, and the United States. The continuous existence of three parties, the clear coalition alignments among them, and the propensity of voters to act consistently over time showed signs of producing commitments of the kind that had so far been missing in postwar Germany. During the 1972 campaign, between 50 and 60 percent of voters exhibited a stable party identification, and this party attachment seemed to influence the voting choice of younger members of the electorate more strongly than that of their elders.[36] In comparison with the behavior of voters in the

---

[34] Thomas Nipperdey, *Die Organisation der deutschen Parteien vor 1918* [The organization of German parties before 1918] (Düsseldorf: Droste Verlag, 1961), p. 398.

[35] Heino Kaack, *Geschichte und Struktur des deutschen Parteiensystems* [History and structure of the German party system] (Opladen: Westdeutscher Verlag, 1971), pp. 482–97.

[36] Kendall L. Baker, "Generational Differences in the Role of Party Identification in German Political Behavior," *American Journal of Political Science*, vol. 22 (1978), pp. 106–29, esp. p. 111. Cf. Manfred Berger, "Parteiidentifikation in der Bundesrepublik" [Party identification in the Federal Republic], *Politische Vierteljahresschrift*, vol. 14 (1973), pp. 215–25.

1960s, voters in the 1970s seemed to be guided by their party preference more than by their preferences on issues. It appeared as if voters were adjusting their positions on the issues to correspond to their newly developing party loyalties.[37] This tendency, if it continued, would lead to the establishment of party loyalty as an influence on voting choice, intervening between social background factors and voting behavior.

Conclusion

A generation after the establishment of the Federal Republic, the German party system shows signs of attaining stability in a form clearly distinguishing it from the party system of the Weimar Republic and the Empire. Only three parties—the cdu/csu, the spd, and the fdp—have serious prospects of gaining voter support; in the 1970s they have gathered over 99 percent of the votes. The three parties offer voters a choice between alternative governments. Thus, they give the electorate the power to select its rulers in the same way as French, British, and American electorates can, a power that German electorates have never before had. The Social Democratic/ Free Democratic coalition, which was confirmed in power at the election of 1976, replaced the Christian Democratic-led coalitions that had governed during the first twenty years of the Republic. Coalitions have in fact alternated in power; all parties have had experience in both government and opposition. Political radicalism has had little support.

These distinguishing characteristics of the new party system are the consequence of the radical destruction of its predecessor through the coercion of a totalitarian dictatorship and the authority of a foreign occupation. The destruction of the old order opened the way for the establishment of a new system, influenced by a new socioeconomic environment and sustained by a new political culture. Habits of mind and behavior in the electorate and organizational inertia among the political activists make it likely that the system will survive the generation of its founding and that it will continue to structure the choices of the German voter, as it did in the election of 1976.

---

[37] Baker, Dalton, and Hildebrandt, "Party Affiliations," pp. 24–26; by the same authors, "Political Stability in Transition: Postwar Germany," paper delivered at the Annual Meeting of the American Political Science Association, San Francisco, California, September 1975, pp. 40–41.

2

The 1976 Campaign and Election: An Overview

David P. Conradt

Elections and the German Political System

The most common and extensive form of political participation in West Germany, as in other industrialized societies, is voting. Indeed, in the absence of any significant plebiscitary components in the Bonn constitution, voting is the West German citizen's major formal means of influence in the policy-making process. Elections were held at the local and state level as early as 1946 in the British and American zones, and the first national election, held in 1949, was a quasi-referendum on the constitution. The subsequent claims by the Bonn government that it was the sole legitimate representative of the German nation were based on the freely elected character of West German governments. Thus, the results of early local, state, and national elections were viewed primarily as indicators of support for the system and of its legitimacy. How many Germans would actually vote? And how many would support the democratic parties? The high turnout and the general rejection of neo-Nazi, Communist, and other extremist parties evidenced in these early elections were seen as securing the legitimation of the postwar system.

The other major functions that elections have for a political system—providing succession in leadership, influencing and controlling the policy decisions of government—were of lesser importance in the early years of the Federal Republic. The elections of the 1950s and even the 1961 poll were largely referenda on Adenauer's leadership; the policy and personnel alternatives of the opposition parties played a subordinate role in these campaigns. Since the mid-1960s, however, the policy, leadership succession, and control functions of elections have become more prominent at both national and

29

state levels. In 1969 the electorate effected the first alternation of government and opposition in the history of the Republic, ending twenty years of Christian Democratic rule. The Christian Democrats' near miss in 1976 continues this pattern of close, hard-fought elections whose outcomes can directly influence the policies and personnel of government.

This chapter will first examine the institutional framework within which the electoral struggle takes place, giving particular attention to the complex German electoral law and its effect upon campaign strategies and voting behavior. The course of the 1976 campaign and the strategies of the major parties together with the system of party and campaign finance will then be described. We will conclude with a brief statistical and comparative analysis of the results and their implications for the parties and the West German political system.

The Institutional Framework: Electoral Mechanics. Elections to the Bundestag must be held at least every four years but can be held sooner if the government loses its majority and requests the federal president to dissolve the Bundestag and call new elections.[1] This occurred in 1972 when the Brandt government, through the defection of several Free Democratic party deputies, lost its majority and the opposition was unable to secure a majority for a new government.

For national elections the Republic is divided into 248 constituencies,[2] with an average size of about 250,000 residents and 170,000 registered voters. Each district must be a contiguous whole while respecting state and, if possible, county boundaries. The size of each district must not deviate by more than one-third from the national average. In 1976, following an extensive reapportionment, the smallest district had about 120,000 voters and the largest approximately 220,000 voters.

The constitution, or Basic Law, as amended in 1970, grants universal suffrage to Germans eighteen years of age or above (passive electoral right) and allows citizens twenty-one years or older to be

---

[1] Elections to the eleven state parliaments (including that of West Berlin), are also held every four years and in some cases every five years, but special elections can be called earlier. Usually state elections are held in "off-years," a provision especially favored by the opposition party at the national level to mitigate "coat-tail effects." There are no by-elections in West Germany. In the event of the death, resignation, or removal from office of a member of Parliament, the next name on the party's list of candidates for the relevant state at the previous election simply assumes the vacated seat. All elections—local, state, and national—are held on Sundays.

[2] Not including West Berlin, which is represented by twenty-two deputies appointed by the city's governing council, the Senat. These Berlin deputies, at the insistence of the Allied occupation powers, have no legal voting right.

elected to public office (active electoral right). West Germany has automatic registration based on residence records maintained by local authorities. If a citizen has officially reported his residence in the constituency (and he is required by law to do so), his name will automatically be placed on the electoral register, providing that he meets the age requirement. Prior to election day, he will then be notified of his registration and polling place.

The Electoral System. The procedures by which popular votes are converted into parliamentary seats are more than just a technical problem best left to constitutional lawyers. Most political scientists and political leaders assume that the electoral law will affect the character and structure of a nation's party system and hence its politics. Generally, there are two basic types of electoral systems: the plurality system, usually with single-member districts, as in the United States and Britain, according to which the party or candidate securing the most votes "takes all"; and the proportional electoral system, by which a party's share of parliamentary mandates is proportional to its percentage of the popular vote. Most political scientists have contended that a plurality system encourages the concentration of popular support among a small number of parties and enables clear decisions to emerge from an election, thus making post-election coalition negotiations unnecessary. The proportional system, on the other hand, is said to produce a fractionalization of the party vote and hence a multiparty system in which no single party secures a majority of the parliamentary seats and government by coalition must result.

The West German electoral system, at first glance, would seem to combine features of both the proportional and plurality systems. Indeed, the present system has been termed a personalized proportional representation system since one-half of the 496 parliamentary deputies are elected by plurality vote in single-member districts and the remaining 248 deputies by proportional representation from state party lists. Each voter casts two ballots—one for a district candidate and a second for a party. The second or party vote, however, is the more important since it is used to determine the final percentage of parliamentary mandates a party will receive. The seats won in the district contests are then *deducted* from this total due the party. Thus, the more district mandates a party wins, the fewer list seats it will receive.

An example, from the 1976 election, should clarify this procedure. As Table 2-1 shows, the Christian Democratic Union/Christian Social Union, with 48.6 percent of the second-ballot vote, was entitled to 243 seats. Since it had won 135 district contests, however, it received only 108 mandates from its state lists. The Social Democratic party, on the basis of its second-ballot percentage, was entitled to 214 seats but, since it won 113 district elections, it received only 101 of its seats from the state lists. Finally, the Free Democratic party won no district contests but received 7.9 percent of the second-ballot vote and was allotted 39 seats, all from its state lists.

In practice, then, this is a proportional representation system with two exceptions to "pure" proportionality: (1) A party must receive at least 5 percent of the second-ballot vote or win three district contests in order to be proportionally represented in Parliament; hence the minor parties in 1976, with only 0.9 percent of the vote and no district victories, received no seats and the four to five mandates they would have been allotted were given to the three parties that secured parliamentary representation. (2) If a party wins more direct mandates than it would be entitled to under proportional representation, it retains these extra seats and the size of the Parliament is increased accordingly. Let us assume, for example, that in 1976 the CDU had won all 248 district contests but had received only 40 percent of the second-ballot vote. In a pure proportional system, the party would be entitled to only 198 seats. According to the existing law, however, it would retain all 248 district seats but receive no mandates from the

TABLE 2-1

DISTRIBUTION OF SEATS IN THE BUNDESTAG, 1976 FEDERAL ELECTION

Party	Vote (in percentages)		Seats		
	First ballot	Second ballot	District contests won	List candidates elected[a]	Total[b]
CDU/CSU	48.9	48.6	135	108	243
SPD	43.7	42.6	113	101	214
FDP	6.4	7.9	0	39	39
Minor parties	1.0	0.9	0	0	0
Total	100.0	100.0	248	248	496

[a] The number of list candidates elected is determined by subtracting the number of district contests won (first ballot) from the total seats won (second ballot).

[b] Calculated, under proportional representation, from the second-ballot vote: each party receives a share of the 496 Bundestag seats proportional to its percentage of the vote on the second ballot.

SOURCE: Federal Statistical Office Wiesbaden, *Wahl zum 8. Deutschen Bundestag 1976* [Election to the eighth German Bundestag, 1976], Wiesbaden.

DAVID P. CONRADT

proportional lists, and the total size of the Bundestag would be increased from 496 to 546. In 1976 no excess mandates were won by any party. The largest number ever won was five in 1961.

Ticket splitting. This electoral system, through its provisions for two ballots and for the possibility that a party might win more seats in the district contests than it would be entitled to under proportional representation, could facilitate a great deal of ticket splitting or "lending" of votes by supporters of two coalition partners or prospective partners. Supporters of one party could cast their first-ballot vote for their coalition partner, thus insuring it a high number of district victories, while voters of the second party could return the favor by casting their second-ballot vote for the coalition partner, thus increasing its share of mandates from the state lists. Only recently, however, has ticket splitting of this type become fairly widespread. As Table 2-2 shows, between 1957 and 1969 second-ballot defections among spd and cdu/csu supporters exceeded 8 percent on only two occasions (cdu/csu in 1965 and spd in 1969). Even fdp supporters, until 1969, remained fairly loyal to their party on both ballots.

TABLE 2-2

Ticket Splitting by Party, 1957–1976

(in percentages)

Party	Election					
	1957	1961	1965	1969	1972	1976
cdu/csu	92.8 (6.6)	92.9 (4.4)	91.9 (6.1)	93.9 (6.6)	96.1 (3.2)	96.9 (2.9)
spd	93.6 (5.0)	93.7 (4.5)	93.6 (5.3)	91.8 (6.6)	89.2 (5.9)	92.9 (5.0)
fdp	86.2 (15.0)	89.9 (13.5)	85.2 (29.7)	72.3 (38.0)	64.3 (61.8)	75.4 (39.1)

Note: The figures in the left-hand column under each year indicate the proportion of first-ballot supporters of the given party who voted for the same party on the second ballot. The right-hand figures, in parentheses, indicate the proportion of second-ballot supporters of the given party who voted for some other party on the first ballot.

Source: Federal Statistical Office Wiesbaden, *Bevoelkerung und Kultur* [Population and culture], Series 8, *Wahl zum 7. Deutschen Bundestag am 19. November, 1972* [Election to the seventh German Parliament on November 19, 1972], "Wahlbeteiligung und Stimmabgabe der Maenner und Frauen nach dem Alter" [Turnout and voting of men and women by age] (Wiesbaden: Kohlhammer Verlag, 1973), p. 20; figures for 1976 from Federal Statistical Office, *Bevoelkerung und Erwerbstaetigkeit* [Population and occupations] Fachserie 1, *Wahl zum 8. Deutschen Bundestag am 3. Oktober 1976* [Election to the eighth German Parliament on October 3, 1976], "Wahlbeteiligung und Stimmabgabe der Maenner und Frauen nach dem Alter" [Turnout and voting of men and women by age] (Wiesbaden: Kohlhammer Verlag, 1977), pp. 22, 52–53.

33

The use of the electoral system to maintain coalitions by splitting ballots began in earnest at state elections after 1969. On several occasions, when the Free Democrats were in danger of dropping below the 5 percent needed for representation in state parliaments, the Social Democrats came to the party's aid and lent it votes. This first occurred on a fairly wide scale at the November 1970 state elections in Hesse and Bavaria. At the 1972 national election, as Table 2-2 shows, ticket splitting was widespread among SPD and FDP supporters: approximately 53 percent of those voters who supported the FDP by voting for its party list (second ballot) voted for the SPD's candidate in their districts, while an additional 8 percent gave the CDU's district candidate their support. Thus, over 60 percent of FDP second-ballot voters did not support the party's local candidate. In 1972, of the 3.13 million voters who supported the FDP with their party-list vote, only 1.20 million supported the FDP's local candidate, while 1.65 million gave their district vote to the SPD and 250,000 to the CDU/CSU candidate. The magnitude of this splitting on the part of FDP voters in 1972 makes it difficult to speak of an "FDP electorate" without distinguishing between the two ballots.[3]

This extensive ticket splitting in 1972 was in part the result of the discreet encouragement given it by the FDP leadership and its tacit acceptance by the SPD. In 1976, however, both parties, but especially the SPD, discouraged ticket splitting among government supporters. But Social Democratic strategists, mindful that Chancellor Schmidt's popularity exceeded that of his party by about 4 million votes, did, in the final phase of the campaign, encourage CDU/CSU, FDP, and undecided voters to split their ballots by, as Schmidt so often requested, "giving me your *Zweitstimme*" (second ballot vote).

Ticket splitting among SPD and FDP supporters in 1976 was not as widespread as in 1972. In 1972 the FDP's district vote amounted to only 57 percent of its total on the party-list ballot. In 1976, however, this increased to 81 percent. While in 1972, 53 percent of FDP second-ballot voters supported the SPD's district candidate, in 1976 only 30 percent of FDP supporters lent their first-ballot vote to a Social Democratic candidate. The proportion of FDP voters who remained faithful to their party in the district contests increased from 38 percent in 1972 to 61 percent in 1976. Likewise, as Table 2-3 shows, there was only a 1.1 percentage point difference between the district and list results for the SPD as compared to a 3.1 percentage point difference in 1972.

---

[3] These figures are projected on the basis of the analysis conducted by the Federal Statistical Office Wiesbaden of a representative sample of all ballots.

TABLE 2-3

MAJOR-PARTY VOTE ON FIRST AND SECOND BALLOTS, 1972 AND 1976

	SPD		CDU/CSU		FDP	
	1972	1976	1972	1976	1972	1976
First ballot	48.9	43.7	45.4	48.9	4.8	6.4
Second ballot	45.8	42.6	44.9	48.6	8.4	7.9
Difference (in percentage points)	3.1	1.1	0.5	0.3	3.6	1.5

SOURCE: See source for Table 2–2.

The district and party-list percentages for the CDU/CSU were virtually the same. The CDU/CSU's intensive publicity campaign during the last two weeks, which was designed to counter the SPD's attempt to encourage CDU/CSU supporters, who preferred Schmidt over Kohl, to split their ballot, was apparently successful.

Nomination and Candidate Selection. The electoral system is also an important structural factor influencing the recruitment and nomination of candidates in Bundestag elections. The party-list section of the ballot allows parties to bring into Parliament, through a high position on the list, representatives of interest groups and experts with specialized knowledge who would for various reasons (personality, background) have a difficult time winning a grass-roots campaign. A district campaign, on the other hand, affords candidates an opportunity to establish their personal vote-getting appeal. A strong district following gives an incumbent a measure of independence from the state or national party organization.

Since the electoral law also allows double candidacies, most major-party candidates (65 percent in 1976) nominated at the district level also seek favorable list positions as a safety net in the event of defeat in their districts. In some cases, a candidate may agree to stand in a hopeless district in exchange for a good list spot.

Constituency or district candidates, by law, must be nominated after a secret-ballot election either by all party members in the district or by a district selection committee which has been elected by the vote of the entire membership. This nomination must be made not more than one year before the election. The official nomination papers must also contain minutes of the selection meeting together with attendance records and voting results. The enforcement of these

35

legal provisions, however, has thus far been left to the parties themselves.

The selection of candidates for state lists takes place at party conventions held from six to eight weeks before election day. The construction of these lists is usually a controversial matter in which the various factions struggle and bargain to receive positions high enough to insure election or, in most cases, reelection.

At the constituency level, the entire process of candidate selection is, according to most observers, a relatively decentralized affair in which local party oligarchies and local issues play a more important role than they do in the construction of state lists. The grass-roots organizations are very sensitive to pressure from above and jealously seek to maintain their power. Indeed, there are reports that candidates of national prominence, especially at recent elections, seeking district nomination, feel themselves at a disadvantage compared with the so-called local matadors and under pressure to prove that they are sufficiently interested in local issues and in touch with the base. Moreover, the local selection process is becoming much more fraught with conflict than in the past. The proportion of district-level incumbents challenged for renomination increased from about 15 percent in 1965 to almost 50 percent by 1972.[4] This development reflects the influence of new members in the local party organizations and the emergence of contending ideological factions at the local level, especially in the SPD between Young Socialists (Jusos) and the established local leadership.

Criteria for selection. How does an aspiring German politico become a candidate for Parliament? Since most nominees are incumbents, the most obvious qualification is previous experience and good performance. In the absence of national experience, however, a good record in some local or state office is an important qualification. About half of all district candidates have held local office, and about a fourth have had some experience at the state level.[5] A reputation for being a good party man, a loyal, hard-working partisan, especially in local party work, also enhances the aspirant's prospects. Since the political culture values expertise, occupational and educational experience is a further qualification. Finally, the degree of interest-

---

[4] Carl-Christian Kaiser, "Jusos—unter ferner liefen" [Young Socialists as "also-rans"], *Die Zeit*, no. 40 (October 6, 1972), p. 3.

[5] See Heino Kaack, *Geschichte und Struktur des deutschen Parteiensystems* [History and structure of the German party system] (Opladen: Westdeutscher Verlag, 1971), pp. 595ff., for an extensive discussion of the candidate-selection process.

group support for a particular candidate and the character of the expected opposition also affect the local nomination process.[6]

A good position on the state list usually requires one or more of the following: state or national prominence, the support of top leaders of interest groups vital to the party (especially important in the CDU/CSU), leadership positions at the state or national level in key auxiliary organizations of the party (youth, women, refugees), and the support of important ideological groupings within the organization. Since the top three names on each party's state list are printed on the ballot, most states place the most prominent national or state leaders in these slots to aid in voter recognition.

The Course of the 1976 Campaign

As in other advanced Western societies, in Germany the style of election campaigns has become strongly influenced by professional advertising and public-relations techniques. All of the major parties contract with agencies for the design of their campaign appeals: slogans, posters, television spots, newspaper and magazine advertisements, all are professionally pretested to achieve, if possible, the desired effect upon the target group of voters. Nonetheless, it would be erroneous to assume that the West German version of Madison Avenue is a behind-the-scenes power in West German politics. The "message" or main themes of a campaign are determined, for the most part, by the parties, the public relations and advertising managers designing the manner in which these themes will be presented.

Preparations for advertising and media campaigns began in early 1976 and, especially in the case of the CDU/CSU, were "tested" in the last state election, held in Baden-Württemberg in April 1976. By June 1976 all the major parties had held their national preelection conventions at which their final election platforms were presented to the nation and the party faithful. The summer vacation season, however, meant that intensive campaigning would not begin until at least mid-August, six weeks before the poll.

In contrast to 1972, when the Brandt government's *Ostpolitik*,

---

[6] The selection process at the district level rarely produces a female nominee. In 1976 fewer than 5 percent of the SPD's district candidates and only about 6 percent of the CDU's nominees were women. The Bavarian affiliate of the CDU did not nominate a single woman for any of the forty-four Bavarian contests. At the state level, however, women candidates were more successful; about 10 percent of the list nominees of the three major parties in 1976 were female. Party leaders and activists apparently have fewer reservations about the vote-getting capacity of female candidates on state lists than at the district level. See *Das Parlament*, no. 39–40 (September 25, 1976), p. 2.

its policy of normalizing relations with Eastern Europe, had been of overriding importance, the 1976 campaign presented no central theme or issue. The opposition, while criticizing the government for being too generous in its relations with the Soviet Union and Eastern Europe, left no doubt that, if elected, it would uphold existing treaties. The rapidly improving economy and generally high level of economic prosperity removed major economic issues from the CDU campaign. Conflicts over the financial viability of the pension system, the presence of radicals in government service, and tax reform were hardly substitutes. In the absence of any overriding issue, much of the campaign revolved around more minor policy questions and the differences in personalities and styles of the candidates and parties.

Campaign Strategies: The Christian Democrats. In 1976, in contrast to 1972, it was the opposition Christian Democrats who conducted the most sophisticated, appealing electoral campaign. The CDU/CSU's campaign was the product of an extensive reorganization and revitalization of the party that had been underway since the disappointing 1972 election. This work of reorganization, in the course of which the party finally adapted to its position as the opposition, was complicated by the unresolved questions of who the party's leader and candidate for the chancellorship in 1976 would be. In addition, conflicts continued between the CDU's more moderate liberal wing and its conservative sister party in Bavaria, the Christian Social Union (CSU), led by the controversial Franz Josef Strauss. But, while the leadership issue and some important policy questions were not resolved until the end of 1975, the CDU, under the direction of its new general secretary, Kurt Biedenkopf, had been busily at work since 1973 attempting to revitalize the party's organization and image. Specifically between 1973 and 1976 the Union was able to (1) double its membership to about 700,000;[7] (2) replace many of its aging county, regional, and state officials with young, aggressive, full-time

---

[7] Most of the CDU party officials interviewed for this study ascribed this sharp gain in membership to the generally increased willingness of Germans to publicly display partisan preferences and to a reaction from those groups (medical doctors, dentists, realtors, pharmacists, and so on) who felt "defamed" by the attacks of the SPD-FDP and especially the Young Socialists (Jusos). The antiparty feeling of the postwar era has subsided and the "burned generation," once so skeptical of party-political commitment because of its Nazi experience, has overcome its inhibitions against formal affiliation with a party. Previously content to vote CDU and contribute money to the cause, these predominantly middle-aged and middle-class Germans have in a sense followed the lead of younger groups who were mobilized during the late 1960s and early 1970s by Socialist and Liberal promises of reform. What Willy Brandt, *Ostpolitik*, and the promised era of *innere Reform* (domestic reform) did for younger people in the late 1960s and early 1970s was

managers, recruited in many cases from government and business by sizable salary increases and the prospect of future government appointments; and (3) develop a sophisticated media and advertising strategy based on extensive public opinion research into the policy preferences of German voters and, above all, their dissatisfaction with the Socialist-Liberal government. There is little doubt that Biedenkopf, with his extensive expertise in management and marketing techniques, played a key role in giving the party this new look.

The CDU sought to project itself in 1976 as a broadly based integrative political force and the SPD as a narrow Socialist party ideologically committed to radical changes in the German economy, polity, and society. Germans were encouraged to vote CDU "out of love for Germany"[8] and for a "new national consciousness," a warm *gemuetlich* feeling towards the *Vaterland*, which would emerge under a CDU government. The party's candidate for chancellor, Helmut Kohl, was portrayed as a generalist who would integrate the narrow, specialized activities of government, and as a warm, open "man you can trust," in contrast to the cold, impersonal Helmut Schmidt. Avoiding specific policy issues, Kohl, in over 140 campaign appearances, spoke in general terms about the need to return to the basic values of home, family, property, achievement, virtue, dignity, authority, partnership, patriotism, and *Vaterland*. This folksy, informal style irritated the opposition and provoked the disdain of intellectuals and apparently most journalists,[9] but it was effective. Survey data show that the electorate perceived Kohl as "more sympathetic" and "warmer" than the chancellor.[10]

The conservatives in the CDU and especially the hard-liners

accomplished for the middle-aged by Helmut Kohl and the specter of Swedish-style socialism in the Federal Republic.

To be sure, we are still dealing with a relatively small number of activists (200,000–250,000) who comprise only a tiny fraction of the electorate, but within the activist strata this mobilization of the "defamed" was an unanticipated consequence of Young Socialist agitation against privileged groups during 1973–1974. Certainly it is not unrealistic to assume, for example, that the Juso demand for the elimination of private real-estate brokers prompted at least some members of this profession to flock to the Christian Democrats.

[8] This slogan was very similar to the "out of love for your laundry" (*Aus Liebe zur Waesche*) once used by the Henkel chemical concern to promote a leading detergent. Biedenkopf was the general manager of Henkel from 1971 to 1973.

[9] See Kohl's interview with the writer Walter Kempowski, "Was lesen Sie, Herr Kohl?" [What are you reading, Herr Kohl?], *Zeit Magazin*, no. 36 (August 20, 1976), p. 4ff. On the response of journalists, see Rolf Zundel, "Bonner Wahlbuehne" [Bonn electoral stage], *Die Zeit*, no. 41 (October 1, 1976), p. 8.

[10] Surveys cited in *Der Spiegel*, no. 37 (September 6, 1976), p. 78; no. 39 (September 20, 1976), p. 52ff., and no. 40 (September 27, 1976), p. 44ff.

around Strauss in the CSU were not satisfied with this strategy and insisted that there had to be a hard, confrontative component in the party's electoral appeal. The conservatives were largely placated by the adoption of the national campaign slogan "Freedom or Socialism," which had been used with success in state elections in Bavaria and Hesse in 1975 and in Baden-Württemberg in 1976. The more liberal elements in the party were able to make a minor modification in the slogan, substituting "instead of" for "or," but even "Freedom instead of Socialism" aroused little enthusiasm in the Kohl-Biedenkopf wing. Nonetheless, during the final weeks of the campaign, Kohl appeared to embrace the hard-line slogan, to the dismay of party liberals. As his chief campaign adviser put it, "one cannot win a campaign as Hamlet."[11]

The disagreement over the content of the party's electoral appeal did not extend, however, to questions of campaign timing and style. In 1976 the CDU began its intensive advertising campaign several weeks before the government and had its enlarged membership out campaigning long before the SPD and FDP had mobilized their adherents.[12] This early start was prompted largely by the findings of the German pollster Elisabeth Noelle-Neumann. After the 1972 election, in a series of articles, Noelle-Neumann had sought to explain the unexpected size of the SPD-FDP victory through the effect that the climate of opinion has on the undecided segment of the electorate, generally estimated at about 15 to 20 percent.[13] She argued that in 1972 the visibility of the SPD-FDP's appeals and the greater readiness of their supporters to express their partisan views had created the impression that the majority of the electorate favored the government even though the actual strengths of the government and the opposition were about equal. The perception that the government was winning had put opposition supporters on the defensive and had made them less likely to express their pro-CDU/CSU opinions. Accord-

---

[11] Nina Grunenberg, "Wer nur den lieben Gott laesst walten" [If thou but suffer God to guide thee], *Die Zeit*, no. 41 (October 1, 1976), p. 2.

[12] Nina Grunenberg, "So schoen wie bei Adenauer" [Just as nice as under Adenauer] *Die Zeit*, no. 37 (September 3, 1976), p. 5.

[13] See especially Elisabeth Noelle-Neumann, "Wahlentscheidung in der Fernsehendemokratie. Eine sozial-psychologische Interpretation der Bundestagswahl 1972" [Electoral decision in a television democracy: a sociopsychological interpretation of the 1972 federal election], in Dieter Just and Lothar Romain, eds., *Auf der Suche nach dem muendigen Waehler. Die Wahlentscheidung 1972 und ihre Konsequenzen* [Searching for the responsible voter: the 1972 electoral decision and its effects] (Bonn: Koellen Verlag, 1974), and Elisabeth Noelle-Neumann, "The Spiral of Silence: A Theory of Public Opinion," *Journal of Communication*, vol. 24, no. 2 (Spring 1974).

ing to Noelle-Neumann, a "spiral of silence" had developed among CDU/CSU partisans, which, combined with the increasing confidence of SPD-FDP supporters, had won over to the government the bulk of the undecided voters, that is, those voters with little political interest who had become aware of the campaign at a late stage and had relied for their information on the media (especially television), chance personal encounters, and exposure to advertisements and posters.

Union strategists, especially the new general secretary, Kurt Biedenkopf, were intrigued by Noelle-Neumann's thesis and sought to make the spiral of silence work to the benefit of the Union in 1976. At the party's convention in Hamburg in December 1973, her findings were presented to the party leaders. In 1974 simplified summaries of the spiral-of-silence concept were given to the party's activists at the local level and a membership drive was initiated that would double the formal membership by 1976. Finally, the decision to begin the Union's nationwide advertising and poster campaigns before those of the SPD was also a result of the Noelle-Neumann thesis, which, in operational terms, meant that the party had to become visible before the SPD campaign could get into full swing.

In 1976 the CDU/CSU was, for the most part, successful in making its appeals and campaign more visible to the general public than it had been in 1972. As the data in Table 2-4 show, the proportion

TABLE 2-4
POPULAR PERCEPTIONS OF PARTY CAMPAIGN ACTIVITY, 1972 AND 1976
(in percentages of responses)

Question: What is your impression: which party's supporters are now the most active in the campaign, which are making the greatest personal effort?

Most Active Party	1972	1976
CDU/CSU	8	30
SPD	44	18
FDP	7	3
All the same	33	42
Undecided	10	9
Total	102	102

NOTE: Figures do not add to 100 because of rounding.

SOURCE: Elisabeth Noelle-Neumann, "Kampf um die oeffentliche Meinung. Eine vergleichende sozialpsychologische Analyse der Bundestagswahlen 1972 und 1976" [The struggle for the support of public opinion: a comparative sociopsychological analysis of the 1972 and 1976 federal elections], unpublished, Institut für Demoskopie, Allensbach, 1977, p. 26.

of the electorate that perceived CDU/CSU supporters to be the most active in the campaign increased from only 8 percent in 1972 to 30 percent in 1976. The proportion of voters who thought that the adherents of the government parties (SPD-FDP) were the most active dropped from 51 percent in 1972 to only 21 percent in 1976. Surveys conducted during the campaign also found that CDU/CSU supporters were more engaged, more ready to "do something" for the party, than SPD and FDP activists.[14]

The contradiction, however, between the "soft" image of Kohl and the "hard" tone of the "Freedom instead of/or Socialism" theme created problems for the Union, especially in the northern and western industrialized districts. Indeed, the implication of the slogan, that freedom and socialism are mutually exclusive, was accepted by little more than a third of the electorate; the remainder either stated that there was "sufficient freedom also under socialism" (39 percent) or were undecided (25 percent).[15] Nonetheless, the focus on Kohl and the well-planned CDU/CSU campaign were major improvements over the diffuse, fragmented team approach used in 1972. Despite the contradiction in campaign image caused by the slogan, the CDU/CSU's real problems in 1976 began *after* the election, not during the campaign.

Campaign Strategies: The Social Democrats. The SPD's campaign, too, was prepared by professional media, public relations, and polling specialists.[16] Unlike the CDU/CSU, however, the SPD, with its larger party organization, was slow to begin the campaign. While the CDU had completed the first wave of its nationwide advertising by mid-August, the SPD's National Executive discovered at its August 25 meeting that much of its initial postering had yet to be completed.[17] Chancellor Schmidt's staff was disappointed at what it perceived to be the lethargic state of the party organization, which in turn was not as enthusiastic about Schmidt's candidacy as it had been about Willy Brandt's in 1972. Generally the coordination between the chancellor's office, the SPD organization, and the government's Press and Information Office was inadequate, at least during the early phases of the campaign. The Young Socialists, to the relief of both the government

---

[14] Arnim von Malinowsky, "Muss Wahlkampf sein?" [Must there be an election campaign?], *Der Stern*, no. 41 (September 30, 1976), p. 33.

[15] Ibid., p. 34.

[16] For an account of the role of public relations firms in the 1976 campaign, see Gunhild Freese, "Wie verkaufe ich Kohl?" [How do I sell Kohl?] *Zeit Magazin*, no. 39 (September 17, 1976), pp. 7–18.

[17] *Frankfurter Allgemeine Zeitung*, September 17, 1976, p. 2.

and the SPD party leadership, maintained a very low profile throughout the campaign.

The SPD's major strategic advantage in 1976, as in 1972, was the chancellor. The "chancellor bonus," that is, the advantage of incumbency, worked to Schmidt's benefit in 1976 just as it had for all chancellors before him.[18] Ever since Kohl had emerged as the CDU/CSU's leader in late 1975, he had been outranked by Schmidt by from ten to fifteen percentage points in the popularity polls.[19] In the final preelection polls, Schmidt was preferred over Kohl for chancellor by 48 percent of the respondents, as against 35 percent who preferred Kohl, a margin of thirteen percentage points. The CDU, however, was the preferred party of about 48 percent of the electorate, while the SPD enjoyed the support of only 40 percent. Thus, Schmidt was more popular than his party, while Kohl's personal support was below that of his party. Schmidt was regarded as more competent, a better speaker, and more a man of the people. Kohl was able to outdistance the chancellor only in the general trust and confidence category ("from whom would you buy a used car?").[20]

The SPD's strategic emphasis on Chancellor Schmidt reached its high point during the last three weeks of the campaign. This "chancellor phase" featured a nationwide advertising campaign in the press stressing that "the better man must remain chancellor" and reminding voters of the importance of the second ballot. In these advertisements the SPD was appealing not only to undecided voters, but also to CDU/CSU supporters who were dissatisfied with their party's candidate. Surveys had found that as many as one out of every four CDU/CSU voters regarded Schmidt as better qualified than Kohl, and the SPD

---

[18] For data from 1961 through 1972, see David P. Conradt, *The West German Party System* (Beverly Hills and London: Sage Publications, 1972), pp. 13 and 48, and David P. Conradt and Dwight Lambert, "Party System, Social Structure, and Competitive Politics in West Germany," *Comparative Politics*, vol. 7 (October 1974), pp. 64–65. It is difficult to separate the culturally induced "chancellor bonus" from the personalities of the chancellor and his opponent. Yet the case of former Chancellor Brandt is certainly indicative of a chancellor effect: as SPD leader, Brandt consistently ranked behind Adenauer (1961–1963), Erhard (1963–1966), and Kiesinger (1966–1969), the first three chancellors of the Federal Republic; yet after becoming chancellor in 1969 he far outranked any CDU/CSU leader. Kohl's popularity rating, however, was greater than that of any other nonincumbent chancellor candidate since public opinion polling on this topic began in the 1950s.

[19] See *Der Spiegel*, no. 37 (September 6, 1976), p. 78, for relevant time-series data from several polling organizations.

[20] Forschungsgruppe Wahlen [Electoral research group], "Bundestagswahl 1976, Eine Analyse der Wahl zum 8. Deutschen Bundestag am 3. Oktober, 1976" [The 1976 federal election: an analysis of the election to the eighth German Parliament on October 3, 1976], unpublished, Mannheim, October 1976, pp. 86–90.

43

was, in effect, inviting these voters to split their ballots, that is, to support CDU/CSU candidates in their districts but vote for Chancellor Schmidt on the second ballot. To be sure, this type of appeal did little to encourage many SPD district candidates, who felt deserted by their national organization, but the fact that Schmidt was more popular than the SPD, and his opponent, Kohl, less popular than the CDU/CSU, left SPD strategists little choice if their prime goal was the return of the Socialist-Liberal coalition with an adequate majority.

In addition to the strong emphasis on Schmidt's superior leadership ability, the SPD and the chancellor stressed several other themes during the campaign: (1) West Germany as a model of economic prosperity and social stability, (2) the government's and the chancellor's skillful handling of the 1974–1976 recession, (3) the dangers posed to social peace and stability by the CDU/CSU's alleged plan to cut back on welfare programs while lowering taxes for business and industrial interests, (4) the continuation of a foreign policy aimed at the normalization of relations and relaxation of tensions with Eastern Europe (including East Germany) and the Soviet Union, and (5) the inexperience of the CDU's candidate Helmut Kohl and his subservience to Franz Josef Strauss, whom the SPD denounced for his foreign and domestic policies and portrayed as a radical threat to West German democracy. The SPD and Schmidt directed their campaign far more against Strauss ("the cook") than Kohl ("the waiter").

Within the context of these major themes, specialized appeals were made to pensioners, women, and that segment of the electorate concerned with educational policy, specifically the question of admission to the universities. The chancellor stressed that CDU/CSU charges of fiscal irresponsibility in the handling of pension funds were unfounded and that the system was in sound financial condition. Women voters were reminded of the government's passage of liberalized divorce and abortion laws as well as changes in the civil legal code that allow a married woman to keep her maiden name and take a job outside the home without her husband's permission. To those concerned about university admissions, the government proposed the elimination of the highly controversial numerical entrance quotas (*numerus clausus*).

In spite of its late start, the SPD campaign was in full swing by mid-September. While unable to match the enthusiasm generated by Brandt in 1972, Schmidt and the SPD generally were able to mobilize the party's proletarian core and prevent significant inroads into major industrial areas. Nonetheless the SPD was on the defensive for most of the campaign, reacting to the initiatives and criticisms of the cdu/csu. There is little doubt that the opposition set the tone during the 1976 campaign. In post-election campaign analyses, the party leadership, including Schmidt, agreed that the SPD campaign had lacked the expressive style and feeling so effectively exploited by Kohl.[21]

Campaign Strategies: The Free Democrats. For the Free Democrats every federal election could be the last. The FDP has not secured a double-digit percentage of the vote since 1965, and the party, in designing its electoral strategy, must above all seek to avoid dropping below the 5 percent needed to secure parliamentary representation. With a minuscule percentage of hard-core voters (about 3 percent), the FDP must attract supporters anew at every election.

In 1976, as in 1972, the FDP pledged at the outset of the campaign that it would, if possible, remain in coalition with the Social Democrats. About two of every three FDP supporters favored the continuation of the alignment with the SPD over one with the cdu/csu. Yet as a small third party, the FDP must avoid becoming identified as merely a satellite of its bigger partner. This necessity to establish its own identity and independence places the party in a position of what might be called intragovernmental opposition, projecting itself as the Liberal corrective to the "unrealistic," if not "radical," policies of the Social Democrats.

In the 1976 campaign the party also emphasized the achievements of its four cabinet ministers: Hans-Dietrich Genscher (foreign affairs), Hans Friderichs (economics), Josef Ertl (agriculture), and Werner Maihofer (internal affairs). These four usually campaigned together and were featured in the party's television spots. Genscher, as vice-chancellor and FDP national chairman, was also given solo exposure in widely distributed posters. The style of the party's campaign and the low-key, factual content of its appeals left little doubt that it was aiming at "critical voters," those of above average education with largely urban, middle-class occupations, moderately concerned with reform, yet suspicious of some of the ideologies within the SPD. The Free Democrats, while generally defending the SPD as preferable to the cdu/csu as a coalition partner, left little doubt that they had differences with the Social Democrats.

Most opinion polls, including many completed just prior to voting day, had predicted that the party would improve on its 1972 performance (8.4 percent). But the FDP, with the most unstable electorate of any party represented in Parliament, lost supporters to the SPD as

[21] *Der Spiegel*, no. 42 (October 11, 1976), p. 21.

the campaign, in its final stages, polarized around the two candidates for chancellor. Also, the FDP received far fewer votes on loan from the SPD than it had in 1972: it probably lost votes as a result of Chancellor Schmidt's "give me your second vote" appeal and his repeated admonition to SPD voters to let the FDP win its votes from CDU supporters. Surveys have also found that for a part of the electorate, estimated at about 5 percent of the total or 10 percent of the combined SPD-FDP vote, the two parties are perceived as almost identical. These voters can shift their support easily and quickly from one party to the other. This exchange had favored the FDP in 1972, but, under the influence of the SPD's last-stage second-vote campaign, it hurt the FDP in 1976.[22]

Effects of the Campaign. As Table 2-5 shows, the general distribution of support for the opposition CDU/CSU and the governing Social and Free Democrats changed little during the campaign. The only significant change was between the coalition partners, with the SPD gaining support, largely from FDP voters, in the latter stages of the race. Between the beginning of September and election day, October 3, support for the FDP dropped from 12 percent to about 8 percent while the Social Democrats increased their support by an almost identical margin.

At the individual level, the campaign apparently did not intensify partisan feelings or polarize the voters. A 1976 panel survey found

TABLE 2-5

INTENDED PARTY VOTE, MID-AUGUST TO LATE SEPTEMBER 1976

(in percentages)

Intended Vote	Survey Date				Election Result, October 3
	Mid-August	Early September	Mid-September	Late September	
CDU/CSU	47.5	48.0	48.0	47.5	48.6
SPD	40.8	39.0	40.5	41.6	42.6
FDP	10.6	11.8	10.5	9.5	7.9
Other	1.1	1.2	1.0	1.4	0.9
Total	100.0	100.0	100.0	100.0	100.0

SOURCE: Surveys conducted by the Institut fuer Demoskopie, reported in *Der Stern*, no. 41 (September 30, 1976), p. 17. The national samples were composed of registered voters.

---

[22] *Allensbacher Berichte* [Allensbach reports], no. 38 (October 1976), p. 4.

that the proportion of German voters who regarded *all* major parties as ones they could conceivably support *increased* during the election campaign from 26 percent to 34 percent.[23] The campaign made some partisans more willing to consider the "other side" as a possible alternative. Even among strong partisans, the opposing party or parties were not evaluated more negatively, but less so, in the course of the campaign.[24] Thus, the often bitter rhetoric of the party leaders, particularly evident in the mammoth three-hour television debate between Schmidt, Genscher, Kohl, and Strauss at the end of the campaign, had little apparent effect among the electorate.

Campaign and Party Finance. The highly professional character of the campaign, the affluence of West German society in the 1970s, the rejuvenated opposition, and public subsidies to the political parties all insured that campaign spending in 1976 would reach an all-time high —and it did. While their American counterparts in 1976 were struggling with the limits imposed by the new presidential campaign financing laws, German party leaders knew no such constraints, though the parties voluntarily "pledged" that expenditures in 1976 would not exceed those made in 1972. In addition to their public relations, advertising, and public opinion advisers, the parties hired professional firms to conduct nationwide poster and advertising campaigns, rather than leaving these to the party faithful. Millions of multicolored posters, stickers, buttons, lapel pins, flags, key chains, T-shirts, bottle openers, dust cloths, umbrellas, and records were distributed to voters by the three Bundestag parties. The SPD even took out a full-page ad in the mass circulation magazine *Der Stern* with a free bumper sticker attached. The printed-media campaign began in earnest in mid-August, although extensive "advitorials" were placed in limited-circulation elite periodicals (*Der Spiegel, Die Zeit, Wirtschaftswoche*) as early as April.

Although all three parties claimed poverty and the two major parties traded accusations about "buying the election," there is no indication that at least the two large parties had any financial problems. As in most other advanced industrial democratic societies, in Germany reliable evidence on campaign spending is difficult to obtain. But most observers put the combined 1972 expenditures of the parties at about DM180 million ($72 million). Officially the parties claimed to have only DM145 million budgeted for 1976, but it has been esti-

---

[23] Forschungsgruppe, "Bundestagswahl 1976," pp. 85–86.
[24] Ibid., p. 86.

mated that the final tab for 1976 will reach DM225 million ($90 million) or 25 percent more than was spent in 1972[25]

Each party received about half of its campaign funds from the public treasury. According to the provisions of the 1967 Party Finance Law as amended in 1976, each party securing more than 0.5 percent of the second-ballot vote (slightly over 200,000 votes) receives DM3.5 (about $1.40) for each vote. The parties may receive advances on this amount to wage the campaign, with a settlement of accounts taking place after the final tally. Thus, in 1976 the parties together received about DM150 million from the state. Their additional funds came from members' dues (especially important for the SPD), including assessments made of party office holders, and contributions, which are crucial to the financial well-being of the middle-class parties (CDU/CSU and FDP).[26]

The Outcome: An Analysis of the Results

The 1976 federal election, the eighth in the Republic's twenty-seven-year history, saw the return of the Socialist-Liberal coalition that has governed Germany since 1969, but with a majority of only ten seats, down sharply from the forty-six-seat advantage the coalition held after the November 1972 poll. The opposition CDU/CSU not only regained its status as Germany's largest party, but also achieved its highest proportion of the party-list vote since 1957 and reversed the steady gains the Social Democrats have achieved at every election since 1957.

In addition, and perhaps more significantly, in 1976 the CDU/CSU won an absolute majority (54 percent) of *direct mandates* for the first time since 1965, while the SPD, which captured 61 percent of the single-member district contests in 1972, lost thirty-nine direct mandates and dropped to 46 percent of the total. Thus, under an Anglo-American electoral system the Christian Democrats would have won an absolute majority of Bundestag seats in 1976.

The Social Democrats were reduced to about their 1969 level, and the slim majority held by the new SPD-FDP government is very similar to the one that emerged from the 1969 election. Unlike the 1969 majority, however, the present SPD and FDP delegations in the Bundestag include few, if any, opponents of the coalition. Thus, it is less

---

[25] Wolfgang Hoffmann, "Strohmaenner fuer Millionen" [Straw men for millions], *Die Zeit*, no. 40 (September 24, 1976), p. 17.
[26] For an excellent study of German party finances through the 1972 election, see Uwe Schleth, *Parteifinanzen* [Party finances] (Meisenheim am Glan: Anton Hain Verlag, 1973).

likely that deputy defections to the CDU/CSU will erode the government's ten-seat majority than it was during the first SPD-FDP coalition government under Willy Brandt.

With just under 8 percent of the party-list vote and thirty-nine parliamentary seats, down slightly from the 8.4 percent and forty-one seats they secured in 1972, the Free Democrats fared somewhat better than their coalition partner. Nonetheless, the result was disappointing to the FDP's leadership and strategists, who had hoped for a double-digit percentage of the poll.

Turnout. The rounded turnout figures for German national elections since 1949 are as follows:

Election	Turnout
1949	79
1953	86
1957	88
1961	88
1965	87
1969	87
1972	91
1976	91

The 1976 figure (90.7) was only slightly below the record 91.1 percent recorded in 1972. The high turnout in 1972 has been attributed to the importance of the campaign issues, above all *Ostpolitik*. In contrast, the 1976 campaign was characterized, according to most observers, by the absence of any gripping theme. How can one explain, then, the continued high turnout? One possible answer (apart from the excellent weather on election day) is that the issues were more important in 1976 than has been assumed. While in 1976, unlike 1972, there was no single dominant issue, a variety of concerns aroused interest of varying intensity in different segments of the electorate. Another possible factor is the greater success of the CDU/CSU in mobilizing its supporters in 1976 in comparison to 1972. The Union's candidate, Kohl, was more popular than Barzel had been in 1972 among Union voters, and the national media campaigns focused exclusively on Kohl, while in 1972 the CDU/CSU campaign had adopted a team approach. In addition, the generally greater visibility of the Union in 1976 and the closeness of the race may have offset the absence of any emotional issue.

Nationally, as in 1972, the SPD was aided slightly by the high turnout. The correlation between the party's 1976 vote and the turnout ($r = +.11$) indicates that at the national level the SPD was helped by the turnout. The relationship between the Union's vote and turnout ($r = -.03$) indicates that the CDU/CSU was neither helped nor hindered in 1976. The Free Democrats, however, with their relatively narrow middle-class base, generally did less well in areas of high voter turnout ($r = -.23$) than they had at the previous election.

Bases of Party Support. By examining the results of the 1976 election in the 248 districts and relating them to the sociodemographic and religious composition of the districts, we can gain a clearer picture of the sources of gains and losses for the parties in 1976. As Table 2-6 indicates, CDU/CSU gains in 1976 were greatest in the 77 metropolitan districts. With 42.3 percent of the party vote in these urban, white-collar areas, the CDU/CSU achieved its best support level since 1957. The Christian Democratic gains in these areas probably came largely from former SPD supporters. The correlation between the CDU/CSU's 1972–1976 change index[27] and that of the SPD in metropolitan constituencies was −.48, indicating a strong competitive relationship, as compared to −.22 in industrial districts and −.19 in the 56 rural constituencies.

Moreover, when we subdivide these seats by their religious composition, we find that in Catholic-metropolitan seats, CDU/CSU gains in 1976 averaged 4.7 percentage points, again an eighteen-year high. These were the same districts which in 1969 went very strongly to the SPD (the 1965-1969 swing to the SPD was 8.2 percentage points).[28] In 1976 the 9.3 percentage-point swing to the CDU/CSU was the largest in any of the nine constituency types (Table 2-7). Generally, as Table 2-7 indicates, the election districts with high proportions of white-collar workers and civil servants were the most volatile between 1972 and 1976, as they were in 1969.[29] Although the Union was still in a minority position in these white-collar areas, its gains in 1976 and its continued exploitation of its south-German Catholic and rural strongholds were the key factors in its 1976 electoral success.

The party change index is a measure of *relative* gains made between two elections in each district. The two-party swing measures the change in the relationship between the two large parties between

---

[27] The party change index for 1972–76 was simply:
$$\text{Index} = \frac{\text{Party Vote 1976} \cdot \text{Turnout 1976}}{\text{Party Vote 1972} \cdot \text{Turnout 1972}} \cdot 100$$
The second-ballot (party-list) total was used for the computation of the index.

[28] "Swing" is here defined as the percentage-point difference between the CDU/CSU and SPD in 1976 minus the percentage-point difference between the two parties in 1972.

[29] Conradt and Lambert, *Social Structure*, pp. 68–69.

1972 and 1976. In Table 2-7 the change indices for the SPD, CDU/CSU, and FDP and the CDU/CSU swing from 1972 to 1976 are presented by district type. While the CDU/CSU increased its support in all districts, its greatest *relative* gains were made in religiously mixed and Catholic

TABLE 2-6
MEAN SHIFT IN MAJOR-PARTY VOTE, 1972–1976, BY DISTRICT TYPE
(in percentage-point gains and losses)

District Classification (number of districts in parentheses)	Shift, 1972–1976		
	SPD	CDU/CSU	FDP
Occupational composition			
Metropolitan (77)	−3.4	+4.0	−0.8
Industrial (115)	−3.0	+3.7	−0.5
Agricultural (56)	−3.2	+3.4	−0.1
Religious composition			
Catholic (86)	−3.6	+3.8	0.0
Protestant (87)	−3.6	+3.4	−0.5
Mixed (75)	−2.9	+3.8	−0.9
Occupational-religious composition			
Metropolitan-Catholic (22)	−4.5	+4.7	−0.4
Metropolitan-Protestant (27)	−2.7	+3.1	−0.6
Metropolitan-mixed (28)	−2.8	+4.2	−1.4
Industrial-Catholic (32)	−3.0	+3.4	0.0
Industrial-Protestant (41)	−3.0	+3.9	−0.6
Industrial-mixed (42)	−3.0	+3.6	−0.5
Agricultural-Catholic (32)	−3.7	+3.5	+0.3
Agricultural-Protestant (19)	−2.3	+2.8	−0.5
Agricultural-mixed (5)	−3.4	+4.2	−0.8
All districts (248)	−3.2	+3.7	−0.5

NOTE: Electoral districts were classified as follows:

(1) According to occupational composition. (a) Metropolitan districts were those in which the percentage of white-collar workers (*Angestellte*) and civil servants exceeded 42 percent; these were all located in cities with populations above 200,000. (b) Industrial districts were those in which the percentage of manual workers exceeded 50 percent; these were in distinctly less urban areas. (c) Agricultural districts were those in which the percentage of self-employed nonmanuals and farmers exceeded 25 percent; in these districts the average number of inhabitants per square kilometer was a very low 117.9. There were no overlapping constituencies.

(2) According to religious affiliation expressed at the 1970 census. (a) Catholic districts were those in which 60 percent or more of the population was Catholic; (b) Protestant districts were those in which 60 percent or more of the population was Protestant; (c) mixed districts were those in which no one sect claimed 60 percent of the population.

SOURCE: Author's calculations based on 1970 census figures and official election returns.

TABLE 2-7
MAJOR-PARTY CHANGE INDEX AND SWING, 1972–1976, BY DISTRICT TYPE

District Classification (number of districts in parentheses)	Party Change Index			Swing
	SPD	CDU	FDP	
Occupational composition				
Metropolitan (77)	92.6	109.2	93.1	7.3
Industrial (115)	93.3	107.9	96.9	6.6
Agricultural (56)	91.5	106.7	101.9	6.6
Religious composition				
Catholic (86)	90.0	106.7	102.7	7.2
Protestant (87)	94.5	108.4	94.8	6.9
Mixed (75)	93.7	109.2	92.4	6.5
Occupational-religious composition				
Metropolitan-Catholic (22)	88.9	109.4	96.8	9.3
Metropolitan-Protestant (27)	94.4	107.8	95.0	5.9
Metropolitan-mixed (28)	94.0	110.3	88.3	7.0
Industrial-Catholic (32)	92.0	105.9	101.8	6.4
Industrial-Protestant (41)	94.0	109.3	94.4	6.8
Industrial-mixed (42)	93.7	108.5	95.5	6.2
Agricultural-Catholic (32)	88.7	105.7	107.6	7.4
Agricultural-Protestant (19)	96.1	107.3	95.6	5.1
Agricultural-mixed (5)	92.1	108.4	89.0	7.7
All districts (248)	92.7	108.0	96.8	6.9

NOTE: For an explanation of the district classifications, see note to Table 2–6.
SOURCE: Author's calculations based on 1970 census figures and official election returns.

metropolitan districts, Protestant and mixed industrial areas, and the five mixed rural constituencies. The SPD lost, in relative terms, most heavily in Catholic metropolitan and rural seats, where its 1976 vote dropped by over eleven percentage points. The SPD's traditionally low percentage of the vote in the rural Catholic districts dropped even more as its junior coalition partner gained at its expense.

The FDP suffered its greatest losses in metropolitan areas, especially those with neither strong Catholic nor strong Protestant majorities. In these twenty-eight districts, the party lost almost 12 percentage points of its 1972 support. In industrial and agricultural districts, however, the party's losses were below the national average, and in Catholic agrarian and industrial districts, the FDP actually made slight gains (although in the Catholic agrarian seats, the FDP's share of the vote had previously been so low—about 5.0 percent—that little significance should be attached to these gains).

Evidence that in 1976 the cdu/csu made new inroads into areas that had previously been dominated by the governing parties is provided in Table 2-8, where the correlations between the Union's 1976 vote and its 1972-1976 change index are presented. While the cdu/csu vote in 1976, as in previous elections, generally is negatively correlated with variables such as the proportion of Protestants in a district, educational level, and variables associated with heavily urban areas (small household size, high proportion of white-collar workers, and high proportion of households with telephones), the Union's 1972-1976 change index is positively related to these variables. This indicates that the party in 1976 was indeed making gains in areas usually associated with low cdu/csu support, the urban white-collar districts. This is also supported by the negative correlation (−.33) found between the change index and the proportion of farmers in the district; the correlation between the cdu/csu's 1976 vote and the proportion of farmers is a strong +.54. Note finally the negative relationship (−.45) between the Union's 1972 vote and its 1972-1976 change index. In those districts where the Union's percentage of the

TABLE 2–8

CORRELATIONS BETWEEN SOCIOECONOMIC VARIABLES AND 1976 CDU/CSU
VOTE AND 1972–1976 CDU/CSU CHANGE INDEX

Variable	Correlation with 1976 Vote	Correlation with 1972–1976 Change Index
Protestants in district	−.63	+.22
Farmers in district	+.54	−.33
White-collar employees in district	−.58	+.34
Residents with academic high school education (*Abitur*)	−.30	+.26
Residents with university-level training	−.17	+.22
Average household size	+.65	−.41
Households with telephones	−.37	+.16
cdu/csu vote, 1972	+.98	−.45

NOTE: Entries are Pearsonian correlation coefficients computed, except for average household size, on the basis of percentages. The unit of analysis is the Bundestag election district ($N = 248$).

SOURCE: Author's calculations based on 1970 census figures and official election returns.

poll in 1972 was low, its 1972-1976 change index was high and, conversely, where the Union did well in 1972, its 1976 gains were lower. Thus, while the 1972 and 1976 Union votes are highly correlated (+.98), the relationship between the 1972 poll and 1976 gains is negative. *The CDU/CSU's greatest relative gains in 1976 were not in its areas of traditional strength; its 1976 gains represent a broadening of the party's social base.*[30]

Age and party choice. While social class and religion remain important determinants of the party vote, since the late 1960s differences in political behavior and attitudes between different age groups have become discernible. At the elections of 1969 and 1972, the SPD or FDP was the choice of most young Germans voting for the first time.[31] According to 1976 survey data presented in Table 2-9, this group (in 1976, between twenty-four and twenty-nine), which supported the governing parties by about a two-to-one margin in 1972, continued to strongly favor the Socialist-Liberal coalition in 1976. The eighteen to twenty-three age group, however, most of whom entered the electorate in 1976, had experienced as adolescents the 1974-1975 recession with its high unemployment for young people, the fall of the Brandt government, and the reduced opportunities for admission to the universities and even vocational education. While 67 percent of the "Brandt generation" (who entered the electorate between 1969 and 1972) intended to support the SPD-FDP alignment in 1976, slightly over 60 percent of the post-1972 cohort had such intentions.

Among older groups, however, the CDU/CSU enjoyed a clear advantage in 1976. The so-called war generation, who were between fifty and sixty-five in 1976 and whose first participation in democratic politics had been, for the most part, at the elections of 1949, 1953, and 1957 (the latter two, decisive CDU/CSU victories) continued its allegiance to the Union, as did respondents who were over sixty-five, most of whom had entered the national electorate in the last stormy years of the Weimar Republic. Over 60 percent of this group intended to support the Union in 1976.

---

[30] The oft-discussed "north-south cleavage" (*Nord-Sued Gefaelle*) in voting behavior—that is, the greater support for the SPD and FDP north of the Main River and the increased strength of the CDU or CSU in districts south of this boundary—was also in evidence at this election. But this regional variation is largely the result of religious and other socioeconomic factors. The southern states are more Catholic, rural, and "old" middle class (independent shopkeepers, artisans) than the Protestant urban-industrial states in the north. In our analysis of the aggregate statistics, the separate effects of region became minimal when the socioeconomic composition of the districts was taken into account.

[31] Conradt and Lambert, *Social Structure*, pp. 70-71.

TABLE 2–9
VOTING INTENTIONS, BY AGE, 1976
(in percentages)

Respondent Intends to Vote For	Age Group				
	18–23	24–29	30–49	50–65	Over 65
SPD or FDP	60.3	67.3	54.1	46.3	38.3
CDU/CSU	37.8	31.3	45.1	52.3	61.2
Other	1.9	1.4	0.8	1.4	0.5
Total	100.0	100.0	100.0	100.0	100.0
Birth date	1953–1958	1947–1952	1927–1946	1911–1926	Before 1911

SOURCE: Adapted from Rudolf Wildenmann, "Wie die Deutschen waehlen" [How the Germans vote], *Capital*, no. 8 (August 1976), p. 39.

Summary. In 1976 the CDU/CSU reversed the trend toward provincialization that had been so noticeable at the 1969 and 1972 elections. In those years the party had lost most of its strength outside the static or declining sectors of the population—farmers, small shopkeepers, independent artisans. But in 1976 the Union, in spite of its conservative wing, made inroads into heavily urban metropolitan areas that had been the domain of the SPD and FDP in 1969 and 1972.

For the Social Democrats, the inability of the CDU/CSU to make greater gains in Protestant areas and the fidelity of manual workers to the party saved it and the government from an even sharper decline. As it had in 1972, the party did best in Protestant and industrial areas. The trend of increasing urban, middle-class support for the Socialists, so apparent in 1969, slowed in 1972 and stopped at the October 1976 election.

The FDP in 1976, in spite of marginal gains in rural and Catholic areas, remained a party of the young, urban middle class with above-average levels of education. Its vote, both in 1972 and 1976, correlates more strongly, for example, with the level of advanced educational training than that of any other party. In metropolitan areas it remains an especially formidable opponent for both Christian and Social Democrats.

Concluding Remarks

The 1976 election continues the trend of closer, more intense party competition first apparent in the mid-1960s and confirmed at the 1969 federal election. The results also certainly indicate that the 1949–1969 hegemony of the Christian Democrats will not, in the foreseeable future, be followed by a comparable period of SPD dominance. Between 1949 and 1969 no stable national government was possible without the participation of the Christian Democrats; the German party system leaned or tilted distinctly to the center-right. The results of the 1976 election make it unlikely that the SPD will soon be in a similar position. Indeed, all three Bundestag parties have now at one time or another been coalition partners with each other, and renewals of past alignments, such as a CDU-FDP coalition, are both numerically and politically possible.

The ability of the CDU/CSU to adapt to its role as opposition party and build an effective extraparliamentary organization is another important development that augurs well for the stability of the party system and the future alternation of government and opposition. In short, the German electorate in eight national elections, in addition to rejecting extremist parties of every coloration, has transformed its party system from a hegemonic system in which "over an extended period of time the same party, or coalitions dominated by the same party, hold governmental power" to what appears to be a "stable turnover system," in which there is "relatively frequent change in the party that governs or the party that dominates a coalition."[32]

The classic problem of achieving a balance between stability and change, conflict and consensus, has been especially difficult in the German experience with democratic politics. During the Weimar Republic, of course, change was frequent and conflict intense; there was little stability or consensus. In the Federal Republic, on the other hand, the Adenauer years (1949–1963) were stable and consensual, but there was little realistic possibility of political change; instead, some have contended, there was an aversion to conflict.[33] Since the mid-1960s, however, Germany has come closer to achieving this balance than ever before in its brief and sometimes tragic democratic political history. In this sense, the narrow victory of the government in 1976 is indicative of the vitality of the electoral and political process in the Federal Republic.

---

[32] Joseph La Palombara and Myron Weiner, "The Origin and Development of Political Parties" in *Political Parties and Political Development*, ed. La Palombara and Weiner (Princeton: Princeton University Press, 1966), p. 35.

[33] Ralf Dahrendorf, *Society and Democracy in Germany* (New York: Doubleday, 1967), pp. 129–41.

3

The Campaign of the Social Democratic Party

Kurt Sontheimer

From Triumph to Insecurity

In the federal elections of 1972 the Social Democratic party of Germany under the leadership of Chancellor Willy Brandt reached its finest result since the foundation of the Federal Republic and the best national election outcome in the party's history of more than a hundred years. The SPD won 45.9 percent of the popular vote and for the first time in the life of the Deutsche Bundestag toppled the CDU/CSU from its traditional position as the strongest party in Parliament. For the first time an SPD deputy was elected president of the Bundestag, since it is a parliamentary convention to elect to the presidency a member of the strongest parliamentary party even if that party does not command an absolute majority or remains in opposition.

Most observers described the 1972 election as a personal triumph for Chancellor Willy Brandt. Although the German election system with its combination of proportional representation and direct constituency elections does not allow for direct contests anything like American presidential elections, in September 1972 the elections to the seventh Bundestag had a markedly plebiscitarian ring. Brandt fought along with the chairman of the Liberal party, Walter Scheel, for the legitimation and continuation of his *Ostpolitik*, which had come under heavy attack from the parliamentary opposition, especially from the Bavarian Christian Social Union led by Franz Josef Strauss. Brandt's main opponent, the CDU/CSU candidate for chancellor, Rainer Barzel, for many reasons proved much less attractive to the majority of the German voters than the acting chancellor and his Liberal coalition partner.

This chapter was written with the assistance of Dr. Wilhelm Bleek.

The 1972 election result gave more than a comfortable governing majority to the renewed coalition of Social Democrats and Liberals and could have been an excellent starting point for the new federal government. Free from the fear that some deputies might cross the floor and join the opposition, thereby reducing the government's majority to nil, as had been the case between 1969 and 1972, the government could indeed have carried out its policies with strong parliamentary backing. In terms of parliamentary politics, there seemed to be every possibility of inaugurating a long-lasting epoch of Socialist-Liberal leadership in the Federal Republic of Germany. Many Christian Democrats and a number of impartial observers were almost sure that the smashing victory of the SPD and, to a lesser extent, of the FDP (which had won 8.4 percent of the total vote compared to 5.4 percent in 1969) would usher in a Social Democratic and Liberal reign at least as long as the legendary Adenauer era which had run from 1949 to 1963.[1] Yet by the middle of the four-year legislative period the prospects for the party looked pretty dim. In most of the state and municipal elections held between 1972 and 1976 the Social Democrats lost a substantial number of votes (for example in Hamburg) or had to form coalition governments with the Liberals (as they did in West Berlin). In some states the Social Democrats even came close to losing their governing position to the CDU; this was the case in North Rhine-Westphalia and in Lower Saxony, where early in 1976 a Christian Democrat was elected minister-president although the SPD-FDP coalition still had a one-vote majority because three Socialist-Liberal deputies (still unidentified) voted for Albrecht of the CDU. Despite the difference between local and national elections, the continuous loss of electoral strength suffered by the SPD between 1972 and 1976 was a clear indication to the party and to all political observers that the SPD no longer had serious hopes of becoming once more West Germany's strongest parliamentary party.

What had happened within the party and the government to turn the tables so soon, making the victory of the opposition over the Socialist-Liberal coalition seem, at least temporarily, probable?

---

[1] In 1973 Werner Kaltefleiter, then director of the Social Science Research Institute of the Christian Democratic Konrad Adenauer Foundation, assumed that the SPD would win an absolute majority in the 1976 election, reflecting a new and probably durable asymmetry of the West German party system. See Werner Kaltefleiter, *Zwischen Konsens und Krise. Eine Analyse der Bundestagswahl 1972* [Between consensus and crisis: an analysis of the Bundestag election, 1972] (Bonn: Eichholz Verlag, 1973), p. 185.

The State of the Party

All of the German parties underwent significant changes in the decade between 1966 and 1976, most of all the FDP, which was transformed from a more or less reliable coalition partner of the conservative CDU/ CSU into a political formation leaning towards governmental coopera- tion with the Social Democrats. Through this realignment the Liberals made possible the important shift in German politics that came about in the autumn of 1969 when Willy Brandt formed his first coalition government with the Liberals under Walter Scheel.

The SPD, however, was transformed almost to the same extent as the FDP.[2] First, its rank and file had to swallow coalition with their former adversary, the CDU/CSU, under the chancellorship of Kurt Georg Kiesinger during the "grand coalition" (1966–1969). The achievements of this coalition were in no way grand, but it is now generally ac- knowledged that it paved the way for further recognition of the SPD among German middle-class voters. This, in conjunction with the transformation of the Liberal party, made possible the Socialist- Liberal government in 1969.

The years of the grand coalition were also the years of student unrest and revolt. They saw the formation of an extraparliamentary opposition that fiercely attacked the alleged autocratic structure of the state and the party system and which brought about a remarkable change in the political and intellectual climate of the Federal Republic. These events had enormous long-term consequences for the party. Many of the young men and women who had been politicized in the years of student protest eventually decided to work within established political parties. Most of them gave their support to the left-wing parties, either the German Communist party or the SPD, in which they automatically belonged to the Young Socialists (Jungsozialisten or Jusos). At the 1973 SPD convention in Hanover, Willy Brandt pointed to the fact that between 1964, when he became party leader, and 1973 the membership of his party had grown enormously, from 650,000 to over 900,000. Of these 900,000, two-thirds had joined the party in the last ten years.[3] The bulk of the newcomers had gone into the

---

[2] The most recent overview of the history, origins, and development of West German parties can be found in Dietrich Staritz, ed., *Das Parteiensystem der Bundesrepublik* [The party system of the Federal Republic] (Opladen: Leske und Budrich, 1976). Susanne Miller, *Die SPD vor und nach Godesberg* [The SPD before and after Godesberg] (Bonn-Bad Godesberg: Verlag Neue Ges., 1974), presents a quasi-official party history of the SPD. See also Kurt Sontheimer, *The Government and Politics of West Germany* (New York: Praeger Publishers, 1973), p. 89 ff.

[3] *Archiv der Gegenwart*, 1973, p. 17822.

Social Democratic party during the first Brandt government, between 1969 and 1972, and most of them were under thirty-five years old. The Young Socialists, to which all Social Democrats under thirty-five belong, recruited its leadership mainly from students who had been politically awakened by the student movement.[4]

The consequence was the revitalization of an ideological debate, first among the Young Socialists, then within the party as a whole. During its long fight in the 1960s for an electoral majority, the SPD had abandoned its emphasis on a long-term program and became a "catch-all party." This strategy was articulated and dictated by the Godesberg program of 1959 in which the SPD had dropped all Marxist formulations of the way to democratic socialism in favor of a program calling for a free market system and more social justice. The revival of the debate over Marxism in the late 1960s and early 1970s broke away from this framework, although the Marxists in the party, young and old, presented their anticapitalist position as a reinterpretation of Godesberg rather than a real departure. They denounced capitalism as the source of all the shortcomings of present-day Germany and called for its gradual elimination and the subsequent transformation of German society. Thus, the debate was between those who would only reform society and those who would transform it. These two positions often produce similar policy stands in the short term, but in the long run the differences in their aims become crucial. The SPD is again, as it was during the Weimar Republic, the forum for an often vehement debate between Marxist and non-Marxist Social Democrats and, even more important, among the different shades of Marxist thought. To accommodate these different points of view has become the challenge and the burden of the party.

The transformation of the party by the influx of substantial numbers of young and ideologically committed party members was, of course, greatest in the party wards of the big cities and the university towns. The Munich SPD, for example, has changed dramatically in the last decade; by 1975 it counted almost as many students as blue-collar workers among its members, and the majority of the party members were white-collar workers.[5] Intellectuals, many of

---

[4] A detailed and sympathetic discussion of the program and politics of the Young Socialists can be found in Volker Häse and Peter Müller, "Die Jungsozialisten in der SPD" [The Young Socialists in the SPD], in J. Dittberner and R. Ebbighausen, eds., Parteien in der Legitimationskrise [Parties in the legitimacy crisis] (Opladen: Westdeutscher Verlag, 1973), pp. 277–306.

[5] See the unpublished analysis of the Munich SPD membership by Peter Glotz, now minister of cultural affairs in Berlin and former deputy chairman of the Bavarian SPD.

them with a new-leftist commitment and a bent for ideology, which they call "theory," occupied positions at all levels of the national party structure. They advocated the party's return to the working-class tradition and to the ideology of the prewar period, although most of them had no links at all with the working class. Indeed, in the last ten years the SPD has become a full-fledged middle-class party with continuing working-class support.

The party's national leadership thus came more and more under attack from different local and other organizations, especially from the youth organization, because it did not carry out the policy of anticapitalist reforms demanded by Jusos. Ideological debate at almost all levels of the party contributed not only to growing internal difficulties but even more to the imprecision and obscurity of the party's broader public image. Even the national leaders of the party now felt themselves compelled to speak of democratic socialism instead of social democracy and of themselves as Socialists rather than merely Social Democrats.

This development within the party, especially its left wing, was certainly not to the taste of the average German middle-class voter. This is probably one of the main reasons for the opposition's success in most of the state elections between 1972 and 1976. In fact, the traditional majority of the parliamentary party, and the government even more, did little to nourish the bourgeois fear that the SPD was moving towards real socialism. Nevertheless, the bitter ideological fight going on in many party organizations gave the opposition and the media an opportunity to warn the public that once the radical left wing of the party gained a majority position, the SPD would be committed to socialism, which Friedrich von Hayek described as the *Road to Serfdom*.

In fact, the left wing succeeded in seizing power only in a relatively small number of local and regional party organizations such as those in Munich and Frankfurt. During the nominations for the 1976 election the leftists were able to drive out established politicians (like Georg Leber in Frankfurt, who was defense minister until early 1978) only in a few districts. In general the pragmatists stood their ground and still represent the overwhelming majority in the parliamentary party. But the few exceptions to this rule were always good news for the opposition, which incessantly tried to persuade the German voters that in the long run they would have to choose between freedom and socialism.

Although the new ideological tension could be felt everywhere, the party still inspired enough confidence among the majority of the

German electorate to win overwhelmingly the Bundestag election of 1972; four years later its image was much less attractive. It certainly was more blurred and confusing than the image of the opposition, the CDU and CSU, although these, too, had allowed their internal conflicts and problems of leadership to become publicly known and discussed.

In 1976 the Social Democratic party was proud to announce that its membership had finally reached 1 million, but apparently the willingness of the party, especially of the younger members, to do everything in their power to make victory at the polls a reality was less marked than in the previous election. The party had demonstrated the traditional party unity at the convention which ratified the *Orientierungsrahmen '85* (General program till 1985) late in 1975 and it proved its solidarity at the numerous public meetings that preceded the election campaign proper. Nevertheless, this expanded membership showed less enthusiasm and less zeal for campaigning than the smaller party of 1972 and even 1969. The SPD campaign of 1976 became a rather official and professional undertaking. This was not only an effect of the many transformations the party had gone through in such a short time; it was also due to the ambivalence of the rank and file toward their own party's government and its performance in the field of reforms.

The Record of the Government and the Role of the Chancellor

Chancellor Brandt's great historic achievement was the reconciliation with Eastern Europe which he negotiated in close partnership with the Western powers.[6] When he formed his second government after the electoral triumph of 1972, everyone expected him to concentrate on his often proclaimed policy of domestic reforms. Yet these not only were slow to come, they also proved to be much less thoroughgoing than most of Brandt's progressive partisans had expected. There were two institutional reasons for this. First, the FDP, seeking to appear truly liberal, was not always an easy partner for the SPD. It seemed to inhibit some of the reforms envisaged by the Social Democratic planners. The FDP, for example, opposed the extension of the system of workers' codetermination from the coal and steel industry to all big enterprises. Second, the CDU/CSU used the Bundesrat, the legislative chamber representing the states, as another and even more effective brake for many of the government's reform proposals. The CDU/CSU commanded a majority in the Bundesrat and used it as an

---

[6] See Roger Tilford, ed., *The Ostpolitik and Political Change in Germany* (Lexington, Mass.: Lexington Books, 1975).

instrument of opposition as best it could. Thus, the conservative parties were able to delay the realization of Social Democratic and Liberal plans for university reform for over five years. The new *Bundeshochschulrahmengesetz* (federal university law) that finally went into effect in 1975 was a shallow compromise between all three parliamentary parties.

During the energy crisis in the wake of the Yom-Kippur War the government unexpectedly had to grapple with totally new and serious problems. Many of the reform proposals looked irrelevant compared with the energy shortage, the economic recession, and growing unemployment. Then Chancellor Brandt suddenly resigned in early summer 1974 after the exposure of an East German spy in his official entourage. Günter Guillaume had been one of Brandt's personal assistants for years and may have informed East Germany of West German plans and tactics in the difficult negotiations with Moscow and East Berlin in the early 1970s. This new development in the intra-German war of espionage was perceived as a setback for détente in general and for the normalization of relations between the two German states. Brandt took it as a blow to his personal integrity. Yet he was even more deeply wounded by the fact that his fellow party leaders doubted his ability to deal with the difficult economic and political situation. These doubts had been most openly expressed by Herbert Wehner, former deputy party leader under Brandt and chairman of the parliamentary party. Brandt seems to have resigned with some relief.[7]

Helmut Schmidt, the new chancellor, differed in many respects from Willy Brandt, politically as well as personally, although the two men tried to work in harmony. Whereas Brandt had in the end been accused of inadequate leadership, Helmut Schmidt was immediately suspected of overassertive leadership and excessive pragmatism. Up until the election of October 1976 Schmidt had to defend himself against the view, widespread particularly in his own party, that he was a pure technocrat, a man of action without much understanding of long-term political aims, let alone ideals; in short, a *Macher*. Schmidt, at the outset of his term, was not much liked by many Social Democrats. Slowly he won respect among them, although he never could fully appease the distrustful left wing of the party.

Brandt's continuing role as chairman of the SPD proved all the more important in that, so it seemed, he alone was able to integrate

---

[7] For Brandt's own account of his resignation, see Willy Brandt, *Über den Tag hinaus. Eine Zwischenbilanz* [Beyond today. An interim report] (Hamburg: Hoffmann und Campe, 1974).

and hold together the diverging wings of the party, still engaged in more or less bitter struggles over doctrine. Schmidt was much less liked than Brandt by the party's intellectuals (and vice versa) and by the Young Socialists, but in the long run they had to acknowledge the fact that within less than two years West Germany's new Social Democratic chancellor had won great respect in the world at large, especially in the United States, Great Britain, and France.

It is difficult to guess what the situation for the SPD would have been if Willy Brandt had stayed on as chancellor. It might well be that without Schmidt's taking over in a period of severe economic difficulties the situation for the SPD in the 1976 election would have been even more difficult than it actually was. Certainly the role Brandt continued to play as leader of the SPD was of great importance (even if, as many claimed, relations between Brandt and the other two leading figures in the SPD, Wehner and Schmidt, were rather cool).

The Federal Republic slowly recovered from the world economic crisis of 1974, which Chancellor Schmidt liked to call the most serious since the late twenties. By 1976 the recovery of the national economy seemed to be in full swing, unemployment was slowly retreating, the prospect for new growth was real, and the climate of crisis and insecurity, so prevalent in 1975, was almost forgotten. It was in this situation that the party organization, assisted by professional campaign advisers and public relations experts, drafted the campaign platform of the SPD. As a governing reform party, the SPD would seek a renewal of its mandate on the basis of its performance in government.

The SPD Platform

The SPD's national preelection convention was held at Dortmund, in the middle of the traditional SPD stronghold of the Ruhr Valley, on June 18 and 19, 1976. Its task was to ratify the party's official campaign platform, outlining a government program for the years 1976–1980.[8] The platform it confirmed showed the strong influence of Chancellor Schmidt, who had insisted on emphasizing above all the achievements and performance of the Schmidt government. The document underlined the government's skill in dealing successfully with a major economic depression and a great number of other problems and presented the Federal Republic of Germany as a model. The

---

[8] *Weiterarbeiten am Modell Deutschland. Regierungsprogramm 1976–80* [Continuing the German model: government program 1976–80] (Bonn: Parteivorstand der SPD, 1976).

emphasis on *Modell Deutschland* was not meant as an exhortation to Germany's European friends and allies to follow the German example, although the chancellor himself occasionally hinted in this direction. Instead it was to be used mainly as a means of information and political enlightenment for the German population, which for months had heard the opposition claiming that Germany was headed for economic and political disaster. The SPD tried to make the most of the international recognition and esteem that Chancellor Schmidt had won and that Herr Brandt continued to have. "Our achievements between 1969 and 1976," the platform said,

> make it clear which model Germany should follow in the future. . . . We have created a Germany of which many are justly proud and which enjoys respect in West and East. Our country owes its eminent position to the many individual achievements of its citizens, to its successful policy of international understanding, to its high economic performance, to its tightly woven net of social security, to its policy of continuous reforms—to the fact that we have taken social solidarity and real individual freedom seriously.[9]

The record looked bright indeed in the party platform, yet it failed to impress people vividly during the campaign. The platform was mainly an enumeration of policies, all of them presented as successful and as warranting therefore a renewal of the voters' confidence. It pledged that the SPD would continue these policies and enunciated vague generalities about further reforms ("Who wants to bring us ahead must have the courage for steady improvements!").[10] Again and again it urged that the results already achieved in the different fields of policy be preserved and the policies extended on the basis of present performance.

The party proclaimed that millions of people in other parts of the world would be happy to live under the material and political conditions that were taken for granted in the Federal Republic, but it did not omit to add: "We know . . . that there remains much to be done, if we want to keep and to secure our place in the world. . . . In a difficult international situation it is of the utmost importance that Chancellor Schmidt remain at the head of the German Government. Helmut Schmidt must remain chancellor!"[11]

---

[9] Ibid., pp. 53–55.
[10] Ibid., p. 27.
[11] Ibid., p. 53.

Campaign Strategy

The SPD campaign can be roughly divided into three phases. The first, extending over the first half of 1976, included the preparation of the platform by different party groups and ended with the Dortmund party convention. The second phase was devoted to the propagation of the *Modell Deutschland* and the Dortmund platform. The government did not hesitate to use funds at the disposal of the Federal Information Office to publicize its performance widely in the German press. The opposition accused the government of using public funds for party purposes, but since this had been common practice under CDU/CSU governments the opposition's attempt at judicial control of the matter did not get very far.[12] The second period ran from June 1976 to the end of August.

Finally, the so-called hot phase. It covered the last five to six weeks before election day and involved intensive campaigning throughout the country. An unusually extensive and costly poster and publicity campaign was supplemented by innumerable election meetings held all over the Republic. Every local and regional party organization tried to be included in the campaign tours of the leading personalities of the party, especially Schmidt and Brandt. In some places the two leading men of the SPD appeared hand in hand to demonstrate publicly the unity of party and government.

More than any other the 1976 campaign showed that only the best-known popular leaders—Brandt and Schmidt, Kohl and Strauss—were sure to attract large crowds, although even these were mainly composed of party followers. The typical SPD campaign meeting, whether organized by the local or the regional campaign committee, was more or less an in-group affair intended to mobilize the rank and file of the party. The Young Socialists, who had been quite active in the 1972 campaign, were more hesitant this time, though not indifferent.[13] In some places the party regulars discouraged Jusos from participating, in the fear that their more radical line might alienate voters.

It was noteworthy, too, that the Social Democratic citizen action

---

[12] The practice of using government material and official public relations agencies and spending public funds in party campaigns was finally outlawed by the Federal Constitutional Court in its decision of March 2, 1977. *Entscheidungen des Bundesverfassungsgerichts*, vol. 44 (1977), pp. 125–97.

[13] For the Jusos' limited support of the party, see the declaration by their chairperson, Heidemarie Wieczorek-Zeul, in the party's theoretical monthly *Die Neue Gesellschaft*, September 1976, p. 716ff.

group known as the Sozialdemokratische Wähler-Initiative, founded in 1969 by the famous writer Günter Grass and joined by a great number of well-known intellectuals and artists, could not gain much ground in the 1976 campaign. Many of those who had joined the Wähler-Initiative to work for Brandt and the SPD in 1969 and who had continued their public support of the SPD in 1972 had reservations about the personality and policies of Helmut Schmidt and therefore no longer spoke up publicly for the SPD. Moreover, since 1969 prominent supporters of the other parties had launched similar action groups. The idea had lost its originality. In 1976 scholars and writers had little appeal as campaign spokesmen. By contrast, all of the parties made use of endorsements by sports celebrities and entertainers: soccer stars of *Bayern München* came out for the CSU, the CDU was supported by popular singers like Dieter "Thomas" Heck, and the SPD won the help of Annegret Richter, at the time the world's best female sprinter. All the parties used gadget publicity too—bumper stickers, buttons, T-shirts, and so on—though in this respect the CDU and CSU far outshone the SPD. Indeed the Social Democrats seemed to be on the defensive right from the beginning of the hot phase of the campaign.

At the beginning of 1976 almost all of the pollsters gave the SPD-FDP coalition a small majority.[14] As the campaign got into full swing in the early summer, however, the figures turned slightly in favor of the opposition. One of the reasons for this reversal was undoubtedly Schmidt's underrating of his rival, Helmut Kohl. Never much interested personally in Kohl, Schmidt always insisted that Franz Josef Strauss was the man to watch and described him as an imminent danger for the Republic should the CDU/CSU come to power. Schmidt and other Social Democrats elevated Strauss to the position of a national bogey, deliberately treating Helmut Kohl as a *quantité négligeable*. As events would show, however, Kohl conducted a rather successful personal campaign.

The Campaign Issues

It is doubtful whether this particular tactic had the intended effect, for only about four weeks before the election it was widely believed by campaign observers that the CDU/CSU was running a better cam-

---

[14] Polls conducted by four institutes (Allensbach, Emnid, Getas, and Infratest) were published in part in *Der Spiegel*, *Stern*, and *Die Zeit* throughout the campaign.

paign than the SPD and was gaining ground.[15] The coalition would have to struggle hard to preserve even a small parliamentary majority. Schmidt, of course, remained confident. One week before the election he predicted that the coalition would gain at least sixteen seats.[16]

The SPD campaign managers hastily tried to turn the tide. They concentrated on mobilizing their traditional supporters—like the millions of industrial workers in the Ruhr Valley—to ensure a high turnout at the polls. Kurt Biedenkopf, then secretary general of the CDU, had launched a massive attack against the "red bastions" in the Ruhr, denouncing the simultaneous accumulation of offices and privileges in the SPD and in the trade unions. This approach seemed to be successful in stirring the voters' doubts about long-term Social Democratic rule in some big cities like Berlin, Bremen, Frankfurt, and Munich—but it alienated the trade unions, which fought more openly against the CDU/CSU. The SPD counterattacked, issuing a new poster inscribed "Den Frieden wählen!" (Vote freedom!), the implication being that a victory of the opposition would endanger international as well as domestic peace.

In the last three weeks of the campaign the SPD concentrated on three issues: (1) Ostpolitik, accusing the opposition of creating security risks by jeopardizing German relations with Eastern Europe; (2) social security, accusing the opposition of planning to weaken the welfare system; and (3) style, denouncing in particular the opposition's slogan "Freiheit oder Sozialismus." In the field of Ostpolitik Chancellor Schmidt tried to interpret some rather militant CSU statements concerning the frontier with East Germany as evidence that the opposition was even prepared to risk war. The future of social security was an issue that the opposition made much of during the whole campaign. Opposition leaders expressed grave doubts that the government would be able to uphold the annually adjusted pension scheme in the near future. Schmidt had to promise that the pensions were safe (the same promise came, by the way, from Helmut Kohl), but his guarantee covered only 1977. These were minor skirmishes, however, compared with the big ideological issue of the 1976 election: the debate over freedom and socialism.

The slogan which Strauss had imposed upon the whole CDU caused anger, criticism, and heated argument within the Social Demo-

---

[15] See for example the series of articles in the August and September editions of the weekly Der Spiegel. On September 6, 1976, the headline of the lead article on the campaign stated: "The SPD is still indecisive," Der Spiegel, no. 37 (1977), p. 21.

[16] Interview with Die Zeit, no. 40 (September 24, 1976), p. 4.

cratic party. The SPD had originally hoped that Kohl and the CDU would not follow Strauss's policy of ideological confrontation. When the slogan became the dominant theme of the opposition's campaign, the SPD was reminded of Adenauer's campaign claim in 1953 that the victory of the Social Democrats would be Germany's downfall (*Untergang*). The great fear of the SPD was that many voters would be unable to see the difference between democratic socialism as intended and practiced by the SPD and bureaucratic state socialism as practiced by the German Democratic Republic and other Communist countries. The SPD claimed on a large new poster that it knew more about freedom than the Union parties (*"Von Freiheit verstehen wir mehr"*). It denounced "Freedom or Socialism" as a divisive formula (*Spalterformel*), as a calculated attempt to split the German people into friends and enemies of freedom. Equally alarming, the slogan persuaded the SPD that the CDU was increasingly under the influence of the "reactionary" forces prominent in the Bavarian CSU.

But the fact is that the slogan *"Freiheit oder Sozialismus"* proved much more effective and impressive than Schmidt's *"Modell Deutschland."*[17] The good results of the CSU in Bavaria and of the CDU in those states where the policy of ideological confrontation as presented by Strauss was most closely followed (Baden-Württemberg and Hesse) seem to indicate that the slogan had a decisive effect. The extremely poor showing of the Bavarian SPD—which lost five percentage points from its 1972 support and fell back to 32.8 of the total vote, compared with a staggering 60 percent for the CSU—was undoubtedly also a consequence of the ideological strife between SPD traditionalists and the new left-wingers, which gave the slogan an inkling of credibility.

Schmidt himself considered the slogan another example of the discrimination the SPD had long suffered at the hands of Hugenberg, Goebbels, and many other former leaders of reactionary forces in Germany. He could be sure that his own governmental policy contained little if anything to justify the reproach that the Federal Republic was moving toward state socialism. He tried to prove that, on the contrary, the Social Democratic party had done much more to secure and safeguard the freedom of individuals than the CDU/CSU, judging its performance on the basis of its legislative proposals to the seventh Bundestag. In fact, aside from the internal party controversy about the best road to democratic socialism, there was not much in the actual record of the government to warrant the opposition's alarmist

---

[17] Forty-five percent of a poll sample knew the Christian Democratic slogan, but only 15 percent that of the Social Democrats. See *Süddeutsche Zeitung*, September 21, 1976, p. 4.

tactics. It was clear even to most members of the CDU/CSU that Schmidt's policies were not very far from what they might have done themselves if they had been in power.

Further, the chancellor saw in the opposition's slogan a dangerous appeal to the emotions. He said in an interview: "The whole campaign of the SPD is much more based on arguments than that of the CDU/CSU. This corresponds to our understanding of democracy. We do not want to appeal to the subconscious, we want to appeal to reason."[18]

Helmut Kohl, Schmidt's rival, had tried from the beginning of his campaign to stage a television debate between himself and the chancellor. The idea was taken from the American television duel between the two presidential candidates. Schmidt stubbornly refused, for two main reasons. First, he had a tacit agreement with FDP leader Genscher not to appear on television in a party contest without him, and Schmidt felt bound by his loyalty to the FDP leader because he knew he could not do without him in the formation of the next government. Second, the chancellor underlined his belief that it would be misleading for Kohl to appear on the screen alone, without Franz Josef Strauss. Kohl nevertheless called Schmidt a *"Kneifer,"* a person who shuns a task because he is afraid of losing face.

But Schmidt had no objections at all to the colossal encounter arranged by the two German television networks between himself, Kohl, Strauss, and Genscher. This was broadcast live three days before the election and lasted more than four hours. No clear winner emerged, with the possible exception of Genscher who got most credit in the press for his thoughtful performance. Certainly Schmidt was not able to tip the balance in his favor. It is likely that the four-hour program had little or no impact upon the attitudes of voters.[19]

Outcome and Assessment

As election day approached, the inner circles of the SPD were hopeful that the party would again be able to form a government together with the Free Democrats, but no one could be totally sure. Election night was filled with tension. The Socialist-Liberal coalition's majority seemed shaky when the first results and computer prognoses came in, and a number of hours passed before the party leaders made any public comment. It was Willy Brandt, as chairman of the Social Demo-

---

[18] *Die Zeit*, September 24, 1976, p. 3.

[19] This was the impression of all professional observers. See the final report on the 1976 campaign by Klaus Dreher in *Süddeutsche Zeitung*, October 2, 1976, p. 3.

cratic party, who appeared first, to declare that his party, although it had registered some losses, had reached its political aim: it would continue the Socialist-Liberal coalition. Helmut Schmidt, who spoke rather late in the night from the chancellor's office, said flatly that Helmut Kohl definitely would not become *Bundeskanzler.* The coalition had won the election and would soon take steps to form a new government under his leadership.

The SPD had lost 3.3 percentage points compared with its outstanding results of 1972. This setback had been expected and was much smaller than some pessimists in the party had feared. Many pollsters had predicted a little less for the SPD but had given a higher rating to the FDP. On the whole, the party, while not particularly proud, was satisfied. There was also some discussion of whether a ten-seat majority would be sufficient to allow the government to carry out the necessary policies, but even the doubters took comfort from the phrase, heard so often during the campaign, "a majority is a majority." The chairman of the party and the chancellor dutifully expressed their gratitude to the party and its voters for all they had done to secure victory for the government. Helmut Schmidt pledged vigorously to continue the policy of peace and social reforms, and Willy Brandt, who had done his best to second the chancellor, assured him of the continuing support of the party in the four years ahead.

Despite victory the SPD had to recognize that it was no longer the strongest political group in Parliament and had suffered losses in all 248 constituencies, ranging from a mild 0.5 percentage points in Emsland (in eastern Lower Saxony) to a dismal 8 percentage points in three election districts in Munich. Moreover, the 1976 election had deepened the structural differences in voting behavior among the northern, central, and southern regions of West Germany. Not only had the SPD won fewest votes in the southern states, Bavaria and Baden-Württemberg, but also the party had suffered its biggest losses in these regions (see Table 3–1). On the other hand, north German states like Schleswig-Holstein, Lower Saxony, and the City of Hamburg not only had remained strongholds of the SPD, but had suffered relatively small losses. In central West Germany the CDU's fulminant attack against the "red bastions" was not too successful. In North Rhine-Westphalia the SPD suffered only a moderate loss, and the Ruhr Valley itself, with a Social Democratic decline of only 2.8 percentage points, once again proved the backbone of Social Democratic support. In Hesse, contrary to all expectations, the scandal-ridden Social Democratic state government did not prompt a major setback for the party.

71

TABLE 3–1

SPD VOTE, BY STATE, 1972 AND 1976

(in percentages and percentage points)

State (from north to south)	SPD Vote		Difference, 1976–1972
	1972	1976	
Schleswig-Holstein	48.6	46.4	−2.2
Hamburg	54.4	52.6	−1.9
Bremen	58.1	54.0	−4.1
Lower Saxony	48.1	45.7	−2.4
North Rhine-Westphalia	50.4	46.9	−3.5
Hesse	48.5	45.7	−2.8
Saar	47.9	46.1	−1.8
Rhineland-Palatinate	44.9	41.7	−3.2
Baden-Württemberg	38.9	36.6	−2.2
Bavaria	37.8	32.8	−5.0
Federal Republic	45.8	42.6	−3.3

SOURCE: *Das Parlament*, October 9, 1976, p. 2.

Overall, the SPD vote declined from north to south. This pattern coincides with the regional origins of the three main competitors (Schmidt comes from Hamburg, Kohl from Rhineland-Palatinate, and Strauss from Bavaria) and, more important, with differences in the economic and social structure of the German regions. The SPD still receives its highest vote in urban areas with a high percentage of trade union affiliated workers, while the CDU and CSU have their strongholds in rural areas where church attendance is high. The above average losses of the SPD in Munich and Frankfurt and their suburbs and its much smaller losses in rural areas do not contradict this general trend. Instead, they are due to structural changes such as the shift from blue-collar to white-collar activities in these cities and to the slow but definite assimilation of rural and urban areas.

A detailed sociological analysis of the 1976 election has yet to be undertaken,[20] but two interesting aspects of the evolution of the SPD electorate deserve mention: (1) the narrowing of differences between male and female voting behavior and (2) the preference of young voters for the Social Democratic party.

The SPD—although responsible for giving women the vote in

[20] For the first analyses see Werner Kaltefleiter, *Der Gewinner hat nicht gesiegt* [The winner did not win], *Aus Politik und Zeitgeschichte*, December 11, 1976, and Manfred Berger et al., *Bundestagswahl 1976: Politik und Sozialstruktur* [Federal election 1976: politics and social structure], *Zeitschrift für Parlamentsfragen*, August 1977, pp. 197–231.

TABLE 3–2
SPD VOTE, BY VOTER'S SEX, 1961–1976
(in percentages)

Voter's Sex	SPD Vote				
	1961	1965	1969	1972	1976
Women	32.9	36.2	40.4	45.7	43.1
Men	39.7	44.0	45.6	46.9	43.6

SOURCE: Federal Statistical Office, *Wirtschaft und Statistik*, 1977, no. 1, pp. 4 and 14–19.

Germany in 1919—had a traditionally male constituency, while female voters tended to support the CDU/CSU. Over the last ten years, however, this gap has been shrinking. It nearly closed in the 1976 election (see Table 3–2). In 1976 the CDU made more than proportionate gains in the male electorate, and the SPD suffered its smallest losses in the female electorate. Clearly, the importance of sex as a determinant of voting behavior is diminishing as a result of social changes that also affect church orientation, role perception, and many other aspects of social life.

Young voters, eighteen to twenty-four years old, had brought the SPD victory in 1972: in this age group the party had scored 54.6 percent, more than eight percentage points above its performance in the electorate as a whole. In contrast, the 1976 setback seemed due to overwhelming losses in this age group. Infas, the institute for applied social sciences affiliated with the SPD, discovered in its poll taken the night before the election that among eighteen to twenty-one year olds only 44 percent had voted SPD, while 45 percent had preferred the CDU/CSU. The next age group (twenty-two to twenty-five year olds), who had cast their first votes in the 1972 "Brandt election," had remained loyal to the SPD (50 percent SPD, 37 percent CDU/CSU).[21]

These findings stirred up discussion in the party.[22] Was the SPD to lose its long-term hope, the allegiance of the young? Some argued that the new generation in the Federal Republic was turning toward conservatism. Others, like the Young Socialist leader, provoked the Social Democratic government by blaming its capitalistic policies for the disaffection of the younger generation. The publication of the

[21] *Süddeutsche Zeitung*, October 6, 1977, p. 6.
[22] See the articles in the November 1976 edition of the party's monthly *Die Neue Gesellschaft*.

official results as well as the random sample statistics cooled this debate and demonstrated the inadequacy of election analysis based on opinion polls. As Table 3–3 shows, the SPD lost 4.8 percentage points among eighteen to twenty-four year olds, but almost 50 percent of these youngest voters still supported the SPD. The party suffered a much more significant setback—6.8 percentage points—among the thirty-five to forty-four year olds. The fact is, the young generation did not turn en masse from the Social Democrats to the conservative parties. What losses the SPD did suffer in this age group were primarily due to nonvoting, which was unusually high among the youngest voters (15.9 percent, compared with 9.6 in the total electorate, and only 6.2 percent among the population over fifty). This presents a general problem for the West German political system: how to integrate and activate the younger generation.

As a whole, the SPD's showing in the 1976 election reflected long-term social change as well as reactions to the political and economic events of the last four years, but it was only minimally affected by the campaign of 1976. The publicity aspect of the campaign had been entrusted to an advertising agency that had proved successful in the previous elections. It had been eager to portray the party in a way that would inspire confidence in a hopeful future under forceful Social Democratic leadership. Some party intellectuals criticized the all too harmonious picture the SPD campaign managers had presented to the public. Some felt that the campaign had been much too rational, not heartwarming enough, and geared too much to the present state of affairs instead of to what they called the "dimension of the future." They missed an emotional undertone and the kind of hopeful message in the midst of gloom that had brought victory to Willy Brandt in 1969 and 1972.

But the party leaders knew that the favorable climate of the late

TABLE 3–3

SPD VOTE, BY AGE GROUP, 1972 AND 1976

(in percentages)

Election	18–24	25–34	35–44	45–59	Over 60	Total Electorate
1972	54.6	47.8	47.9	44.2	42.2	46.3
1976	49.8	44.8	41.1	42.4	42.0	43.3

SOURCE: Federal Statistical Office, *Wirtschaft und Statistik*, 1977, no. 1, pp. 4 and 14–19.

sixties and early seventies could not be restored. The then general secretary of the SPD, Holger Börner, mentioned some organizational problems that would have to be solved more efficiently. He pointed to the financial superiority of the opposition (although judging by the SPD's campaign, his own party was by no means poor).[23] The party monthly, *Sozialdemokrat Magazin*, explained the party's weak results in Bavaria and Baden-Württemberg at least in part by the SPD's numerical and financial inferiority in these regions. And it was sensitive to the possibility that the party's image had been tarnished by charges of corruption and cronyism.[24]

Thus, it was not the campaign as such—either the party's platform or its strategy—that was blamed for the more disappointing aspects of the election outcome. Rather, it was the management of the campaign that received the most criticism. Whether the technical aspects of a campaign are decisive for an election outcome can be questioned. More important determinants of the outcome would appear to be the record of the government (if the party is in power), the state of the party, the quality and reputation of its leaders, the general climate of opinion, and last but not least the strength of the competing parties, in particular of the opposition. Whatever the determinants, had the coalition lost the election, the management of the campaign would have been criticized much more bitterly than in fact it was. After all, the coalition attained its most important aim: the continuation of the SPD in a government with the FDP. Victory, even if the margin is small, seldom leads to serious self-criticism and significant change. Instead, it is defeat that drives political parties to drastic reassessment of their policies, their campaign, and their management. In 1976 this was the experience not of the SPD, but of the CDU and CSU, which had lost the election despite winning more votes than either the SPD or the FDP.

---

[23] See Börner's letter of October 13, 1976, to the directorate of the party offering his resignation from the party's management, in *Die Neue Gesellschaft*, December 1976, pp. 973–74. Börner became minister-president of Hesse.

[24] *Sozialdemokrat Magazin*, October 1976, pp. 8–10.

4

The FDP in the German Party System

Heino Kaack

The Strategy of Self-Sufficiency

Any discussion of the Free Democratic party is necessarily a discussion of the party system of the Federal Republic.[1] None of the Bundestag parties has been as dependent on the general development of the German party system as is the FDP. This is above all a consequence of the relative strength of the German parties within the German party system.[2]

In 1949 the FDP was already the third strongest party in the Bundestag. It has maintained this position to the present, but the party system has changed considerably. In the early 1960s, the multiparty system of the 1950s, whose dominant structural trait had been a dichotomy between the middle class and the socialist camps, became a party oligopoly as the majority of the supporters of the smaller middle-class parties shifted their allegiance to the CDU/CSU and the SPD gave up its rigid policy of opposition based on a tenacious commitment to socialism.[3] This structural change was perceived by the

[1] For an introduction to the historical development of the FDP in the context of the party system, see Heino Kaack, *Zur Geschichte und Programmatik der Freien Demokratischen Partei. Grundriss und Materialien* [On the history and program of the free democratic party: outline and materials], Studies on the Political System of the Federal Republic of Germany, vol. 18 (Meisenheim: Hain, 1976).

[2] See Heino Kaack, "Die Liberalen. Die FDP im Parteiensystem der Bundesrepublik" [The liberals: the FDP in the party system of the Federal Republic], in Richard Löwenthal and Hans-Peter Schwarz, eds., *Die zweite Republik. 25 Jahre Bundesrepublik Deutschland—Eine Bilanz* [The second republic: 25 years of the Federal Republic of Germany—a summary] (Stuttgart: Seewald, 1974), p. 408 ff.

[3] In general, for the development of the German party system, see Heino Kaack, *Geschichte und Struktur des deutschen Parteiensystems. Ein Handbuch* [History and structure of the German party system: a manual] (Opladen: Westdeutscher Verlag, 1971).

FDP only after the formation of the grand coalition between the CDU/CSU and the SPD in late 1966. Under the direction of Erich Mendes, the FDP saw itself as a distinctly middle-class party even after the SPD had substituted the "people's party" concept[4] for the middle-class versus socialist cleavage and had formulated a strategy aimed at SPD participation in government.

Further, the FDP considered itself a "corrective" for the CDU/CSU—according to circumstances, either a brake or a motor. Its opponents were inclined to dismiss it as a rump of the Christian Democrats, but they could not ignore its position as swing party, its power to tip the balance in stalemates. Since 1957, neither the CDU/CSU nor the SPD has had an absolute majority,[5] and since 1961 only three party groupings have been represented in the Bundestag; under these circumstances the swing party often achieved disproportionate influence. One consequence was that the media rarely defined the FDP on its own merits, but presented it instead primarily in terms of its relations to the other parties. Although the FDP was accorded a "hinge function" beyond the rump-dimension after the 1969 change in government—after all, FDP coalition support enabled Brandt to form the new SPD-FDP government—shortly thereafter the view of the FDP as a rump, this time of the SPD, once again dominated public opinion.[6]

Particularly under the leadership of Hans-Dietrich Genscher, the FDP tried to counter this image by becoming self-sufficient.[7] One of the components of this strategy was the deliberate adoption of the label Liberal, intended to undermine the view that all Bundestag parties are essentially Liberal and that the FDP consequently had no philosophical identity of its own. The primary purpose of the strategy of self-

---

[4] For a criticism of this development, see Wolf-Dieter Narr, *CDU-SPD. Programm und Praxis seit 1945* [CDU-SPD: program and practice since 1945] (Stuttgart: Kohlhammer, 1966).

[5] See Kurt J. Körper, *FDP: Bilanz der Jahre 1960–1966. Braucht Deutschland eine liberale Partei?* [FDP: summary of the years 1960–1966. Does Germany need a liberal party?] (Cologne-Lindenthal: Wison-Verlag, 1968) and Rüdiger Zülch, *Von der FDP zur F.D.P.—Die dritte Kraft im deutschen Parteiensystem* [From the FDP to the F.D.P.—the third force in the German party system] (Bonn: Eichholz, 1973). Both authors, as proponents of the two-party system, have basic reservations about the FDP which this author does not share.

[6] See Christian Fenner, "Das Parteiensystem seit 1969—Normalisierung und Polarisierung" [The party system since 1969—normalization and polarization] in Dietrich Staritz, ed., *Das Parteiensystem der Bundesrepublik* [The party system of the Federal Republic] (Opladen: Leske, 1976), p. 194 ff.; the "hinge function" of the FDP is referred to on p. 197.

[7] For further reference, see the speeches of Hans-Dietrich Genscher at the national and state conventions since his takeover as chairman at the Hamburg convention in early October 1974.

sufficiency was to persuade people to think of the party not on the basis of its coalition position, but on the basis of its political principles and problem-solving initiatives. The coalition question, Genscher believed, should become a purely functional issue: the FDP would align itself with whatever partner seemed most able to implement a Liberal policy in any given situation.

The self-sufficiency of the FDP as the party of organized liberalism has important historical roots. Indeed, liberalism has a longer tradition than does socialism or Christian conservatism and a somewhat different philosophical orientation. "Although elements of Liberal thought were assimilated by conservative and Socialist groups in that they were retained as common political property, they have remained peripheral to policy, often not more than alibi formulas."[8] This assertion of the nonliberalism of the competing parties rests on the theory formulated by Karl-Hermann Flach, a prominent leader of the FDP, that liberalism is not committed to one social model and logically cannot be fulfilled historically, but must constantly be developed through its application in a changing political environment.[9] The FDP's adoption of liberalism as a political theme and its espousal of the Liberal tradition in Germany, of course, cannot completely substantiate the claim of self-sufficiency of the FDP. Nevertheless, numerous traditional Liberal principles defended by the FDP are not to be found in the same combination in other parties of the Federal Republic. The antibureaucratic, anticlerical, individualistic tendency of the old Liberal tradition has been retained despite substantial changes in the Liberal parties in the last hundred years. These principles have always resulted in specific constitutional, legal, and cultural policy initiatives and have produced permanent tension between Liberal economic and social policies.[10] The political content of the FDP's autonomous position can therefore be seen as significant in light of the fact that ideologically the established parties in the Federal Republic differ from each other only in degree and not in principle anyway.

In addition, democratic theory plays an important role in the self-image and rhetoric of the FDP. The Liberals hold the inadmissi-

---

[8] F.D.P.—Arbeitshandbuch, I. Strategie der Eigenständigkeit [F.D.P.—working manual I. strategy of self-sufficiency] (Bonn 1976), Section I/2, p. 5.

[9] Karl-Hermann Flach, Noch eine Chance für die Liberalen. Oder: Die Zukunft der Freiheit, Eine Streitschrift [Another chance for the liberals or the future of freedom: a dissent] (Frankfurt/Main: S. Fischer, 1971), p. 8 ff., particularly p. 13.

[10] For a recent history of the FDP platform, see Peter Juling, Programmatische Entwicklung der FDP 1946 bis 1969. Einführung und Dokumente [Programmatic development of the FDP from 1946 to 1969: introduction and documents], Studies of the Political System of the Federal Republic, vol. 19 (Meisenheim: Hain, 1977).

bility of any one party's having an absolute majority, and not only out of self-interest; this principle is also an expression of the fundamental distrust with which Liberals view power agglomerations that might threaten minority rights. It is in addition an expression of the fact that liberalism is inimical to all-encompassing, hard and fast solutions. At least as defined by Flach, liberalism teaches above all the necessity of constant reexamination and adaptation in the political sphere, a field of action in which there cannot and must not be final solutions.[11]

The primary goal of the strategy of self-sufficiency, then, was to define the role and function of the FDP in the Federal Republic in terms of political content and democratic principles and not, as has been the case in the past, in terms of power or coalition politics.

There are structural reasons for the high electoral stability in the Federal Republic, most notably the clear dominance of the two major parties, the CDU/CSU and the SPD, but also the clear lead of the FDP over all of the smaller parties. These characteristics will be explained here only insofar as they relate to the conduct of the CDU/CSU or SPD on the one hand and the FDP on the other. There are several reasons for the structural imbalance between the FDP and the two major parties.[12]

(1) In the churches and the unions, the CDU/CSU and SPD have political bases from which the greater number of their steady voters are recruited. The FDP has no comparable political base in society as a whole. Although the Liberal party competes with the CDU/CSU for support among sectors of the entrepreneurial and middle class, the latter clearly dominates. This fact affects the attractiveness of the FDP to the voters.[13]

(2) State financing of political parties tends to reinforce existing power relations because the level of financial support is determined by the number of votes received. Since none of the Bundestag parties is in a position to meet the costs of personnel and organization from membership dues alone, it is unavoidable that, with the more limited state subsidization of the FDP relative to the CDU/CSU, it trails the other

---

[11] Flach, p. 13.

[12] See *Liberales Forum*, March 1974, p. 5.

[13] It was generally agreed that the farmers were essentially satisfied with the agrarian policy implemented since 1969 by Joseph Ertl, the Liberal agriculture minister. Nonetheless, the FDP lost votes among those voters, who are usually position oriented and in sympathy with the CDU-CSU, as are their leading organization officials.

parties in organizational presence. While the CDU/CSU and SPD have been able to build strong organizations from the neighborhood to the state level, the FDP has no organizational presence in numerous communities of the Federal Republic.[14]

(3) Since the war the German party system has become increasingly concentrated. In the Bundestag elections of 1949 the two major parties won 60 percent of the vote; by 1972 their share had risen to over 90 percent, where it remained in 1976. As a result, the media have tended to refer to a de facto two-party system, and the voters have tended to think in either-or terms.[15] Political alternatives are consistently presented and assessed in terms of clear pros and cons, yes or no, "red" or "black." In addition, compromise has negative connotations in German political culture.[16] It is difficult for the mass of voters to sympathize with a party that tends to be perceived as a disturbing factor in such a scenario.

(4) The dominant concern of the electorate is the striving for security. It can hardly approve of a party whose very existence is constantly threatened. With only slightly more than the 5 percent of the vote necessary for inclusion in the Bundestag, the FDP radiates insecurity. The relativism implicit in its Liberal principles only reinforces the fact that such a party is not attractive to voters whose political orientation is based on a striving for security.

As a result of this structural framework, the FDP has been favored primarily by educated and highly skilled minorities. An analysis of the FDP electorate according to sociostructural criteria shows that the FDP voter is of above-average education, above-average political interest, and above-average social and geographic mobility. Nevertheless, all analyses of the FDP support base suggest that its sociological composition is relatively diffuse. This is apparently due to the significantly

---

[14] With reference to party financing, see: Heino Kaack, "Die Finanzen der Bundestagsparteien von 1968 bis 1975" [The finances of the Bundestag parties from 1968 to 1975] in Heino and Ursula Kaack, eds., *Parteien-Jahrbuch 1975. Dokumentation und Analyse der Entwicklung des Parteiensystems der Bundesrepublik Deutschland im Jahre 1975* [Party yearbook 1975: documentation and analysis of the development of the party system in the Federal Republic of Germany in 1975], Studies of the Political System of the Federal Republic of Germany, vol. 16 (Meisenheim: Hain, 1977).

[15] On the concentration of the party system, see the attempt at typology by Werner Kaltefleiter, "Wandlungen des deutschen Parteiensystems 1949–1974" [Changes in the German party system 1949–1974] in *Aus Politik und Zeitgeschichte*, vol. 14/75, April 5, 1975.

[16] Compare with Theodor Wilhelm, *Traktat über den Kompromiss. Zur Weiterbildung des politischen Bewusstseins* [Treatise on compromise: on the further development of political consciousness] (Stuttgart: Metzler, 1973).

higher voter turnover of the FDP as compared to the CDU/CSU or SPD,[17] which itself can be explained if one differentiates between FDP voters according to their motives for party preference. One can distinguish the following types of voters: (1) those who temporarily endorse the FDP in order to withhold their votes from the CDU/CSU and SPD—in essence, undecided two-party-system voters; (2) those who prefer the FDP on democratic grounds, particularly because of their basic reservations about an absolute majority of any one party; (3) those who are attracted to FDP national leaders on grounds of personality or competence; (4) those whose class identification and interests align them with the FDP, for example high civil servants and managers, usually in the upper-middle and upper class; and (5) those who prefer the FDP on the grounds of party platform, believing their own liberal convictions to be actively represented by the FDP.

It is obviously difficult to separate and evaluate quantitatively these motives. But overall, it could be said that secondary and temporal motives clearly predominate.

The structural problems of the FDP we have outlined are all the greater when the party's behavior deviates from prevailing expectations. In the mid-1960s most people expected the FDP to be a reliable and consistent partner of the CDU/CSU and to participate with the Union in government. This was true not only for the electorate, but to an even greater extent for the party members and officers. Within the FDP, factional cleavages were always closely related to coalition policy. Traditionally, discussion of coalition policy supplanted debate within the FDP over substantive political issues. Any substantive differences between factions inside the FDP were less conspicuous than their vows of loyalty to the coalition.

In late 1966 the FDP, fully unprepared, was forced into the opposition after the formation of the grand coalition between the CDU/CSU and the SPD. Shortly thereafter, a majority within the FDP began to push for a reorientation of the party.[18] By 1968–1969 the change of coalition partners had become a symbol of this reorientation of political content. As the party leadership around Walter Scheel became more convinced of the wisdom of an alliance with the Social Demo-

---

[17] Another reason is "The evolution of a party through the quadrants of the party system with a new policy position in the span of five years," from 1967 to 1972. See Max Kaase in *Politische Vierteljahresschrift*, vol. 14, no. 2 (1973), p. 167.

[18] See Kaack, *Die Liberalen* [The liberals], p. 420 ff., and Kaack, *Zur Geschichte und Programmatik der Freien Demokratischen Partei* [On the history and program of the Free Democratic party], p. 33 ff.

crats, the resistance of those who still favored a coalition with the CDU/CSU became more vocal. In practice, the habit of defining the party through its coalition preference allowed for only one form of intraparty compromise, that is, indecision with regard to any coalition commitment whatever. The FDP could only emerge from this structural dilemma if the coalition question were assigned a low priority in the party platform. The strategy of self-sufficiency postulated by Hans-Dietrich Genscher performed this function by providing room for the development of the FDP as an independent party despite its inclusion in the Socialist-Liberal coalition.

Landtag Elections and Coalition Policy

The background to the 1976 Bundestag election cannot be limited to the 1972–1976 period, but must include developments since 1969. The premature Bundestag election of 1972 was seen (and not only by the parties of the Socialist-Liberal coalition) as reinforcing, not contradicting, previous results; the 1969–1976 period is clearly a unit. Thus it is not by accident that the progress report of the FDP regarding the 1976 Bundestag election refers to the period 1969–1976. In the 1976 election, both the government and the opposition measured the achievements of 1972–1976 against the goals set in 1969–1972.

After it entered the Willy Brandt government, between 1970 and 1972, the FDP suffered a serious internal crisis characterized by the disaffection of numerous politicians who had been prominent in the more conservative wing of the party.[19] These internal disturbances were associated with a remarkable decline in membership[20] and seriously threatened the existence of the party and the Socialist-Liberal coalition. They also had considerable effects on the conduct of the FDP between 1972 and 1976. One can almost speak of a stability trauma: after the 1972 Bundestag election, at which the FDP fared far better than it had expected, the party's strategy was aimed at demonstrating the reliability of the FDP to the voters. At the same time efforts were made to widen support for the party's policy of favoring the Socialist-Liberal alliance despite the fact that through the ratification of the Freiburg Theses at the party conference in the fall of 1971 the

---

[19] For details see Heino Kaack, "Landtagswahlen und Bundespolitik 1970–1972" [Landtag elections and federal policy 1970–1972] in *Aus Politik und Zeitgeschichte*, vol. 13 (March 30, 1974), p. 6 ff.

[20] For the development of the constituent levels see Kaack, *Zur Geschichte und Programmatik der F.D.P.* [On the history and program of the F.D.P.], p. 51.

FDP's political platform had acquired a distinctly Socialist-Liberal slant.[21]

Consequently the off-year, 1973, was to be used for strengthening the party's organization and further developing the platform. The general secretary elected at the Freiburg party convention, Karl-Hermann Flach, was considered a symbol of the renewal of the FDP as a party of democratic and social liberalism.[22] But the FDP leaders almost without exception were committed to support for the coalition government and cooperation between the party caucuses. After the 1972 Bundestag election, this applied even to Flach, who had become a Bundestag delegate and deputy chairman of the FDP parliamentary group. Shortly thereafter, in August 1973, the general secretary who had outlined the Liberal posture in its contemporary political context in his polemic, "Another Chance for the Liberals," died. This left a vacuum in the party leadership, the effects of which became increasingly noticeable the more the Socialist-Liberal coalition encountered internal difficulties.

The energy crisis which broke in October 1973 as a consequence of the OPEC oil boycott further sharpened the economic policy problems of the relatively stable Federal Republic. To the excessive rates of price inflation was added a perceptible rise in unemployment, a phenomenon which had been virtually unknown in the Federal Republic for twenty years. But in the final analysis, the internal party disputes, particularly within the SPD, contributed more to the erosion of the chancellor's authority and the coalition than did the economic difficulties.

Survey analysis in the course of 1973 showed consistent losses in sympathy for the Social Democrats from their favorable position in late 1972. These were largely balanced by gains in sympathy for the FDP.[23] Overall the results of the Hamburg state election in early March 1974 confirmed this general trend: the SPD suffered losses while

[21] Party speeches and theses in Karl-Hermann Flach, Werner Maihofer, Walter Scheel, *Die Freiburger Thesen der Liberalen* [The Freiburg theses of the liberals] (Reinbek: Rowohlt, 1972).

[22] See Karl-Hermann Flach, *Liberaler aus Leidenschaft* [Liberal by passion] (Munich: C. Bertelsmann, 1974) with a preface by Flach and a collection of important speeches and writings by Flach.

[23] See Reinhold Roth, "Die Parteien in der Wählermeinung 1973/74" [Voter opinion on political parties 1973/74] in Heino and Ursula Kaack, eds., *Parteien-Jahrbuch 1973/74: Dokumentation und Analyse der Entwicklung des Parteiensystems der Bundesrepublik Deutschland in den Jahren 1973 und 1974* [Party yearbook 1973/74: documentation and analysis of the development of the party system in the Federal Republic of Germany in the years 1973 and 1974], Studies on the Political System of the Federal Republic of Germany, vol. 11 (Meisenheim: Hain, 1977), p. 38 ff., particularly p. 47.

the FDP gained. The extent of the Social Democratic losses, however, and even more the fact that the FDP, though it gained considerably over its showing in the 1970 state elections in Hamburg, did not match its results in the 1972 Bundestag election, caused some surprise.[24] Some national party spokesmen attempted to explain this by claiming that the Hamburg FDP had adopted a stance that placed it distinctly to the left of the national party.

In any case, having failed to take steps to improve the long-term competitive position of their party in 1973, FDP leaders were now preoccupied—as were SPD leaders—with crisis management after the Hamburg election. In May 1974 a spy affair implicating Willy Brandt sparked the resignation of the chancellor, and the previous FDP chairman and foreign minister, Walter Scheel, was elected president. The interior minister, Hans-Dietrich Genscher, who had been considered a potential successor to Scheel as party chairman, moved into the foreign office. The change within the Social Democratic party proceeded equally smoothly; Helmut Schmidt succeeded Willy Brandt, who retained his position as party chairman. Strategists in both of the coalition parties hoped that this reshuffling of leadership would end the losses of sympathy their parties had experienced and eventually win back previous Socialist-Liberal voters.[25]

On June 9, 1974, elections to the state legislature (Landtag) of Lower Saxony were held. The results corresponded only conditionally to these expectations. Although the losses of the Social Democrats lagged behind those in Hamburg, the trend of the Hamburg election was reinforced in principle in that the FDP was again unable to reach its 1972 results (see Tables 4–1 and 4–2). On the other hand, the Liberals could explain this new disappointment in terms of the particular difficulties they faced in Lower Saxony, where the FDP had not been represented in the Landtag for four years.

Responsible FDP politicians could no longer resort to this sort of self-justification when the party once again suffered defeats in the Hesse and Bavarian Landtag elections on October 27, 1974. Even if its readmission to the parliament of Lower Saxony could be seen as a success, the losses in Hesse were a clear portent: they were large in

---

[24] See Table 4–1. A short analysis of all 1974 Landtag elections and further references can be found in Reinhold Roth, "Die Landtags- und Kommunalwahlen 1973/74" [The Landtag and district elections 1973/74], Heino and Ursula Kaack, eds., *Parteien-Jahrbuch 1973/74* [Party yearbook 1973/74], p. 17 ff.

[25] See Ursula Kaack, "Die Koalitionspolitische Konstellation im Parteiensystem der Jahre 1973 und 1974" [The coalition policy constellation in the party system of the years 1973 and 1974], Heino and Ursula Kaack, eds., *Parteien-Jahrbuch 1973/74* [Party yearbook 1973/74], p. 292 ff.

comparison with both the Bundestag election of 1972 and the Landtag election of 1970. In Bavaria, the FDP won the same proportion of the votes as it had in the 1970 election, but because of a change in the counting procedure it lost the organizational and financial privileges of a formally recognized parliamentary group, which seriously limited the effectiveness of the party. Since the Social Democrats simultaneously suffered considerable losses, the view spread within the FDP that the Liberals would be dragged down along with the SPD and would only be able to save themselves by changing their coalition partner. This, however, was contrary to the political strategy of the party leadership, which gave low priority to the coalition question.

It was precisely this strategy that Hans-Dietrich Genscher reiterated in his speech to the FDP party convention in late September 1974 when he was elected party chairman. Genscher had concluded from the historical experiences of the party that the FDP must always clearly present its coalition intentions to the voters.[26] In the present instance, a coalition commitment should be made before the electoral campaign to avoid any appearance of uncertainty or disunity on this point and to clear the way for the substantive political ideas that the FDP must make central to its campaign.

In the 1972 Bundestag election, the coalition caused no debate since this election was held for the explicit purpose of reinforcing the Socialist-Liberal alliance.[27] By then, the national political polarization extended completely to the states. The beginning of the end for the FDP-CDU state governments had come immediately after the 1969 Bundestag election when Kurt George Kiesinger, then CDU chairman and chancellor, had responded to the FDP's alliance with the SPD by threatening that the CDU would throw the Liberals out of the state governments. At the time there were FDP-CDU coalitions in three of the eleven states. In two of these, the coalitions came to an end when the FDP was unable to gain access to the respective Landtags in 1970 and 1971. In the third, Baden-Württemberg, the coalition ended when the CDU achieved an absolute majority in the spring of 1972. With the elimination of this last CDU-FDP coalition at the state level, FDP coalition policy became consistent throughout the country.[28]

---

[26] See the speeches of Genscher at the national and state conventions in 1974 and 1975.

[27] See, among others, Werner Kaltefleiter, *Zwischen Konsens und Krise. Eine Analyse der Bundestagswahl 1972* [Between consensus and crisis: An analysis of the Bundestag election 1972] (Köln: Heymanns, 1973); and *Zeitschrift für Parlamentsfragen*, March 1972 and January 1973.

[28] See Heino Kaack, *Zur Geschichte und Programmatik der F.D.P.* [On the history and program of the F.D.P.], pp. 32 and 46.

Although the 1972 election gave the Socialist-Liberal coalition a clear majority in the Bundestag, the states governed by the CDU or the CSU retained their majority in the Bundesrat.[29] Since the Bundesrat could influence legislation on many issues by either postponing or vetoing measures, the Landtag elections during the 1974–1976 period gained importance because of their potential impact on majority control in the Bundesrat. The state party organizations of the FDP consequently were pressured to take account of the national interests of the party. Coalition policy decisions rested with the state conventions, but the state central committees (Landeshauptausschüsse) and particularly the executive committees (Landesvorstände) often issued strong recommendations. The national committee of the party (Bundesvorstand) could not prescribe policy for the state parties since within the FDP nationally the state organizations carry more weight than does the national one. However, this situation was in turn affected by numerous interlocking memberships among the leading elite on the national and state levels.[30]

Furthermore, it must be noted that in many states the FDP had no coalition policy alternative. It would hardly have been understandable for the voter had the Liberals in Hamburg and Hesse failed to endorse the continuation of the coalition with the Social Democrats given the polarization in those states between the FDP and SPD on the one hand and the CDU on the other. Likewise in Bavaria a CSU-FDP coalition was hardly plausible considering the long-lived and vigorous disputes between the two parties, particularly in the area of educational policy—not to mention the fact that the CSU had a stable absolute majority in the Landtag. It was only in Lower Saxony that the FDP had a choice between the CDU and SPD in terms of state policy, and the decision within the state organization was contested accordingly. Not least because of national policy considerations, a majority ultimately favored alliance with the Social Democrats.[31]

Although a majority was formed by the Socialist-Liberal alliance in the Landtag of Lower Saxony and Hesse, the SPD lost its position as the strongest party in both states. The CDU consequently denounced

---

[29] The number of votes for the states governed by the CDU or CSU: Bavaria 5, Baden-Württemberg 5, Rhineland-Palatinate 4, Schleswig-Holstein 4, Saar 3 (total 21); the number of votes by the states governed by the SDP: North Rhine-Westphalia 5, Lower Saxony 5, Hesse 4, Hamburg 3, and Bremen 3 (total 20); Berlin has 4 votes but only conditional voting rights.

[30] See Heino Kaack, *Geschichte und Struktur* [History and structure], p. 673 ff.

[31] See Klaus Wettig, "Die niedersächsische Landtagswahl vom 9. Juni 1974" [The Lower Saxony Landtag election of June 9, 1974] in *Zeitschrift für Parlamentsfragen*, vol. 6, no. 4 (1975), p. 404 ff.

the SPD-FDP coalition as an alliance of losers and argued that the electoral success of the CDU expressed the will of the voter to replace the SPD with the CDU as the leading government party. If the FDP were to remain allied with the SPD, according to this view, it would be acting contrary to the will of the voter and would furthermore be showing that it had become the rump of the SPD. This argument probably was not without effect on voters wavering between the CDU and the FDP, although it was untenable on constitutional grounds and questionable in terms of democratic theory. It did, however, expose a weak point in the FDP's strategy: the prior announcement of a coalition preference narrowed the ability of the party to adapt to electoral results. The practical effect was to heighten awareness of the relationship between trends in the SPD and the FDP vote.

The electoral results in Hesse and Bavaria were considered especially disappointing, but they had only indirect effects on the FDP's coalition decisions in the states where elections were to take place in the course of 1975.[32] In Berlin and Schleswig-Holstein the decision favoring a coalition with the SPD had already been made. In North Rhine-Westphalia there was no alternative to a continuation of the SPD-FDP coalition that would not simultaneously jeopardize the Socialist-Liberal coalition in Bonn. There is an almost infallible rule in the Federal Republic that the existence of different coalitions in Bonn and Düsseldorf (the capital of North Rhine-Westphalia) compromises the effectiveness of both governments to the point that such an arrangement can only be temporary. In the Saar and Rhineland-Palatinate, on the other hand, the situation was considerably more open since there was a longstanding tradition of CDU-FDP alliances. However, internal developments in the Saar FDP, which since 1970 had not been represented in the Landtag, led to a surprisingly unambiguous preference for cooperation with the Social Democrats. The same weekend, January 11–12, 1976, after a lively internal debate, the FDP in the Rhineland-Palatinate gave preference to a CDU alliance by a slim majority.[33]

This vote was the first FDP coalition statement in favor of the CDU/CSU since 1972. It was considered particularly significant because the minister-president of the Rhineland-Palatinate, Helmut Kohl, was also national chairman of the CDU. In the internal CDU/CSU dispute Kohl was the chief opponent of Franz Josef Strauss and an advocate

---

[32] For a short analysis with further source references for the 1975 Landtag elections, see Robert Graeff, "Die Landtags- und Kommunalwahlen 1975" [The Landtag and district elections 1975] in *Party Yearbook 1975*.

[33] See the daily press of January 13, 1975.

of taking over the federal government by means of an alliance with the Free Democrats. On the other hand, the FDP organization in the Rhineland-Palatinate was considered comparatively conservative so that the leadership of the national party was able to credibly represent this divergent vote as a unique state policy decision. Simultaneously national leaders could adduce it as proof that the FDP in no way wanted to bind itself exclusively to the SPD, but would decide with which major party it would cooperate according to the demands of given situations at the state and national levels.

The FDP vote for an alliance with the CDU in the Rhineland-Palatinate did not, however, have any national or state policy implications. On the one hand the CDU reacted cautiously to the FDP's overture, and on the other the alliance became superfluous after the CDU succeeded in renewing its absolute majority in the Landtag. The fact that the FDP not only lagged behind its 1972 goals in the state but also fell short of its results in the 1971 Landtag election cast further doubt on the wisdom of its coalition policy there.

The elections that followed made the joint decline of the SPD and FDP seem less inevitable than it had previously. Although the SPD clearly did not repeat the results it had achieved in 1972 when Willy Brandt had led the party to victory (a victory that increasingly appeared to have been an isolated phenomenon), the Social Democrats were able to limit their losses to narrower margins at the state level and even began to speak of a reversal. Then in the Saar, on May 4, 1975, they finally surpassed their previous Landtag election results. The FDP, meanwhile, lagged behind its election goals only in the Rhineland-Palatinate and in Berlin, where special circumstances, in particular the kidnapping by anarchists of the CDU city-state chairman Peter Lorenz, easily explained its defeat. In the 1974 elections the FDP had clearly trailed behind the results forecast by the polls, but in 1975 its showings corresponded to realistic expectations and could be considered as stabilizing its position. Its gains in North Rhine-Westphalia were a particularly pleasant surprise since the polls had given the CDU a good chance of achieving an absolute majority there and of expanding its majority in the Bundesrat. Instead, the FDP's gains balanced the light losses of the SPD.[34] In Schleswig-Holstein the CDU was barely able to defend its absolute majority, and on the same day that the Socialist-Liberal coalition won a victory in North Rhine-Westphalia, the SPD

---

[34] For the FDP election results, see Tables 4–1 and 4–2. With reference to the polls, see Elizabeth Noelle-Neumann, ed., *Allensbacher Jahrbuch der Demoskopie 1976* [Allensbach yearbook of public opinion research 1976] (Wien: Molden, 1976), p. 118.

and FDP together won as many seats as the CDU in the Saar, taking twenty-five of the fifty seats the CDU had previously held.

This situation naturally put to the test the FDP's strategy of announcing its coalition commitment. In accordance with its electoral platform, the Saar FDP, which had received three seats in the Landtag, refused to enter an alliance with the CDU. Such an alliance would have given the CDU-FDP twenty-eight seats and the SPD opposition twenty-two, thus creating a stable coalition majority. Even a coalition with the FDP would not have given the SPD a majority, and the CDU government was forced to remain in office as a minority government (since according to the state constitution the CDU's term of office did not depend on election returns but on an adverse vote in the legislature). Finally, the FDP endorsed a policy of constructive opposition and thereby facilitated the passage of the state budget after it had won several concessions.[35] In the Bundesrat the CDU/CSU retained its majority even if in individual cases the Saar CDU government would not vote with the other CDU governments because of its dependence on FDP "toleration."

In the second half of 1975 few changes occurred that influenced the position of the FDP within the national party system. The Liberals achieved their greatest success of the period in the Bremen state elections, but since Bremen is the smallest federal state and is heavily pro-SPD, no inferences for national politics could be drawn from the outcome there (see Tables 4–1 and 4–2).

Overall, the FDP as well as the Socialist-Liberal coalition appeared to have stabilized by late 1975. Although the governing parties expected to lose some of their lead over the CDU/CSU in the 1976 Bundestag elections, the progress of the CDU/CSU toward an absolute majority in the Federal Republic seemed to have been checked. Even so, the governing parties had increasing difficulty in implementing their announced reform policy as economic and financial conditions had decreased their room for maneuver. At the same time the contrast between the two governing parties became sharper in the second period of the Socialist-Liberal alliance. This was particularly true in the area of economic and social policy; the end of *Ostpolitik*, meanwhile, meant that foreign policy no longer played an integrating role.[36]

---

[35] See Adolf Kimmel, "Ende der CDU/CSU-Mehrheit im Bundesrat oder Anfang vom Ende der 'Blockparteien'?" [End of the CDU/CSU majority in the Bundesrat or beginning of the end of the "bloc parties?"] in *Zeitschrift für Parlamentsfragen*, vol. 6, no. 3 (1975), p. 281 ff.

[36] Reinhold Roth, *Aussenpolitische Innovation und politische Herrschaftssicherung. Eine Analyse von Struktur und Systemfunktion des aussenpolitischen Entscheidungsprozesses am Beispiel der sozialliberalen Koalition 1969 bis 1973* [Foreign policy innovation and safeguarding of political authority: An analysis

Faced with these constraints, the government left many promises un-fulfilled. It stemmed the price rise but could find no effective solution to the rising unemployment rate, and as a result it had very little with which it could oppose the CDU and CSU. This was partially because it could alter little in the international framework, but also because the two Christian parties could not agree about an opposition strategy. While Franz Josef Strauss—and with him the CSU and parts of the CDU—pleaded for unconditional confrontation and insisted on an absolute majority as a prerequisite for governing, the majority of the CDU under Helmut Kohl tended toward a more flexible course and were prepared to consider the FDP a potential ally. This disagreement over opposition strategy was evident in the nomination process of the CDU/CSU before the 1976 Bundestag election.[37] The extent and form of the controversy gave fuel to the FDP's argument that the CDU/CSU was too irresolute to be a viable coalition partner.

In mid January 1976 the scenario changed considerably in favor of the CDU/CSU, when the opposition candidate, Ernst Albrecht, was unexpectedly elected minister-president of Lower Saxony following the premature resignation of Alfred Kubel of the SPD. The CDU did not have a majority in the Lower Saxony legislature. Yet, in a secret ballot, the CDU's leader, Albrecht, received a majority of the votes. He be-came minister-president but of a minority government since only the CDU members would openly acknowledge having voted for him.[38] This considerably strengthened the position of the CDU in the Bundesrat, while the FDP was confronted by a particularly difficult situation since it was suspected that some of the dissidents from the ranks of the Socialist-Liberal coalition who had voted for Albrecht were members

of the structure and system function of the foreign policy decision process using the example of the Socialist-Liberal coalition 1969 to 1973], Studies on the Political System of the Federal Republic of Germany, vol. 14 (Meisenheim: Hain, 1976).

[37] See Robert Graeff, "Auseinandersetzungen um Oppositionsstrategie und Führungspositionen" [Disputes over opposition strategy and leadership positions], in *Party Yearbook 1975*.

[38] Albrecht received 78 out of 155 votes on January 15, 1976, in spite of the fact that his party had only 77 seats in the Landtag, while Helmut Kasimir, the nominee of the Social Democrats for the Socialist-Liberal coalition, received only 74 votes. Consequently Albrecht became minister-president, but his cabinet needed the support of a majority of the Landtag in an open vote. The dissidents of the SPD and/or the FDP were not willing to publicly endorse Albrecht. Therefore Albrecht was forced to put himself up for election again after he had failed to form a cabinet endorsed by a majority within twenty-one days. In this vote on February 6, 1976, Albrecht received 79 votes and was thereby elected because the approval of the Landtag was no longer necessary for the formation of his cabinet.

of the FDP. The situation was exacerbated by the fact that the call went out to the FDP to assume the responsibility of forming a majority government and entering into an alliance with Albrecht after there was apparently no longer a basis for the continuation of a Socialist-Liberal coalition in Lower Saxony. However, the FDP chose—as it had in the Saar—the course of constructive opposition.

Since the FDP chairman and foreign minister Hans-Dietrich Genscher needed the support of a majority of the Bundesrat for the ratification of the treaty signed with Poland, and since this majority could only be achieved with the participation of the CDU states of the Saar and Lower Saxony as well as of the state governments led by the SPD, the public quickly began to perceive a connection between coalition policy and voting conduct. Genscher proposed more cooperation among all Bundestag parties, particularly in the field of foreign affairs, and in this context demanded a relaxation of the polarization between the Bonn government and the opposition parties.[39] He immediately received a critical response to this proposition—primarily from within the party—since it was suspected that this would pave the way for a general change in coalition policy. Although the states governed by the CDU and CSU finally endorsed the treaty with Poland, this did not contribute to a rapprochement between the parties.

One of the main causes for this was the hotly contested Landtag electoral race in Baden-Württemberg which had been dominated by the polarization issue although—or maybe because—the FDP had long remained undecided on the question of whether and in whose favor to make a coalition statement.[40] The state party convention of the FDP finally decided, against the will of the state chairman, Martin Bange-

---

[39] See the press coverage in February and March in the national dailies and weeklies, for example Gerhard E. Gründler, "Genscher gewinnt eine Alternative" [Genscher wins an alternative], *Vorwärts*, February 2, 1976; Rolf Zundel, "Die Liberalen pokern hoch" [The liberals bid high], *Die Zeit*, February 13, 1976; Heino Flottau, "Auflockerung heisst die Parole der Freien Demokraten" [The password with the Free Democrats is relaxation], *Süddeutsche Zeitung*, February 24, 1976; "Freie Demokraten wollen die Fronten zwischen den Parteien auflockern" [Free Democrats want to relax the polarization between the parties], *Stuttgarter Zeitung*, March 9, 1976; Hans Schuster, "Auflockerung—ein liberales Angebot" [Relaxation—a liberal offer], *Süddeutsche Zeitung*, March 26, 1976.

[40] See Hans-Peter Biege, Hans-Joachim Mann, Hans-Georg Wehling, "Die Landtagswahl vom 4. April 1976 in Baden-Württemberg" [The Landtag election of April 4, 1976 in Baden-Württemberg] in *Zeitschrift für Parlamentsfragen*, vol. 7, issue 3, 1976, p. 329 ff.; Research Group Elections: *Wahl in Baden-Württemberg. Eine Analyse der Landtagswahl am 4. April 1976* [Election in Baden-Württemberg: An analysis of the Landtag election of April 4, 1976], Bericht der Forschungsgruppe Wahlen e.V. Mannheim, Nr. 8, vom 7. April 1976 [Report of the Research Group Elections, Inc., Mannheim, Number 8, April 7, 1976].

mann, to take up coalition negotiations with the Social Democrats after the elections, providing none of the parties received an absolute majority. The focus of the controversy was the statement in the CDU platform that the issue of this election was the choice between a "democratic state" and a "socialistic society," a forerunner of the slogan that would dominate the CDU/CSU campaign in 1976. The FDP was counted almost without exception as a member of the Socialist camp. This confrontation in Baden-Württemberg sufficed to revive the polarization between the parties and to make any demands for flexibility—at least in 1976—remain moot.

The 1976 Bundestag Campaign of the FDP

By mid-1975, after the elections in North Rhine-Westphalia and the Saar, the FDP knew that the 1976 Bundestag election would be an attempt to win the voters' endorsement for a continuation of the Socialist-Liberal coalition. At the FDP's annual federal convention, which took place in October 1975 in Mainz, the party leadership clearly indicated that it did not see an alliance with the CDU/CSU as a viable alternative and announced that a clear statement of coalition preference would be forthcoming at the opening of the party's nominating convention in May 1976.[41]

From the outset the main strategic problem was not the coalition question, but the development of an interim initiative which would minimize the imbalance between the FDP and the major parties in a context of self-sufficiency[42] and which would stabilize or even expand the FDP electorate in the short term.

In preparing for the campaign, party officials placed great emphasis on vote analysis. The "1976 Business Report" issued by the FDP national headquarters made the following points:[43]

The party's election research program had been initiated in December 1973 to provide for a series of representative public opinion polls on the state and federal levels in preparation for the

---

[41] Speech of Hans-Dietrich Genscher to the twenty-sixth regular FDP convention in Mainz, October 27, 1975.

[42] Compare above (pp. 80–81) and footnote 12.

[43] F.D.P.—Die Liberalen: Geschäftsbericht 1976 [F.D.P.—The Liberals: activities report 1976], Bonn, 1976, p. 30.

Landtag elections. This had been continued for North Rhine-Westphalia, Rhineland-Palatinate, Schleswig-Holstein, and the Saar in the second half of 1974. Investigations had already been made in Lower Saxony, Hamburg, Bavaria, and Hesse. In addition, on the basis of all of the state polls conducted in 1974, a cumulative evaluation of the results on the federal level had been made in 1975.

The results of this analysis were first examined in a federal study in October 1975 and completed and made more accurate on the basis of widened investigation. Then in January 1976 a study was undertaken of the FDP's potential electoral support followed by a second survey in May 1976 of the same panel participants who had been interviewed for the 1975 federal study. The main goals of all these studies were the following: the determination of the potential size of the FDP vote according to the number and sociological structure of the votes available; the determination of the target groups besides the "hard core" of loyal FDP voters; and analysis of the stability of the electorate and of the potential for change in sociostructural and political terms.

In this connection it must be noted that the FDP had to overcome a number of difficulties in its voter analysis that did not affect the CDU/CSU and the SPD: while sensitive measures of potential sympathy for the major parties could be obtained using samples of only 1,000 persons, an analysis of potential support for the comparatively tiny FDP had to be based on much larger samples involving higher financial expenditures.

One of the main findings of all of the surveys conducted since 1973 was the discovery that "Liberal" was viewed as a considerably more positive label than "Conservative" or "Socialist," although its precise meaning remained obscure for the voter. Furthermore, it was determined that the adjective Liberal clearly was used with reference to the FDP. This encouraged the Free Democrats to fill out the content of their Liberal image.

The first preparations for the electoral campaign are also described in the FDP's 1976 Business Report:

The plans and preparations began in February 1975 at the Bundesgeschäftsstelle. It developed a voluminous blueprint which contained not only ideas about the content, conduct, and implementation of the 1976 electoral campaign, but also suggestions for the formation and activity of a prospective commission. (The plan was passed with amendments in May.)

Under the direction of the general secretary and the Bundesgeschäftsstelle chairman a campaign group was formed consisting of staff workers of the Bundesgeschäftsstelle, the parliamentary group, and personnel from the four FDP ministries, as well as friends of the party and professional advertisers. In March the presidium decided that there should be a briefing for a competition among three advertisement agencies and two public relations agencies and the campaign group proceeded to develop it. At preliminary meetings early in July 1975, the campaign group discussed with these agencies the standard written briefing, and the preliminary presentations took place in the presidium on July 11. The result was that two of the three advertising agencies and both public relations agencies were asked to prepare major presentations by August 18, 1975. After additional talks between the campaign group and the agencies in the summer of 1975, the presidium on September 16, 1975, chose the advertising agency Baums, Maug & Zimmermann (BMZ) and the public relations agencies Time Public Relations and Irlenborn & Partner.

On October 3, 1975, the presidium informed the national central committee about the status of the preparations for the Bundestag electoral campaign. The central committee for the most part approved the preliminary decisions that had been made. (Martin Bangemann resigned as general secretary in the same session.)

The national central committee drew up a daily calendar for the campaign. Simultaneously on September 30, 1975, the managers of the state party organizations were asked to review all important measures. It was proposed to the state central committees that they be informed of campaign developments through the Bundesgeschäftsführer or deputy manager. Several state parties took advantage of this. One essential consideration was quick communication and mobilization within the party.[44]

This early planning allowed the FDP to begin its public campaign in the last quarter of 1975, well before the other Bundestag parties. The FDP opened its campaign in October 1975 with a series of advertisements prepared by the Friedrich-Naumann foundation, of which the tradition of political liberalism was the theme. This was the first step

---

[44] Ibid., pp. 32–33.

toward implanting in the public mind the equation Liberal $=$ FDP.[45]

The opinion polls showed that the four FDP cabinet ministers were more popular than the Social Democratic ministers. They were evaluated in predominantly positive terms and were ranked not only as sympathetic, but also as particularly competent. At the same time the problem-solving ability ascribed to the FDP by the voter had risen. From this two conclusions were drawn for campaign strategy: (1) the personal role of the four ministers should be stressed, particularly since they represented departments responsible for particularly important tasks, and (2) the emphasis should be on achievement, first the proven achievements of the FDP and particularly its ministers, and second the necessary correlation between freedom and progress.[46]

The FDP's slogan was "Freedom-Progress-Achievement" and its main campaign brochure invited the public to "Vote for Achievement." The FDP's successful governmental and parliamentary activities were reviewed in a thirty-two-page prospectus with the motto "Liberal Achievement." Other brochures were specifically aimed at young and women voters. In the latter, the party tried to make the most of the fact that in comparison to the other federal parties it had not only the highest proportion of women members, but also the greatest number of women among its main candidates. This brochure spotlighted the careers of Liselotte Funcke, Hildegard Hamm-Brücher, Ingrid Matt-häus, and Helga Schuchardt, who had run in important list posi-

---

[45] The Friedrich-Naumann foundation is the publicly funded foundation allied with the FDP; see Chapter 8, p. 206 and footnote 25. In addition to the series of advertisements, a twenty-four-page brochure was published. With reference to this campaign, the "creative director" of the agency BMZ, Peter Zimmermann, was quoted as saying: "In the preliminary phase, when nobody was yet campaigning, we brought out the advertising campaign for the Friedrich-Naumann Foundation, which was to inform the citizen about the accomplishments of liberalism in Germany. It was signed 'the Liberals.' This concept was then simply taken over to the FDP in order to make it clear that the FDP was the only Liberal party in Germany which still advocated these goals." *Form 75* (Seeheim), third quarter, 1976, p. 30.

[46] See the speech of Werner Maihofer at the Mainz national convention, October 29, 1975, "Die liberale Position in der Gesellschafts- und Staatspolitik" [The Liberal position in social and state policy] (Brochure of the Bundesgeschäfts-stelle of the FDP, Bonn, 1975/76). Obviously the emphasis on achievement was contested within the party; with reference to this, see the remarks of Peter Zimmermann of the BMZ agency in *Form 75*, p. 28: "Our concept is that this is a small but agile party, a party of doers. They do something for the voters. This small party with its four ministers achieves more than its size would indicate; therefore, voters, strengthen it! Vote for achievement. And there is another slogan: 'Freedom, Achievement, Progress.' We don't think it is good; it is too interchangeable, and does not sufficiently describe the party. But it exists because some people within the party oppose the achievement slogan and need an alternative."

tions and had filled prominent offices within the party or parliamentary group, largely outside the areas that are typically considered women's concerns. Since there had been much public discussion of the discrepancy between the prevailing demands for emancipation and the small proportion of women in positions of political leadership in the Federal Republic, it was hoped that this appeal would be effective.[47]

In its main brochure, of which 2 million copies were published,[48] the FDP attempted first to clarify its function in the system and thereby appeal particularly to the voter who had reservations about a pure two-party system.[49] The party's self-image was then sketched in nine points, before the central theme of the brochure, "The Liberal Program of Achievement 1976–1980," was addressed. The program was outlined by policy area, with reference to the FDP leader associated with each: foreign policy and national security (Hans-Dietrich Genscher), economic policy (Hans Friderichs), domestic policy (Werner Maihofer), agricultural and nutritional policy (Josef Ertl), education (Hildegard Hamm-Brücher), social policy (Liselotte Funcke), and welfare policy (Wolfgang Mischnick).

The brochure itself was based on the platform that had been passed by the national convention in Freiburg on May 31, 1976.[50] After a preamble that sketched the party's Liberal principles and political bases, this document dealt with the various issue areas in the following order: state policy (domestic, legal, and cultural), educational policy, social policy, economic policy, agricultural policy, and foreign policy. The weighting that this order suggests probably corresponds to the importance of each area for the definition of a Liberal position. (Agricultural policy, for example, is considered a branch of economic policy in this context.)

The campaign platform was passed after discussions at working sessions before the convention and at the convention itself, where over 100 proposed amendments to the original draft were considered

---

[47] The proportion of women in the German Bundestag declined continuously from 9.2 percent in 1957 to 5.8 percent in 1972. See Heino Kaack, "Zur Personalstruktur und Führungsauslese im Parteienstaat" [On personnel structure and leadership selection in a party state] in *Parteien-Jahrbuch 1973/74* [Party yearbook 1973/74], p. 307 ff. For the Bundestag election in 1976, the FDP nominated women candidates in 23 of the 248 electoral districts (the SPD and CDU-CSU by contrast had only twelve each). Ten percent of the FDP members elected in 1976 were women, the largest proportion of any parliamentary group.

[48] *F.D.P.—Die Liberalen: Geschäftsbericht 1976* [F.D.P.—The Liberals: activities report 1976], p. 45.

[49] See above p. 82.

[50] Reprinted in Heino Kaack, *Zur Geschichte und Programmatik der F.D.P.* [On the history and program of the F.D.P.], p. 230 ff.

and numerous changes made. The extent of debate over the platform was exceptional by German standards, the general rule being that campaign platforms are swiftly adopted by party conventions with little or no amendment and often by unanimous vote.

But the FDP could afford a degree of internal controversy under the circumstances. It had been considered far more homogeneous than the other parties, and it was fully in keeping with the strategy of self-sufficiency that attention be shifted from the coalition to substantive political issues. The party convention thus set the stage so that Genscher's coalition formula—a strong public preference for the SPD—could be decided on without discussion and with only one dissenting vote. Nevertheless, an analysis of the minutes of the convention indicates that the change of emphasis from coalition to political substance was not altogether successful. This surely was due partially to the routine reporting of the press, but primarily to the statements of the campaign platform, although less to individual statements than to the general form of the statements, which was the same for all parties and thus did not call attention to the FDP's attempted change of emphasis.

In a recent study of the 1976 election campaign the following interesting conclusions were drawn:[51]

> The campaign publicity distributed to the media by the four major parties suggests that none of the parties designed its campaign to help the citizen make an educated judgment. All of them subordinated discussion of political content, substantive arguments, and concrete alternatives to a strategy aimed at persuasion. Each party's strategy was carefully planned and attuned to the other parties. Each was directed not to the politically thinking and acting citizen, but against him.
>
> At the normative level, a number of characteristics of campaigns oriented toward persuasion rather than rational choice can be identified:
>
> (1) The voter is encouraged to endorse values in the abstract, not in relation to substantive issues ("Vote Freedom").
>
> (2) Each party claims a monopoly over certain values and political goals and simultaneously implies that these values would be jeopardized by a victory for its opponent.

---

[51] Hans-Georg Helwerth, Wolfgang Niess, Rolf Sülzer, Bettina Wieselmann, Michael Zeiss, "Wahlkampf und politische Bildung" [Election campaign and political education] in *Aus Politik und Zeitgeschichte*, vol. 9/77 (March 5, 1977), p. 14 ff.

(3) Each party forces the voter to think about politics in terms of stereotypes, to identify with the party's stand on issues without asking questions about the actual content of the party's policies.

(4) Simple deprecation is the major weapon used against the opposing parties.

(5) Polarization occurs and produces fear.

(6) Policy is equated with leadership figures; the personal qualities of individuals are emphasized to detract attention from the shortcomings of the platform.

In summary, the public is not informed of the effects of political decisions during the campaign. It is impossible for the voter to determine from campaign publicity how particular aspects of a given party are linked with specific desired measures. The relationships between various actions are not exposed. The concrete difficulties of implementation inherent in the plans of the party are not discussed. The desired aims are presented as feasible, and the demands of the population are translated into election promises as if they could be fulfilled. The fact that in a complex society a constant tradeoff takes place, that power and governing claims must be fought for, that limited finances must be distributed according to particular priorities—all these aspects are ignored.

This normative model points out several basic shortcomings of the campaigns of the German parties in 1976, although two of the six characteristics listed above do not apply to the FDP campaign. Deprecating statements about political opponents and the generation of fear were avoided in the official campaign. In fact, the stronger the personal polemic between the leading candidates of the CDU/CSU and the SPD became, the more the FDP concentrated on appearing pointedly factual and fair. This was particularly clear in the televised debates between Schmidt, Kohl, Strauss, and Genscher three days before the election on October 1, 1976.[52] The polarization that occurred during the campaign was forced by the CDU/CSU slogan "Freedom instead of Socialism." The Social Democrats rightfully saw in this slogan a fallback to the anti-Communist campaigns of the 1950s, which had bluntly equated Socialists and Communists, the internal opponent and the external enemy.

---

[52] For the text of the program see Press and Information Center of the Federal Government, Overview of Television and Radio Commentary, Part I, No. 199a, October 1, 1976.

In its campaign the cdu/csu did not differentiate between the spd and the fdp. The Liberals felt defamed not only by the equation of the fdp with the Social Democrats but also by the attempt of the cdu/csu to present itself as the truly Liberal party, sole guarantor of individual rights against all foes. The Free Democrats' attempts to dent this aspect of the cdu/csu's image—largely through the defensive formula "in this country no party has a monopoly on freedom"—were not successful.[53]

One of the key points of the campaign model outlined above is the suggestion that the voter is not offered alternative assessments, that neither the pros and cons of given policies nor the limits of their feasibility are presented. In evaluating this critique, one must realize that the past process of political socialization in the Federal Republic has not fully prepared either the parties or the voters to play such an idealized national role in an electoral campaign. The analysis of the content of the most important supraregional and local media in itself reveals numerous barriers to the realization of a completely rational campaign. Yet the fdp in particular might be expected to favor the articulation of alternatives in accordance with the Liberal outlook described early in this chapter and because the fdp aims not at winning an absolute majority but at winning a particular qualified and highly motivated minority. As a government party, however, the fdp could hardly undertake an open assessment, since this would imply criticism of the status quo for which the government is always held responsible.

Election campaigns are determined not only by strategic considerations, but also by financial and organizational limits. In the case of the fdp these were of considerable consequence. Despite the electoral success of 1972, the fdp carried heavy debts in 1973 and 1974 which were only paid after the change in office of the national party treasurer in the fall of 1974 through the implementation of rigorous fiscal restraint. This fiscal restraint required above all a considerable reduction of the personnel of the national party office but also the limitation of the 1976 campaign budget to the 1972 level. Consequently, the fdp had at its disposal for the 1976 election only DM 10 million, while the cdu and spd each could count on four times that sum. The cdu candidate campaigning exclusively in Bavaria had funds roughly equal to the total available to the fdp.[54]

The fdp was thus forced to concentrate its limited means at focal

---

[53] Ibid., p. 6.

[54] For the official campaign budgets of the parties, see zaw Service, vol. 4, no. 46, 1976, p. 2 published by Zentralausschuss der Werbewirtschaft-zaw, Bonn.

points in order to be able to compete with the major parties in at least some areas. On the other hand, it had to provide coverage in a minimal number of Bundestag election districts, although in contrast to the other Bundestag parties it could not establish a campaign office in each of the 248 electoral districts. The organizational difficulties were amplified by a lack of cooperation among the individual party organizations described in a report issued by the national headquarters:

For the 1976 Bundestag election regional priorities for the use of campaign resources were developed on the basis of survey results and a detailed district analysis. The local FDP would mount the best campaign it could in each of the 248 districts, and the national party would provide additional support (for example, speakers) in those districts where the greatest additional benefit could be expected. After consultation with the state FDP organizations, however, this plan was modified to reflect the differing organizational strength and regional interests of the state organizations. Beginning in October 1975 fifty campaign offices were established in the Federal Republic. The national party paid monthly contributions toward the personnel costs of these offices and provided each with a campaign car, a small bus equipped with a speaker system, and the materials necessary for information stands and a street campaign. The buses were used as mobile units for street campaigning for an average of five districts each, the offices as depots for campaign materials to be distributed to those in charge of specific campaign tasks. These resources were used with varying effectiveness.[55]

Several points can be made about the 1976 FDP campaign overall.

(1) The focus of the FDP's self-image was liberalism—whence the party's main slogan, "FDP—the Liberals."

(2) A further accent was placed on achievement.

(3) The campaign was personalized to a great extent; the FDP ministers were represented as "the four on whom the future depends."

(4) The polarization between the CDU/CSU and the SPD remained a dominant pattern of the campaign. Its political substance could be minimized but not eliminated.

(5) The Liberals' position as a government party as well as their limited financial, organizational, and personal resources left the FDP little margin for unconventional electoral initiatives.

---

[55] *F.D.P.—Die Liberalen: Geschäftsbericht 1976* [F.D.P.—The Liberals: activities report 1976], pp. 30–31 and p. 34.

(6) During the campaign, neither political developments nor the FDP's campaign itself produced any new reasons for the voter to choose the Liberals.

Thus, the FDP's campaign was essentially defensive, aimed at stabilizing the Liberal vote. It was not apt to win over new voters.

The Election Results

On election night, the FDP's showing was perceived as the biggest surprise of the election. The Liberals had won a mere 7.9 percent of the second-ballot votes, trailing 0.5 percentage points behind their 1972 results (see Tables 4–1 and 4–2). Most observers had expected the FDP vote to rise, and some had given it a good chance of exceeding the 10 percent mark. These expectations had been based on polls and on developments during the campaign.

Opinion surveys using the question "Which party would you vote for if federal elections were held next Sunday?" taken between 1973 and 1975 had shown the FDP's share of the responses to be higher than its 1972 election results; in a 1974 survey the Liberals' share was

TABLE 4–1

FEDERAL AND STATE ELECTION RESULTS OF THE FDP, 1972–1976
(in percentages of second-ballot votes)

	Election		
State	Bundestag, 1972	Landtag, 1974–1976	Bundestag, 1976
Schleswig-Holstein	8.6	7.1	8.8
Hamburg	11.2	10.9	10.2
Lower Saxony	8.5	7.0	7.9
Bremen	11.1	13.0	11.8
North Rhine-Westphalia	7.8	6.7	7.8
Hesse	10.2	7.4	8.5
Rhineland-Palatinate	8.1	5.6	7.6
Baden-Württemberg	10.2	7.8	9.1
Bavaria	6.1	5.2	6.2
Saar	7.1	7.4	6.6
Berlin	—	7.2	—
Federal Republic of Germany (without Berlin)	8.4	6.9	7.9

SOURCE: Federal Statistical Office Wiesbaden, Series A: *Bevölkerung und Kultur* [Population and culture], Reihe 8, Stuttgart and Mainz, 1961.

TABLE 4–2

COMPARISON OF THE NATIONAL AND STATE FDP ELECTION RETURNS,
1970–1976

(in percentage point gains and losses)

State	*Elections Being Compared*			
	Landtag, 1974–1976 and Landtag, 1970–1972	Landtag, 1974–1976 and Bundestag, 1972	Bundestag, 1976 and Bundestag, 1972	Bundestag, 1976 and Landtag, 1974–1976
Schleswig-Holstein	+3.0	−1.5	+0.2	+1.7
Hamburg	+3.8	−0.3	−1.0	−0.7
Lower Saxony	+2.7	−1.5	−0.6	+0.9
Bremen	+5.9	+1.9	+0.7	−1.2
North Rhine-Westphalia	+1.2	−1.1	± 0	+1.1
Hesse	−2.7	−2.8	−1.7	+1.1
Rhineland-Palatinate	−0.3	−2.5	−0.5	+2.0
Baden-Württemberg	−1.1	−2.4	−1.1	+1.3
Bavaria	± 0	−0.9	+0.1	+1.0
Saar	+3.0	+0.3	−0.5	−0.8
Berlin	−1.3	—	—	—
Federal Republic of Germany (without Berlin)	+0.5	−1.5	−0.5	+1.0

SOURCE: Calculated from statistics given in Table 4–1.

as high as 14 percent.[56] The party's poorer showings in the 1974 Landtag elections had suggested that the Liberals were not making full use of their potential sympathizers, but in 1975 the discrepancy between the poll results and the election returns had been milder. In part this could be explained by the fact that the FDP was less attractive at the state level than at the national level. Consequently, the FDP's ratings in the 1976 polls for the national elections, while considered somewhat exaggerated, were on the whole regarded as realistic. All of them forecast a neck-and-neck race between the government and

[56] See Elisabeth Noelle-Neuman, ed., *Allensbacher Jahrbuch* [Allensbach yearbook], pp. 118–119.

the opposition parties as well as clear losses for the SPD, partially balanced by a slight rise in the proportion of FDP votes.[57]

During the campaign it seemed increasingly likely that the FDP would do well despite the overwhelming influence of the polarization between the two governing parties and their leading representatives. Many were convinced that voters would choose the FDP as a way of avoiding the harsh choice called for by the major parties' campaigns and of promoting political consensus. This possibility—presumably reinforced by the impact of the television debate between the four party leaders—was much overrated.[58]

At any rate, events in the last phase of the campaign obscured the known fact that the FDP always loses sympathizers during the final weeks of a campaign when there is a sharp polarization between the two major parties. This helped make the discrepancy between the results and expectations on election night particularly great.

Yet the leading FDP candidates, though disappointed, were hardly crushed. The FDP and SPD had reached the goal of renewing their mandate to continue the governing coalition. Furthermore, the Liberals could point to the fact that they had succeeded in narrowing the margin between their first- and second-ballot results. While the FDP had won only 4.8 percent of the first-ballot vote in 1972, in 1976 it won 6.4 percent, an increase of 1.6 percentage points.[59] Its first-ballot results amounted to 81 percent of its second-ballot results. As sample statistics showed, 60.7 percent of the voters who cast their second ballot for the FDP also voted for the FDP on the first ballot, while 29.9 percent voted for the SPD and only 6.8 percent for the CDU. Overall, the votes split the same way as in 1972: the splitting took place largely between the SPD and FDP whereas in 1969 splitting between the CDU/CSU and the FDP had predominated (see Table 4–3). A comparison of several Bundestag elections shows clearly that more vote splitting occurred in the 1972 election than in any other election and that consequently 1972 must be seen as a special case. Thus the high proportion of FDP first-ballot votes in 1976 as compared to 1972 not only was a consequence of the redoubled efforts of the FDP to capture first-ballot votes,

---

[57] See, for example, the polls published in *Stern*, no. 36 (August 26, 1976), p. 17 and no. 41 (September 30, 1976), p. 17.

[58] See the daily press in the Federal Republic, October 2, 1976.

[59] Statistisches Bundesamt Wiesbaden, *Bevölkerung und Kultur* [Population and culture], series 8, "Wahl zum 8. Deutschen Bundestag" [Election of the eighth German Bundestag], October 3, 1976, issue 5: *Endgültige Ergebnisse nach Wahlkreisen* [Final results according to electoral districts] (Stuttgart and Mainz: Kohlhammer, 1976), p. 4.

TABLE 4–3

VOTE SPLITTING AMONG SECOND-BALLOT FDP VOTERS, 1957–1976
(in percentages)

Party Supported on First Ballot	Second Ballot for the FDP					
	1957	1961	1965	1969	1972	1976
SPD	3.8	3.1	6.7	24.8	52.9	29.9
CDU/CSU	7.5	8.1	20.9	10.6	7.9	8.0
FDP	85.0	86.5	70.3	62.0	38.2	60.7
Others/invalid votes	3.7	2.3	2.1	2.6	1.0	1.4

SOURCE: Federal Statistical Office Wiesbaden, *Bevölkerung und Kultur*, Reihe 8, and *Bevölkerung und Erwerbstätigkeit*, Fachserie 1.

but equally suggested that the 1972 elections must be classified as atypical.

But the coalition only barely reached its election goal. The SPD lost 16 seats, and its total dropped from 230 in 1972 to 214. The FDP lost 2 seats, which reduced its total to 39. Moreover, the coalition's lead over the opposition declined from 46 to 10 seats—smaller than the Brandt/Scheel coalition's lead after the 1969 election. Both in 1969 and in 1976 the CDU/CSU had a majority in the Bundesrat. Nevertheless, the SPD-FDP majority was relatively stable. Doubts about the loyalty of the FDP had been largely allayed by the firm commitment to the Socialist-Liberal alliance made by the FDP convention in May 1976.

An inquiry into the changes in the FDP electorate from 1972 to 1976—necessarily tentative at this point given the state of information available on the 1976 election—may begin with an analysis of the election results by state.

The changes in the FDP vote at the state level between 1972 and 1976 range from +0.7 to −1.7 percentage points (see Table 4–2). In Rhineland-Palatinate and the Saar the FDP's share of the votes changed exactly as much as the national average, −0.5 percentage points; in Lower Saxony the losses slightly exceeded the national average, −0.6 percentage points. A clear negative tendency was evident in Hamburg (−1.0), Baden-Württemberg (−1.1), and above all in Hesse (−1.7). In these states the difference between first- and second-ballot votes had been particularly great in the 1972 election. The extremely high level of vote splitting between SPD preference (first ballot) and FDP preference (second ballot) pointed out that many of those who voted FDP on the second ballot in 1972 were SPD sympathizers who had voted FDP in order to safeguard the coalition; in 1976 they returned to the ranks of the SPD because they believed the position of the SPD to be in jeopardy. This hypothesis is supported by the fact that in numerous areas where the FDP recorded excessive losses the SPD did relatively well.

The FDP's results were relatively good in North Rhine-Westphalia (where the party's good showing in the 1975 Landtag election was indirectly reinforced), Bavaria, Schleswig-Holstein, and Bremen. In Bavaria the FDP obviously profited from the fact that in the Liberal Diaspora areas the continued presence of the FDP as a national government coalition party had stabilizing effects. Munich was a special case: extremely high SPD losses due to internal party conflicts favored the FDP, although they were even more helpful to the CDU. In Schleswig-Holstein and Bremen, on the other hand, the relatively good showing of the FDP was the product of its own state party organizations.

Overall the FDP's national vote was one percentage point higher than the average it achieved in Landtag elections from 1974 to 1976. This confirmed the fact that the FDP generally achieves a greater proportion of the votes on the national than on the state level. However, the long-term trends in the various states are very different. Quite evident is the fact that the restructuring of the FDP into a party of chiefly democratic and social liberalism was effected rather differently in the various state party organizations. The state differences are reflected in the differences between state and national vote averages (see Table 4–4). It is also useful to note that between 1965 and 1975 the FDP improved its relative position in Schleswig-Holstein, Hamburg, Bremen, North Rhine-Westphalia, and Bavaria, while it declined in Lower Saxony, Hesse, Rhineland-Palatinate, Baden-Württemberg, and the Saar.

With the exception of Bavaria, the states where the FDP's results improved are those in which the young age groups (eighteen to thirty-five) are overrepresented by national standards. It is not coincidental that a distinctly conservative state organization like that of Rhineland-Palatinate had least response among the eighteen to twenty-five year-olds (see Table 4–5).

Once again, in 1976 the FDP achieved its greatest proportions of the vote in areas with a high proportion of civil servants and white-collar workers as well as in metropolitan areas, although it also registered its largest losses in these areas. The FDP could assert itself in the predominantly Catholic regions, but lost by comparison in the Protestant strongholds (see Table 4–6). Thus, overall, a leveling of

TABLE 4–4

Deviation of the fdp State Results from National Averages, Bundestag Elections, 1961–1976

State	1961	1965	1969	1972	1976
Schleswig-Holstein	+1.0	−0.1	−0.6	+0.2	+0.9
Hamburg	+2.9	−0.1	+0.5	+2.8	+2.3
Lower Saxony	+0.4	+1.4	−0.2	+0.1	±0.0
Bremen	+2.4	+2.2	+3.5	+2.7	+3.9
North Rhine-Westphalia	−1.0	−1.9	−0.4	−0.6	−0.1
Hesse	+2.4	+2.5	+0.9	+1.8	+0.6
Rhineland-Palatinate	+0.4	+0.7	+0.5	−0.3	−0.3
Baden-Württemberg	+3.8	+3.6	+1.7	+1.8	+1.2
Bavaria	−4.1	−2.2	−1.7	−2.3	−1.7
Saar	+0.1	−0.9	+0.9	−1.3	−1.3

Source: Same as in Table 4–1.

the fdp's share of the vote took place, involving losses in the fdp strongholds and stabilization in the Diaspora areas.

One of the most significant changes in the fdp electorate in 1976 as compared with 1972 was in the voting behavior of the sexes. While the Free Democrats lost 0.7 percentage points among males, they fell short of their target vote among women by only −0.1 percentage point. Women between the ages of eighteen and forty-five voted for the fdp in greater proportions than in 1972 (see Table 4–7).

On the whole, the fdp electorate changed only slightly from 1972 to 1976. Above all, the fdp's position in the party system remained relatively unchanged. As polls and representative statistics prove, a clear majority of the fdp voters preferred the Social Democrats to the cdu/csu.

The Consequences of the Election for the FDP and for the German Party System

After the election the fdp was forced to recognize that its position in the German party system had not improved. The quantitative discrepancy between the Liberals and the major parties was maintained. Moreover, the fdp had not bettered the 5 percent limit by enough to

107

TABLE 4–5

OVER- AND UNDERREPRESENTATION OF AGE GROUPS IN THE
FDP ELECTORATE, BY STATE, 1976 BUNDESTAG ELECTION
(in percentages and percentage points)

State	FDP Vote, 1976[a]	Age Groups[b]				
		18–25	25–35	35–45	45–60	Above 60
Schleswig-Holstein	8.8	+2.9	+2.8	+1.4	± 0	−3.6
Hamburg	10.0	+2.0	+5.1	+2.5	+0.1	−4.2
Lower Saxony	7.6	+1.0	+2.5	+1.0	−0.3	−2.3
Bremen	12.5	+0.7	+4.1	+1.0	+0.9	−3.5
North Rhine-Westphalia	7.8	+1.3	+3.1	+0.7	−0.4	−2.8
Hesse	8.6	+0.5	+2.9	+1.4	−0.1	−2.7
Rhineland-Palatinate	7.2	−0.1	+1.4	+0.7	−0.1	−1.4
Baden-Württemberg	9.2	± 0	+2.9	+1.4	−0.7	−2.5
Bavaria	6.0	± 0	+2.0	+1.0	−0.3	−1.6
Saar	6.5	+0.9	+1.3	+0.5	−0.4	−1.5
Federal Republic of Germany	7.8	+0.7	+2.7	+1.1	−0.3	−2.4

[a] This is the percentage of second-ballot votes for the FDP in the 1976 Bundestag elections based on a random poll; there were only slight differences between the results of the sampling and the actual results; compare with Table 4–1.

[b] These figures are percentage-point deviations among age cohorts from the FDP state average based on random poll results.

SOURCE: Statistisches Bundesamt Wiesbaden, Fachserie A, Heft 8, *Wahlbeteiligung und Stimmabgabe der Männer und Frauen nach dem Alter* [Voter participation and voting of men and women according to age], Stuttgart and Mainz, 1977.

feel that its existence was safe. But it found comfort in the fact that its position had stabilized. Indeed, the rise in the level of first-ballot votes pointed to an enlargement of the party's permanent base, a hypothesis confirmed by surveys about party identification. Even so, the FDP has a higher rate of voter turnover than the CDU, the CSU, or the SPD.

Despite its losses at the second ballot, the FDP reached its election goal—the continuation of the Socialist-Liberal coalition. The announcement of a coalition preference before the election had not been without risk for the Free Democrats in view of the closeness of

TABLE 4–6

INFLUENCE OF SOCIAL VARIABLES ON THE FDP's SECOND-BALLOT VOTE,
1976 AND CHANGE 1972–1976
(in percentages and percentage points)

	FDP Vote	
Social Group	1976	Change from 1972
Lowest segment of blue-collar pop.	9.0	−1.0
Middle segment of blue-collar pop.	7.3	−0.6
Upper segment of blue-collar pop.	6.3	−0.2
Lowest segment of civil servant pop.	5.1	−0.2
Middle segment of civil servant pop.	7.3	−0.3
Upper segment of civil servant pop.	9.2	−0.9
Lower segment of professional pop.	8.1	−0.7
Middle segment of professional pop.	8.2	−0.3
Upper segment of professional pop.	5.5	−0.5
Lower segment of Catholic pop.	8.9	−0.8
Middle segment of Catholic pop.	8.4	−0.8
Upper segment of Catholic pop.	5.1	0.0
Cities with populations less than 5,000	6.0	−0.3
Cities with populations from 5,000–250,000	7.7	−0.5
Cities with populations above 500,000	9.1	−0.7
Federal Republic of Germany	7.9	−0.5

SOURCE: Forschungsgruppe Wahlen [Election Research Group], *Bundestagswahl 1976. Eine Analyse der Wahl zum 8. Deutschen Bundestag am 3. Oktober 1976* [1976 Bundestag elections, an analysis of the eighth Bundestag election, October 3, 1976], Mannheim, October 7, 1976.

the race between the SPD and FDP on the one hand and the CDU/CSU. If the election had produced a tie, 248 to 248, in the Bundestag, a tedious process of political negotiation could not have been avoided and either outcome would have been detrimental to the FDP.

After the 1976 election both government parties soon realized that their position had become harder rather than easier. This was a result not only of the narrowing of the coalition's majority in the Bundestag and the CDU/CSU's continued majority in the Bundesrat, but also, and above all, of the persistent political pressure on the government. For the time being, crisis management was its major task. On

TABLE 4–7

FDP VOTE ACCORDING TO AGE AND SEX OF VOTERS, 1976
AND CHANGE 1972–1976
(in percentages and percentage points)

Age Groups	Men 1976	Men Change 1972–1976	Women 1976	Women Change 1972–1976	Men and Women 1976	Men and Women Change 1972–1976
18–25	8.5	(−1.1)	8.6	(+0.1)	8.5	(−0.6)
25–35	10.3	(−0.2)	10.7	(+0.6)	10.5	(+0.2)
35–45	9.0	(+0.1)	8.7	(+0.4)	8.9	(+0.3)
45–60	7.7	(−1.2)	7.4	(−0.3)	7.5	(−0.7)
60–	5.7	(−1.0)	5.2	(−0.5)	5.4	(−0.7)
Federal Republic of Germany	8.1	(−0.7)	7.6	(−0.1)	7.8	(−0.4)

SOURCE: Same as Table 4–5. Because of the exclusion of absentee ballots, the random sample deviates slightly from the actual results.

the other hand, the fact that the CDU and CSU were preoccupied with internal disputes left the government some room for maneuver.

The conviction has grown in the FDP, however, that the Socialist-Liberal coalition needs support on the state level. The FDP state organizations in the Saar and Lower Saxony rescinded their reservations about an alliance with the CDU after the 1976 Bundestag election and entered the state cabinets to help CDU minister-presidents form majority governments. The effects of this coalition decision on the voting in the Bundesrat cannot yet be predicted.

Two lines of development, equally possible given the present party system and the present state of individual parties, should be noted: the continuation of the existing polarization, or the shifting of coalition fronts to either the grand coalition (CDU/CSU-SPD) or to the CDU/CSU-FDP coalition. Either alternative could come about as a matter of chance. Only one thing is certain: in the immediate future no party will be as dependent on the development of interparty relations within the party system as the FDP.

5

Winning Without Victory: The 1976 CDU Campaign

Werner Kaltefleiter

In 1976 the CDU/CSU won a resounding 48.6 percent of the total vote in the federal election. But this success, second only to the Adenauer triumph of 1957, failed to produce an absolute majority (249 seats) in the Bundestag. Short of a majority by six seats, the CDU/CSU nevertheless became once again the strongest party in the Bundestag—and the strongest opposition party ever. The campaign that ultimately led to this result began the night of the Union's great defeat in the general election of November 1972 (see Table 5–1).

Preelection Campaigning

In 1972 the CDU/CSU won 44.9 percent of the vote, but the coalition partners, the SPD (45.8 percent) and the FDP (8.4 percent), celebrated a great triumph. This election had followed the first dissolution of the German Parliament in the history of the Federal Republic.[1] The thin six-seat majority won by the SPD and FDP in 1969 had eroded by the spring of 1972. Using the so-called constructive vote of no-confidence,* in April 1972 the CDU/CSU parliamentary group had tried to elect Rainer Barzel chancellor of the Federal Republic. Their failure is still unexplained, and the possibility that two votes were bought by the coalition has not been laid to rest.

The CDU/CSU—which at the time still believed itself to be the

---

* Editor's Note: As stipulated in the Basic Law of 1949, the constructive vote of no-confidence is a procedure whereby the Bundestag declares its lack of confidence in the federal chancellor only by electing a successor. There is a forty-eight-hour delay between the motion and the vote; in order to pass, the motion must secure a majority of the total membership of the Bundestag.

[1] For details see Werner Kaltefleiter, "Zwischen Konsens und Krise" [Between consensus and crisis], in *Verfassung und Verfassungswirklichkeit Jahrbuch 1973* [The living constitution, yearbook 1973] (Cologne: Heymanns, 1973).

TABLE 5-1

RESULTS OF GERMAN FEDERAL AND STATE ELECTIONS, 1965–1976

Party	Federal Election, 1965	State Elections, 1966–1968[a]	Federal Election, 1969	State Elections, 1970–1972[a]	Federal Election, 1972	State Elections, 1974–1976[a]	Federal Election, 1976
CDU/CSU	47.6	42.9	46.1	49.5	44.9	50.7	48.6
SPD	39.3	41.5	42.7	40.9	45.8	40.0	42.6
FDP	9.5	7.7	5.8	6.2	8.4	7.2	7.9
Other parties	3.6	7.9	5.5	3.4	0.9	1.9	0.9
Turnout[b]	86.8	89.2	86.7	77.9	91.1	82.2	90.7

[a] Cumulative and weighted election results.

[b] In percentages of registered voters.

SOURCE: Federal Statistical Office, *Statistische Jahrbuecher der Bundesrepublik Deutschland* [Statistical yearbooks of the Federal Republic of Germany], Wiesbaden, appropriate years.

natural government party, forced into opposition by a kind of deception on the part of the Free Democratic party in 1969—felt sure of victory in 1972. This expectation, supported by quite a few favorable results in the previous state elections, was the basis for the party's gloomy view of the 1972 electoral result. For the first time in the history of the Federal Republic, the CDU/CSU was no longer the strongest party in the Federal Parliament. The Union's reaction to this defeat is conveyed in an observation made by Max Weber in his analysis of the parliamentary system more than fifty years ago: "The majority of deputies function as followers of the leader or of the small group of leaders who form the cabinet and obey them blindly as long as they are successful."[2] The defeated Rainer Barzel immediately lost his authority and the question of a new party leader was raised the very night of the election.

A few weeks later, the minister-president of Rhineland-Palatinate, Helmut Kohl, who had already challenged Rainer Barzel at the previous party convention, announced his candidacy for the chairmanship of the party at the forthcoming party convention. Meanwhile Rainer Barzel was reelected leader of the parliamentary opposition. But this job, the springboard from which Barzel had captured the leadership of the party in 1971, had also started the erosion of his power. Barzel had been the most successful parliamentary leader of the CDU/CSU for more than eight years, yet he had slowly lost control over his colleagues. It was only a question of time until the erosion of his authority became obvious. The fatal moment came in May 1973 when he was unable to unite his party on the question of the Federal Republic's joining the United Nations. The majority of the parliamentary party voted against his proposal to accept the governmental decision, and Barzel resigned.[3] After a short internal struggle, Karl Carstens was elected parliamentary leader. This came as a surprise since Carstens, who had served as undersecretary in the Foreign Office, the Ministry of Defense, and the Chancellor's Office, had been elected to the Bundestag only six months before his election as leader. But his easy victory over former Minister Gerhard Schröder demon-

---

[2] Author's translation. See Max Weber, *Wirtschaft und Gesellschaft* [Economy and society], 2nd half-volume, 4th ed. (Tübingen: I.C.B. Mohr, 1956), p. 861; "Die ganze breite Masse der Demokraten fungiert nur als Gefolgschaft für den oder die wenigen 'leader' welche das Kabinett bilden, und gehorcht ihnen blind, solange sie Erfolg haben."

[3] See Friedrich Karl Fromme, "Barzels Entschluss" [Barzel's decision], *Frankfurter Allgemeine Zeitung*, May 10, 1973, and Alfred Rapp, "Barzels Weg an die Spitze—und wohin nun?" [Barzel's way to the top—and where to now?], *Frankfurter Allgemeine Zeitung*, May 11, 1973.

strated the desire for new leadership and new faces within the party.[4]

For a few weeks, Barzel concentrated on his position as chairman of the party and tried to give the party the leadership it needed, hoping in this way to survive the challenge that would come from Helmut Kohl at the forthcoming party convention. Barzel tried to introduce new, progressive elements into the political thinking of the party that could move it slightly to the left and started to prepare the party convention along these lines.[5] But soon he realized that there was no chance of his remaining chairman. He resigned from this office, and shortly thereafter a party convention was organized to elect a new chairman. In June 1973, only eight months after the election defeat, Helmut Kohl was elected leader of the party and his nominee, Kurt Biedenkopf, was elected general secretary. Together with Carstens, Kohl and Biedenkopf symbolized the "new" CDU.

On the CSU side, there was no new leadership. The different development of the two allied parties has to be explained by the fact that the 1972 election was not perceived as a defeat inside Bavaria. In 1972, for sociological reasons (including the percentage of Catholics and people living in rural areas) the outcome of the CSU (56 percent) was high in absolute terms, though compared with the level of support the CSU can expect to receive, it was no better than the outcome of the CDU in the rest of the country. Politicians always tend to confuse a high absolute result with a high realization of the potential vote, which in Bavaria must be regarded as about 65 percent for the CSU.[6] In any event, since the Bavarian result was not perceived as a defeat, it did not generate a demand for new leadership of the CSU. In the post-1972 period it became obvious that the lack of new leadership in the CSU was the major problem facing the Union.

The change in the CDU's leadership was a first step towards its relative success in 1976.[7] Surveys conducted in 1976 show that Kohl, Stoltenberg, and the CDU got high sympathy scores, were respected as competent, and were viewed by the electorate as close to the political

[4] See "Chancen fuer Carstens weiter gestiegen" [Chances for Carstens have further improved], *Sueddeutsche Zeitung*, May 17, 1973, and Klaus Dreher, "Schneller Sieg fuer den Unverschlissenen" [Speedy victory for the newcomers], *Sueddeutsche Zeitung*, May 16, 1973.

[5] See Rainer Barzel's speech to the National Governing Board of the CDU on May 12, 1973, published by the National Headquarters of the CDU, Bonn, 1973.

[6] This figure is based on the author's regression analysis of socioeconomic and political data.

[7] Eduard Neumaier, "Erneuerung aus dem grossen Krach? Eine Anatomie der Unions-Krise" [Renewal out of controversy? An anatomy of the Union crisis], *Die Zeit*, May 18, 1973.

center (see Tables 5–2, 5–3, and 5–4). By contrast, Strauss and the csu got low sympathy ratings and a rather extreme rating on the left-right dimension, although their competence was not questioned. The nomination and election of Kurt Biedenkopf had an especially important impact on the image of the cdu. During the Christian Democrats' long period in power, especially after 1965, the party had come to be thought of as a rural, confessional party, unattractive to intellectuals. The election of the eloquent professor to the job of general secretary hardly fit the image of the cdu. Biedenkopf, a professor of law at the newly founded University of Bochum, had joined the management of the well-known Henkel Company in 1971. He was cheered by the rank and file of the party and was cordially treated even by the most critical representatives of the mass media. Both expected that he would give the party intellectual leadership and pro-

TABLE 5–2

RESPONDENTS' PERCEPTIONS OF THE POSITIONS OF PARTIES AND POLITICIANS ON THE LEFT-RIGHT DIMENSION, 1976

Party or Politician Evaluated	Respondent Group			
	Total electorate	SPD sympathizers	CDU/CSU sympathizers	Potential floating vote
SPD	l 2.27	l 1.57	l 3.11	l 2.14
CDU	r 1.52	r 1.62	r 1.71	r 0.85
FDP	l 0.98	l 0.45	l 1.49	l 1.19
CSU	r 1.96	r 2.10	r 2.06	r 1.43
Schmidt	l 1.55	l 0.97	l 2.08	l 1.67
Kohl	r 1.33	r 1.36	r 1.61	r 0.74
Genscher	l 0.84	l 0.33	l 1.32	l 1.13
Brandt	l 2.78	l 1.99	l 3.67	l 2.63
Stoltenberg	r 1.35	r 1.54	r 1.57	r 0.57
Friderichs	l 0.73	l 0.27	l 1.10	l 0.93
Wehner	l 3.53	l 2.91	l 4.21	l 3.43
Strauss	r 2.28	r 2.49	r 2.46	r 1.47
Respondents	l 0.23	l 1.17	l 1.00	l 0.79

NOTE: 'l' indicates distance from the center to the left, 'r' indicates distance from the center to the right, on a left-right dimension where the extreme left and the extreme right are valued at five points each and the center is valued at zero.
SOURCE: All of the opinion poll results reported in this chapter are taken from six preelection surveys conducted by the author in 1976. Each sample consisted of 1,500 respondents. For details see Werner Kaltefleiter, Vorspiel zum Wechsel [Prelude to change] (Berlin: Duncker and Humblot, 1977).

TABLE 5–3

RESPONDENTS' SYMPATHY FOR PARTIES AND POLITICIANS, 1976

Party or Politician Evaluated	Total Electorate	SPD Sympathizers			CDU/CSU Sympathizers			Potential Floating Vote
		Total	Strong identifiers	Weak identifiers	Total	Strong identifiers	Weak identifiers	
SPD	5.5	8.3	8.9	7.8	2.9	2.2	3.5	5.5
CDU	5.9	3.8	3.2	4.2	8.3	8.8	8.0	5.8
FDP	4.8	5.6	5.7	5.4	3.7	3.2	4.1	4.6
CSU	4.4	2.1	1.4	2.6	7.0	7.6	6.6	4.1
Schmidt	6.6	8.6	8.9	8.3	4.6	4.2	4.9	6.5
Kohl	6.0	4.5	3.9	4.9	8.0	8.5	7.6	5.9
Genscher	5.1	5.8	5.9	5.8	4.2	4.0	4.5	5.0
Brandt	4.4	7.0	7.4	6.7	2.1	1.5	2.6	4.1
Stoltenberg	5.3	4.0	3.5	4.3	6.9	7.3	6.6	5.1
Friderichs	5.1	5.6	5.8	5.5	4.5	4.1	4.8	5.0
Wehner	2.9	5.0	5.7	4.5	1.1	0.8	1.4	2.7
Strauss	3.8	1.6	1.2	1.2	6.4	7.1	5.9	3.6

NOTE: Respondents were asked to evaluate each party and politician according to a ten-point scale where zero indicates no sympathy and ten indicates strong sympathy.
SOURCE: See Table 5–2.

vide efficient management and organization—an expectation that was not fulfilled.[8] In several speeches Biedenkopf tried to analyze the basic values of liberty and solidarity and their meaning for policy formation within a Christian Democratic party.[9] People listened to

[8] Since the late days of Konrad Adenauer, the history of the CDU has involved a continuous struggle for more effective organization. Under Adenauer the party was led to a very large degree from the Chancellor's Office. Since 1969, when the party was thrown into opposition, remarkable change has occurred. Nevertheless, many problems remain unresolved, largely because in a parliamentary system only a fusion between the leadership of the parliamentary party and the party organization will improve efficiency. See W. Kaltefleiter, "Instrumente demokratischer Regierungsweise?" [Instruments of the democratic form of government?], and Wolfgang Falke, "Partei und Fuehrung" [Party and leadership], both in Die politische Meinung, special issue (April 1974), pp. 9–21 and pp. 21–62.
[9] See Biedenkopf's speech, "Die Politik der Unionsparteien—die freiheitliche Alternative zum Sozialismus" [The policy of the Union parties—the free alternative to socialism], delivered at the Catholische Akademie, Bavaria, on September 9, 1973, and printed by the National Headquarters of the CDU, Bonn, 1974. See also Kurt H. Biedenkopf, "Eine Strategie fuer die Opposition" [A strategy for the opposition], Die Zeit, March 16, 1975.

TABLE 5–4

RESPONDENTS' PERCEPTIONS OF THE COMPETENCE OF PARTIES AND
POLITICIANS, 1976

Party or Politician Evaluated	Total Electorate	SPD Sympathizers			CDU/CSU Sympathizers			Potential Floating Vote
		Total	Strong identifiers	Weak identifiers	Total	Strong identifiers	Weak identifiers	
SPD	5.9	8.1	8.7	7.7	3.8	4.3	4.3	5.8
CDU	6.4	5.1	4.9	5.2	8.1	8.5	7.8	6.1
FDP	5.0	5.9	6.1	5.7	4.1	3.7	4.3	4.6
CSU	5.0	3.3	2.9	3.7	7.0	7.5	6.7	4.6
Schmidt	6.9	8.7	9.2	8.4	5.3	5.1	5.5	6.9
Kohl	6.3	5.2	5.0	5.3	7.8	8.2	7.5	6.2
Genscher	5.5	6.2	6.6	6.0	4.6	4.4	4.9	5.2
Brandt	4.6	6.8	7.2	6.4	2.6	2.1	3.0	4.4
Stoltenberg	5.5	4.5	4.2	4.8	6.9	7.4	6.6	5.4
Friderichs	5.5	6.0	6.2	5.9	4.9	4.6	5.1	5.2
Wehner	3.5	5.4	6.1	4.9	1.8	1.5	2.1	3.4
Strauss	5.5	4.2	4.0	4.3	7.3	7.9	6.9	5.1

NOTE: Respondents were asked to evaluate each party and politician according to a ten-point scale where zero indicates no competence and ten indicates high competence.
SOURCE: See Table 5–2.

his reflections, but the rank and file, who failed to really understand them, simply assumed that he was doing a good job and that there was no longer need for them to worry about what was coming in 1976. The media equally failed to appreciate the substance of Biedenkopf's concerns, but, impressed by their sophistication, accepted the new style.[10]

The increasing popularity of the CDU/CSU coincided with an upcoming government crisis. It was becoming more and more obvious that Willy Brandt was unable to provide effective leadership as chancellor. The internal struggle in the SPD between the Socialists and the Social Democratic wing hurt the image of the party. The situation became more critical when inflation was expected to increase to 9 percent in 1974—a higher rate than could be attributed merely to the

[10] See "CDU: Vormarsch nach rueckwaerts. Die politischen Leitlinien des Generalsekretaers Kurt Biedenkopf" [CDU: backward march, the political guidelines of General Secretary Kurt Biedenkopf], *Der Spiegel*, n. 8 (February 18, 1974).

increase in the price of oil.[11] One and a half years after the SPD's great
election victory in 1972, the scenario had changed completely. The
first election since the federal election of November 1972 was held in
the state of Hamburg in March 1974 and ended in disaster for the
Social Democratic party. Municipal elections held at the same time in
Rhineland-Palatinate, Schleswig-Holstein, and the Saar produced the
same result: large electoral gains for the CDU and substantial losses for
the Social Democratic party.[12] In a speech delivered to the governing
board of his party after the Hamburg election, Helmut Schmidt, then
minister of finance, analyzed the situation of the party and made very
clear that only a change in leadership would solve its problems.[13] In
short order the spy affair implicating Willy Brandt offered the SPD the
opportunity it needed. Two days after the SPD's disaster in the municipal election in the Saar, Willy Brandt resigned, and very quickly
Helmut Schmidt was elected chancellor of the Federal Republic. Less
than one year after the resignation of Rainer Barzel, the SPD in turn
demonstrated the aptness of Max Weber's insight.

Subsequent elections in Lower Saxony, Hesse, Bavaria, and finally
Rhineland-Palatinate showed the impact of this new leadership on the
Social Democratic party. The gains of the CDU/CSU were comparable
with those in Hamburg and the municipal elections mentioned above,
but the losses of the Social Democratic party were substantially
smaller. This time, however, the SDP's coalition partner, the FDP, also
suffered. It became clear that Helmut Schmidt was able to win back
former SPD votes from the FDP but not to hurt the CDU/CSU (see Tables
5–5, 5–6, 5–7).

State elections in Schleswig-Holstein, North Rhine-Westphalia,
and the Saar in the spring of 1975 changed this. The CDU gained over
its 1972 showing, but compared to expectations based on the previous
state and municipal elections its outcome was rather poor. On the
other hand, the Social Democrats and the Free Democrats did much
better than expected. There were two main reasons for this development: In the spring of 1975, for the first time in about two years, the
general perception of the economic situation improved, and in the
process the main source of support for the opposition disappeared. In
addition, an inflammatory speech delivered by Franz Josef Strauss

[11] See Ursula Hohmeyer, "Inflation und Energiemangel gemeinsam bekaempfen"
[To jointly combat inflation and the energy shortage], Sueddeutsche Zeitung,
November 8, 1974.
[12] See Werner Kaltefleiter, "Landtagswahlen und Bundespolitik. Eine Analyse der
Landtagswahlen von 1974/75" [Landtag elections and federal policy: an analysis
of the Landtag elections of 1974–75], Transfer, no. 2 (1974/75).
[13] Klaus Dreher, "Warten auf die starke Hand" [Waiting for the strong arm],
Sueddeutsche Zeitung, March 15, 1974.

received wide publicity.[14] Addressing a group of Bavarian politicians in Sonthofen, a little Bavarian city, the day after the election in Rhineland-Palatinate, Strauss attacked the government: "We have to drive them to the point where they must present legislation to guarantee the security of the budget or declare the bankruptcy of the state or introduce a drastic raise in taxes, any of which would have decisive and negative consequences for the economy." On noneconomic matters he was just as outspoken:

> The debate must revolve around fundamental issues. We must not shy away from confrontation in this area. . . . We must always identify the others with socialism and the opposite of freedom, with the idea that they represent collectivization and the rule of bureaucrats and that their policies will eventually result in the hegemony of the Soviet Union over Western Europe.

Strauss's rhetoric reached its apotheosis in his tactical recommendations:

> We must say that the SPD and FDP are handing this state over to criminal and political gangsters. There is not the slightest difference between criminal and political gangsters—they are all criminals. If we come and clean up, none of these bandits will dare to open their mouths in Germany again, even if we can't exactly keep our promise. We must however create the impression. . . . And now to tactics: just accuse and warn but don't offer concrete solutions.

It was the tone of Strauss's remarks—not uncommon in Bavarian politics—that produced an outcry from the coalition and from critics in the media, who considered this new proof of Strauss's irresponsibility. The most important effect of this episode was the revitalization of the SPD's party activists, who are the party's greatest campaign asset.[15]

---

[14] See "Aufraeumen bis zum Rest dieses Jahrhunderts. Franz Josef Strauss ueber die Strategie der Union" [Cleaning up for the rest of the century: Franz Josef Strauss—on the strategy of the Union], *Der Spiegel*, n. 11 (March 10, 1975).

[15] If one considers the effect that one party member can have on three strong identifiers in his immediate environment, the mobilization of about 1 million members means to put into motion 4 million people. If each of these contacts four more people you get roughly the total electorate of the SPD. It seems clear that the 1 million activists within the SPD are much more willing to work for their party than the activists of the other parties. This was first realized by the Cologne Elections Study Group of 1961; an overview of this study by G. Edler, is given in Erwin K. Scheuch and Rudolf Wildenmann, "Zur Soziologie der Wahl" [Sociology of the election], *Koelner Zeitschrift fuer Soziologie und Sozialpsychologie*, special issue 9 (1965). Unfortunately Edler never published the data of the study group in full.

TABLE 5-5

CDU/CSU Election Results: State and Municipal Elections of 1974–1976 Compared to National Elections of 1972 and 1976

(election results in percentages; differences in percentage-point gains and losses)

| Date of State Election[a] | State | CDU/CSU | | | | |
| | | Result | | | Difference | |
		State election	N1976	N1972	N1976	N1972
Phase I						
March 3, 1974	Hamburg (S)	40.6	35.8	33.3	+ 4.8	+ 7.3
March 17, 1974	Rhineland-Palatinate (M)	51.6	49.9	45.9	+ 1.7	+ 5.8
March 24, 1974	Schleswig-Holstein (M)	53.3	44.1	42.0	+ 9.0	+11.1
May 5, 1974	Saar (M)	50.4	46.2	43.4	+ 4.2	+ 7.0
Phase II						
September 6, 1974	Lower Saxony (S)	48.9	45.7	42.7	+ 3.2	+ 6.2
October 27, 1974	Hesse (S)	47.3	44.8	40.3	+ 2.5	+ 7.0
October 27, 1974	Bavaria (S)	62.1	60.0	55.1	+ 2.1	+ 7.0
March 9, 1975	Rhineland-Palatinate (S)	53.9	49.9	45.9	+ 4.0	+ 8.1

Phase III

April 13, 1975	Schleswig-Holstein (S)	50.4	44.1	42.0	+ 6.3	+ 8.4
May 4, 1975	North Rhine-Westphalia (S)	47.1	44.5	41.0	+ 2.6	+ 6.1
May 4, 1975	Saar (S)	49.1	46.2	43.4	+ 2.9	+ 5.7
September 28, 1976	Bremen (S)	33.8	32.5	29.6	+ 1.3	+ 4.3

Phase IV

| April 4, 1976 | Baden-Württemberg (S) | 56.7 | 53.3 | 49.8 | + 3.4 | + 6.9 |

| Average, Federal Republic of Germany | | 51.4 | 48.6 | 44.9 | + 2.8 | + 6.5 |

a Willy Brandt was federal chancellor during phase I, Helmut Schmidt during phases II, III, and IV.

NOTE: The types of election have been abbreviated as follows: S, state election; M, municipal election; N, national (Bundestag) election.

SOURCE: Federal Statistical Office, Jahrbuecher.

TABLE 5–6

SPD Election Results: State and Municipal Elections of 1974–1976 Compared to National Elections of 1972 and 1976

(election results in percentages; differences in percentage-point gains and losses)

Date of State Election[a]	State	Result		SPD	Difference	
		State election	N1976	N1972	N1976	N1972
Phase I						
March 3, 1974	Hamburg (S)	44.9	52.6	54.4	− 7.7	− 9.6
March 17, 1974	Rhineland-Palatinate (M)	35.4	41.7	44.9	− 6.3	− 9.5
March 24, 1974	Schleswig-Holstein (M)	35.6	46.4	48.6	−10.8	−13.0
May 5, 1974	Saar (M)	37.3	46.1	47.9	− 8.8	−10.6
Phase II						
September 6, 1974	Lower Saxony (S)	43.0	45.7	48.1	− 2.7	− 4.9
October 27, 1974	Hesse (S)	43.2	45.7	48.5	− 2.5	− 5.3
October 27, 1974	Bavaria (S)	30.2	32.8	37.8	− 2.6	− 7.6
March 9, 1975	Rhineland-Palatinate (S)	38.5	41.7	44.9	− 3.2	− 6.4

Phase III

April 13, 1975	Schleswig-Holstein (S)	40.1	46.4	48.6	— 6.3	— 8.9
May 4, 1975	North Rhine-Westphalia (S)	45.1	46.9	50.4	— 1.8	— 5.3
May 4, 1975	Saar (S)	41.8	46.1	47.9	— 4.3	— 6.1
September 28, 1976	Bremen (S)	48.8	54.0	38.1	— 5.2	— 9.3

Phase IV

| April 4, 1976 | Baden-Württemberg (S) | 33.3 | 36.3 | 38.9 | — 3.0 | — 5.6 |
| Average, Federal Republic of Germany | | 39.9 | 42.6 | 45.8 | — 2.7 | — 5.9 |

[a] Willy Brandt was federal chancellor during phase I, Helmut Schmidt during phases II, III, and IV.

NOTE: The types of election have been abbreviated as follows: S, state election; M, municipal election; N, national (Bundestag) election.

SOURCE: Federal Statistical Office, *Jahrbuecher*.

TABLE 5-7

FDP ELECTION RESULTS: STATE AND MUNICIPAL ELECTIONS OF 1974–1976 COMPARED TO NATIONAL ELECTIONS OF 1972 AND 1976

(election results in percentages; differences in percentage-point gains and losses)

Date of State Election[a]	State	FDP Result: State election	Result: N1976	Result: N1972	Difference: N1976	Difference: N1972
Phase I						
March 3, 1974	Hamburg (S)	10.9	10.2	11.2	+ 0.7	− 0.3
March 17, 1974	Rhineland-Palatinate (M)	8.7	7.6	8.1	+ 1.1	+ 0.6
March 24, 1974	Schleswig-Holstein (M)	9.0	8.8	8.6	+ 0.2	+ 0.4
May 5, 1974	Saar (M)	7.4	6.6	7.1	+ 0.8	+ 0.3
Phase II						
September 6, 1974	Lower Saxony (S)	7.1	7.9	8.5	− 0.8	− 1.4
October 27, 1974	Hesse (S)	7.4	8.5	10.2	− 1.1	− 2.8
October 27, 1974	Bavaria (S)	5.2	6.2	6.1	− 1.0	− 0.9
March 9, 1975	Rhineland-Palatinate (S)	5.6	7.6	8.1	− 2.0	− 2.5

Phase III

April 13, 1975	Schleswig-Holstein (S)	7.1	8.8	8.6	− 1.7	− 1.5
May 4, 1975	North Rhine-Westphalia (S)	6.7	7.8	7.8	− 1.1	− 1.1
May 4, 1975	Saar (S)	7.4	6.6	7.1	+ 0.8	+ 0.3
September 28, 1976	Bremen (S)	13.0	11.8	11.1	+ 1.2	+ 1.9

Phase IV

April 4, 1976	Baden-Württemberg (S)	7.8	9.1	10.2	− 1.3	− 2.4
Average, Federal Republic of Germany		6.9	7.9	8.4	− 1.0	− 1.5

[a] Willy Brandt was federal chancellor during phase I, Helmut Schmidt during phases II, III, and IV.

NOTE: The types of election have been abbreviated as follows: S, state election; M, municipal election; N, national (Bundestag) election.

SOURCE: Federal Statistical Office, *Jahrbuecher.*

One further element in the party conflict at this period should be mentioned. In 1974 the coalition had passed a law legalizing abortions performed during the first three months of a pregnancy. The states governed by the CDU/CSU brought the matter before the Federal Constitutional Court and the law was declared unconstitutional. Especially in the Protestant north the CDU was blamed for having adopted a strong Catholic position on the abortion issue and thus having opened itself up to the old charge of confessionalism.[16]

These events had an important impact on the internal power struggle in the CDU/CSU. The election of Helmut Kohl as party chairman had not resolved the issue of who would be the CDU/CSU candidate for chancellor in 1976. Helmut Kohl had a strong rival in the person of the minister-president of Schleswig-Holstein, Gerhard Stoltenberg, who had been a member of the Bundestag from 1957 until 1971. Stoltenberg had accepted a request from the Schleswig-Holstein party to lead it in the 1971 state election and had won with an absolute majority. During his time in Bonn, Stoltenberg had been a member of the Ways and Means Committee and had served as minister for technology, first in the Erhard government and then under the Grand Coalition. After the defeat in 1969 he had become spokesman of the parliamentary party for economic affairs, and since 1969 he had served as vice-chairman of the CDU.

In public opinion polls Gerhard Stoltenberg always rated very high, sometimes slightly ahead of Helmut Kohl (see Figure 5–1). In particular, Stoltenberg was regarded as more experienced in federal politics and more competent to compete with Schmidt, who was perceived as highly efficient. In the winter of 1974–1975 the situation seemed to be quite open and it was generally accepted that the outcome of the state elections in March in Rhineland-Palatinate, where Helmut Kohl was minister-president, and in April in Schleswig-Holstein would have a decisive impact on the leadership of the CDU/CSU. The election in Rhineland-Palatinate again showed large CDU/CSU gains, but a few weeks later Stoltenberg's showing in Schleswig-Holstein and the outcomes in the other states were disappointing. Though it became obvious that Stoltenberg had suffered from the effects of the economic improvement, the Strauss speech, and the abortion controversy, the party quickly rallied around Helmut Kohl, who was considered to have the larger vote-getting capacity. Franz Josef Strauss opposed Kohl to the last,[17] but finally gave way. At the

---

[16] See, for example, Friedrich Karl Fromme, "Nach dem Abtreibungs-Urteil" [After the abortion decision], *Frankfurter Allgemeine Zeitung*, February 27, 1975.

[17] W. Hertz-Eichenrode, "Kohl vor der Bewaehrungsprobe" [Kohl on probation], *Die Welt*, April 28, 1975.

FIGURE 5-1

VOTERS' SYMPATHY FOR AND EVALUATION OF PERFORMANCE
OF CHANCELLOR SCHMIDT AND KEY CDU/CSU LEADERS, 1974

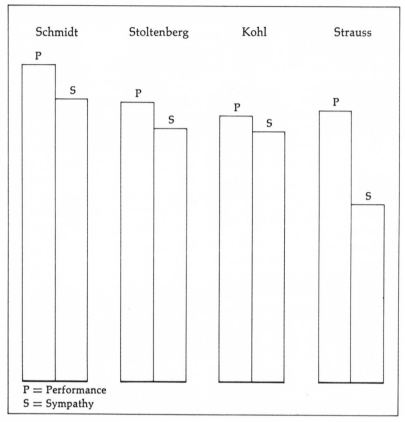

SOURCE: Werner Kaltefleiter, "Mit Blick auf 1976" [Looking toward 1976], *Politische Meinung*, November 1974, p. 9.

party convention in Mannheim in June 1975, Kohl became the party's candidate for chancellor in 1976.[18]

This party convention was another important step in the preparation of the 1976 election. One of the major themes of the convention was "the new social question," brought to the attention of the party

---

[18] See Thomas Meyer, "Schwache Stellen im Lack der Einmuetigkeit" [Cracks in the veneer of unanimity], *Frankfurter Allgemeine Zeitung*, June 26, 1975, and Ruediger Moniac, "Jetzt kommt Kohls Stunde" [Kohl's hour has come], *Frankfurter Allgemeine Zeitung*, August 2, 1975.

by Kurt Biedenkopf.[19] He conceived this as essentially a constitutional question: the problem of effective government control of the power of pressure groups, which is fundamental in modern industrial societies.[20] But the problem as posed by Biedenkopf did not interest the relevant groups within the party, who saw minorities and pressure groups above all as blocs within the electorate to be wooed and won. The core of the internal coalition behind Helmut Kohl consisted of the left wing, women, and the youth organization. These groups agreed that the party had to move to the left in order to regain power. Under their influence the "new social question" was reduced to a new emphasis on "marginal groups and minorities" (the elderly, women, and so on) who believed they were not sharing adequately in the economic strength and social benefits of modern German society.

In the end, the party followed essentially the line proposed by Rainer Barzel during his last days as party chairman. It tried to move to the left at a time when two changes had occurred: First, German public opinion in general had reached a more conservative understanding of politics; not only the large gains of the CDU/CSU during the state elections but also quite a few other indicators, such as the mood of young people in universities and high schools, demonstrated this complete change in public opinion.[21] And second, in the summer of 1975 a financial crisis in the public budgets[22] became obvious and the request for more social benefits outlined in the platform drawn up at the Mannheim convention contrasted sharply with the problems of the day. The "new social question" was quickly forgotten, and the summer and fall of 1975 were characterized by a protracted struggle between the CDU and CSU over a common platform for 1976, ending in the general acceptance of Kohl's position and candidacy by the CSU.[23]

19 See Bundesvorstand der CDU, 1976, *Mannheimer Erklaerung* [Mannheim declaration], November 12, 1975.
20 See Kurt H. Biedenkopf, "Moeglichkeiten und Grenzen der Beeinflussung der unternehmerischen Willensbildung durch gesellschaftliche Gruppen" [Possibilities and limits of influencing the decisions of managers by social groups], in *Die Bedeutung gesellschaftlicher Veraenderungen fuer die Willensbildung in Unternehmen* [The meaning of social change in the decisions of managers], Horst Albach and Dieter Sadowski, eds., Schriften des Vereins für Sozialpolitik. Gesellschaft für Wirtschafts- und Sozialwissenschaften [Writings of the Association for Social Policy. Society for Economics and Social Sciences], vol. 88 (Berlin: Duncker & Humblot, 1976).
21 See Werner Kaltefleiter, "Die gespaltene Generation" [The divided generation], in *Politische Meinung*, June 1974, p. 34.
22 See *Monatsberichte der Deutschen Bundesbank* [Monthly reports of the German Federal Bank], volume 28, n. 5 (May 1976), pp. 21–23.
23 Characteristic of this struggle was the debate following a remark made by Kurt Biedenkopf, in which he described the rather leftist "Ahlener Programm" from 1947 as one of the fundamental bases of CDU politics. For more details on

Even so, it remained obvious to the German electorate that Strauss considered himself the more competent man and better candidate.[24]

Early in the election year, events in Lower Saxony brought new support to the CDU. The respected Social Democratic minister-president, Alfred Kubel, had decided to resign by the end of 1975 to give his successor an opportunity to gain public support before the next state election in 1978. But to the general surprise, the SPD-FDP majority (seventy-five seats against seventy-three held by the CDU) twice failed to elect a Social Democratic candidate, and the CDU candidate, Ernst Albrecht, was elected. It is still unknown which members of the coalition voted in favor of Albrecht. He immediately formed a minority government, which increased the majority of the CDU/CSU in the Bundesrat.

Also during the early months of 1976 a treaty with Poland was under discussion. In this treaty the Federal Republic of Germany agreed to pay Poland 2.3 billion DM and the Polish government guaranteed the emigration of at least 125,000 German natives to the Federal Republic.[25]

In the aftermath of the debate over *Ostpolitik*, this treaty became a crucial issue. Finally, the CDU/CSU-governed states allowed the treaty to pass in the Bundesrat, after additional clarifications and confirmations had been given by the Polish foreign minister. As far as the campaign is concerned, these events offered the CDU leaders, including the newly elected Minister-President Albrecht of Lower Saxony, prime-time television appearances for quite a few days. In addition, the FDP, led by Foreign Minister Genscher, was much more sympathetic to the demands of the CDU/CSU than the chancellor and the SPD. This suggested to many that in foreign policy as well as in economics the FDP and the CDU/CSU had become closer.[26]

this debate see Ernst-Guenter Vetter, "Die Versoehnungsthese des Generalsekretaers" [The reconciliation theme of the general secretary], *Frankfurter Allgemeine Zeitung*, October 25, 1975, and Ludolf Herrmann, "Kurt Biedenkopf—ein Mann in der Krise" [Kurt Biedenkopf—a man in the midst of crisis], *Deutsche Zeitung*, October 17, 1975.

[24] See Eduard Neumaier, "Eine Rechnung, die nicht aufging" [An equation that did not balance], *Die Zeit*, November 21, 1975.

[25] Up to 1969, about 70,000 people were allowed to emigrate to the Federal Republic of Germany from Poland annually. This was stopped after the beginning of the new *Ostpolitik*, and the figures sank to 5,626 in 1970, 25,243 in 1971, 13,476 in 1972, 8,903 in 1973, 7,827 in 1974, 7,041 in 1975. The new treaty reestablished the situation that had ended in 1969 and instituted the payments mentioned above. These figures were provided by the general secretary of the German Red Cross, Bonn.

[26] On economic issues the positions of the CDU/CSU and the FDP were traditionally rather close. See W. Kaltefleiter, "Der Schwanz wackelt mit dem Dackel" [The tail wags the dog], *Wirtschaftswoche*, n. 25 (June 18, 1976), pp. 30–31.

The state election in Baden-Württemberg in April 1976 was the last important event before the campaign. The short period of economic optimism in the spring of 1975 had ended. By the following winter, for the first time since the mid-fifties, more than 1 million people were unemployed. The Sonthofen speech was forgotten, and in the predominantly Catholic south the abortion question was not an issue. Under these conditions, Hans Filbinger, minister-president of Baden-Württemberg, extended the large gains the CDU and CSU had made in 1974. More important was another element of the CDU campaign in Baden-Württemberg. In his opening speech in Freiburg, Filbinger stated that Germany was confronted with a choice: "a democratic state or a Socialist society."[27] The rank and file reacted favorably to this campaign appeal, which was precisely the line pursued by Franz Josef Strauss. A few weeks later the slogan "Freedom or Socialism" was born. Nobody really knows who first used this phrase, but it was quickly adopted by the CSU and many CDU militants.

The leaders of the CDU, Helmut Kohl, Gerhard Stoltenberg, and Kurt Biedenkopf, were very reluctant to accept this slogan. The CDU's success in Baden-Württemberg, however, where Filbinger's opponent was the left-wing Social Democrat Erhard Eppler, put so much pressure on them that they finally accepted it at least for the preelection campaign, with one modification: they replaced the Bavarian "Freedom or Socialism" with "Freedom instead of Socialism."[28]

This was the theme of the party convention of the CDU in May in Hanover. Kohl and Biedenkopf tried to make sure that the slogan was only being used to give momentum to the campaign and that a more sophisticated formula would be adopted for the final campaign.[29] The Social Democrats reacted very strongly,[30] and the media made sure that the slogan would bring the opposition into the news during the summer. The fact is that the CDU/CSU's black-and-white view of things did not correctly describe the reality of the Federal Republic, especially when the Social Democratic party was led by

27 W. Hertz-Eichenrode, "Stuttgarter Barometer" [Stuttgart barometer], Die Welt, April 3, 1976.

28 Ruediger Moniac, "Die Wahl '76: 'Freiheit oder Sozialismus' " [The 1976 election: 'freedom or socialism'], Die Welt, May 15, 1976. See also Georg Schroeder, "Alternative '76," Die Welt, May 17, 1976, and Karl Feldmeyer, "Die CDU stimmt sich auf den Wahlkampf ein" [The CDU is tuning up for the election campaign], Frankfurter Allgemeine Zeitung, May 22, 1976.

29 Karl Feldmeyer, "War Hannover fuer die CDU ein Erfolg?" [Was Hanover a success for the CDU?], Frankfurter Allgemeine Zeitung, May 28, 1976.

30 W. Hertz-Eichenrode, "Bilanz der Parteitage: Die SPD in der Defensive" [Balance sheet of the party conventions: the SPD on the defensive], Die Welt, June 28, 1976.

Helmut Schmidt who (in contrast to Eppler) had the image of being part of the Social Democratic right wing and had a fine record of criticizing leftist elements in his own party.[31]

The 1976 Campaign

October 3 was fixed as election day by the government. The implication of this decision was that the campaign would be divided by the summer break. Vacation periods are staggered in the various German states to avoid chaos on the highways and hopeless crowding in the main recreational areas, and as a result the vacation period for the country as a whole is very long. In 1976 it started in mid-June in the north and ended early in September in Bavaria. Since German politicians assume that campaigning during vacation time is ineffective and may be counterproductive, the real campaign could not start before mid-September. This reduced the so-called hot phase of the campaign to about three weeks, but also prompted a kind of "pre-hot-campaign" phase before the summer break.

All of the major parties held their conventions in May. The CDU used this opportunity not only to inaugurate the "Freedom instead of Socialism" slogan but also to hold a "Day of Europe," when the leaders of the major conservative parties in Europe joined with the CDU in calling for a new approach to European unity. It was the British Conservative leader Margaret Thatcher who was most enthusiastically cheered by the delegates when she attacked the Socialists for creating a "pockey-money society."[32] All of the major European conservative party leaders joined the CDU in endorsing the slogan "Freedom instead of Socialism."

The campaign publicity that had already taken shape by May, however, under the auspices of the national party bureaucracy, struck quite a different note. For one thing, it made the most of Helmut Kohl's personal image. People trusted Kohl, and in the sympathy polls he was rated higher than any previous candidate for chancellor, including Erich Ollenhauer, Willy Brandt (in three elections), and Rainer Barzel. At various times during the campaign Kohl was compared with Jimmy Carter: a native of Rhineland-Palatinate, he had no connection

---

[31] In a speech before the state party convention in Hamburg in September 1974, Schmidt accused the leftist elements in the SPD of discussing the "crisis in their own brain." See "Helmut Schmidt gegen SPD-Theoretiker" [Helmut Schmidt against the SPD theoreticians], *Neue Zuercher Zeitung*, September 23, 1974.

[32] Friedrich Karl Fromme, "Viele europaeische Zungen rufen auf zur Verteidigung der Freiheit" [Many European voices call for the defense of freedom], *Frankfurter Allgemeine Zeitung*, May 26, 1976.

with the dirty aspects of Bonn politics; he was a man from whom you would buy a used car.[33]

Pursuing this theme, the campaign planners had put together an appeal based on sympathy and trust. They came up with the slogan "Out of Love for Germany" and used the national colors, black, red, and gold, to stimulate patriotic feeling. They also designed a bumper sticker incorporating the "D" (for Deutschland) that appears on German cars with a "C" and a "U."

These preparations were disrupted by the convention's adoption of "Freedom instead of Socialism" as the party's main slogan. The hard-line slogan was incompatible with the "Love for Germany" one and also with the image of the main party spokesmen, Kohl, Stoltenberg, and Biedenkopf; it fitted the image only of Franz Josef Strauss. Moreover, sufficient to mobilize the activists, it was less attractive to the potential floating vote. A survey analysis just before election day showed that "Freedom instead of Socialism" was the best-known slogan of the campaign and that it was accepted by 80 percent of CDU/CSU identifiers, but rejected by two-thirds of the potential floating vote as well as 90 percent of the Social Democratic identifiers. Thus the slogan's mobilization effect was even stronger among the Social Democrats than among the CDU/CSU (see Table 5–9). Its most positive effect was to force the SPD and Chancellor Schmidt onto the defensive: the opposition acted, the government reacted.

In the final phase of the campaign the CDU introduced the slogan "Vote Freedom," again in conjunction with "Out of Love for Germany." Avoiding the term socialism, this slogan was not as provocative as the first, but it came too late and was practically unknown on election day. The same was true of the two posters used by the CDU to promote Helmut Kohl: On one side a walking Helmut Kohl was described as "the man you can trust"; on the other he appeared as "Chancellor of Germany." In addition, it should be mentioned that the CDU used a third picture of Helmut Kohl to announce rallies with the candidate. A number of additional posters represented, for example, "Women for the CDU."

The most important part of the CDU publicity campaign was a highly professional series of ads in which different people were shown explaining why they were voting for the CDU. The pictures were mostly taken in real life situations and the captions were short and to the point, for example: "Why do I vote for the CDU? Because I want a stable economy again."

---

[33] See Hans Reiser, "Kohl setzt auf Sympathiewerbung" [Kohl gambles on garnering sympathy], *Sueddeutsche Zeitung*, May 26, 1976.

TABLE 5–8

VOTERS' SYMPATHY FOR PARTIES AND POLITICIANS, BY PARTY IDENTIFICATION AND REGION, FEBRUARY AND SEPTEMBER 1976

| Party or Politician | All Respondents | | Respondent's Party Identification | | | | | | Respondent's Region | | | | | |
| | | | SPD Identifiers | | CDU/CSU Identifiers | | Non-identifiers | | North | | Central | | South | |
	Feb.	Sept.	Feb.	Sept.	Feb.	Sept.	Feb.	Sept.	Feb.	Sept.	Feb.	Sept.	Feb.	Sept.
SPD	5.5	5.7	8.3	8.5	2.9	3.0	5.5	5.4	5.7	5.7	5.8	6.0	5.3	5.3
CDU	5.9	5.9	3.8	3.7	8.3	8.4	5.8	5.6	5.8	5.7	5.6	5.5	6.2	6.2
FDP	4.8	5.0	5.6	5.9	3.7	3.8	4.6	5.0	4.9	5.6	5.0	5.0	4.6	4.7
CSU	4.4	4.6	2.1	2.3	7.0	7.4	4.1	4.3	3.6	4.3	3.9	3.9	5.1	5.5
Schmidt	6.6	6.4	8.6	8.7	4.6	4.2	6.5	6.3	6.8	6.5	6.6	6.6	6.4	6.0
Kohl	6.0	6.0	4.5	4.2	8.0	8.0	5.9	5.8	5.8	5.7	5.9	5.6	6.3	6.4
Genscher	5.1	5.3	5.8	6.1	4.2	4.3	5.0	5.2	5.5	5.5	5.1	5.2	4.9	5.1
Brandt	4.4	4.4	7.0	6.8	2.1	2.0	4.1	4.4	4.7	4.5	4.8	4.8	4.0	3.9
Stoltenberg	5.3	5.3	4.0	4.0	6.9	6.9	5.1	5.1	5.6	5.5	5.1	4.9	5.4	5.5
Strauss	3.8	4.3	1.6	1.8	6.4	7.1	3.6	3.9	3.4	3.9	3.4	3.8	4.4	4.9

NOTE: Respondents were asked to evaluate each party and politician according to a ten-point scale where zero indicates no sympathy and ten indicates strong sympathy.

SOURCE: See Table 5–2.

133

The same basic approach was used in the television spots. In Germany, the parties receive gratis two-and-a-half minutes after the news for advertising, the number of spots allocated to each party being determined on the basis of its outcome at the previous election. The CDU had this opportunity ten times and the CSU four times. The CDU spots always started with attractive pictures suggesting the German way of life accompanied by stimulating music. These shots—in color—were contrasted with black-and-white pictures, many of them from the German Democratic Republic, showing Social Democrats "joining the smiling campaign of aggressive world communism" or attacking aspects of government policy. This part was intended to underline the "Freedom instead of Socialism" concept. A very short statement by Helmut Kohl followed, again in a real life setting, showing the candidate walking through crowds, playing with his children, and so on. Finally, different people were shown testifying that they would vote for the CDU and for Helmut Kohl and briefly explaining their reasons.

These television spots typified the ambiguity of the whole CDU campaign: the positive beginning and the final appeal for sympathy were combined with hard attacks on the government in the vein of "Freedom or Socialism." The campaign in the media was accompanied by innumerable rallies. Helmut Kohl, an extremely active campaigner,[34] held about 140 rallies, and Gerhard Stoltenberg more than 100.[35] All were very different from the CDU's rallies in 1972. There were practically no hecklers. The few who did appear were Communists (mostly Maoists), not Social Democrats, and they tended to stimulate the audiences more than they were able to disturb the speakers. All of the CDU leaders drew large crowds. Another contrast between 1972 and 1976 lay in the use of bumper stickers and buttons: in 1972 the SPD's display had outnumbered the CDU's by three or four to one, while in 1976, if either party was ahead it was the CDU.

What were the issues? The topics covered in CDU campaign speeches and publicity always tended to revolve around the "Freedom or Socialism" theme—the dangers of Socialist détente policy, the failure of Socialist experiments in education, the disastrous consequences of Socialist misconceptions of economic policy, and so on.

---

[34] See, for example, "Drei Wahlkampf-Reisende im Sonderzug [Three campaign workers in a special train], Die Welt, September 25, 1976, and "Die erstaunliche Wirkung des Doktor Helmut Kohl" [The remarkable impact of Doctor Helmut Kohl], Die Welt, September 9, 1976.

[35] See "1200 oeffentliche Kundgebungen" [1200 public rallies], Deutsches Monatsblatt, n. 7/8 (July/August 1976), Bonn.

TABLE 5–9

Voters' Assessment of the Slogan "Freedom instead of Socialism," by Party Identification, Voting Intention, and Region, Late September 1976
(in percentages)

Response	All Respondents	Party Identification			Voting Intention			Region		
		SPD	CDU/CSU	None	SPD	CDU/CSU	FDP	North	Central	South
Do you identify with the slogan?										
Yes	36.5	6.6	82.3	33.9	6.7	77.9	10.0	35.4	30.3	42.6
No	62.7	93.4	17.2	64.5	92.9	21.3	88.3	63.9	69.7	56.6
Which party uses the slogan?										
SPD	2.4	2.9	0.5	3.3	2.7	0.8	1.7	3.5	3.7	1.1
CDU/CSU	97.5	96.7	99.5	96.7	96.9	99.2	98.3	95.8	96.3	98.9
FDP	0.2	0.4	—	—	0.4	—	—	0.7	—	—

Source: See Table 5–2.

Nevertheless, the electorate perceived it as a campaign without issues. As long as the economic situation was perceived as deteriorating, economic issues—especially fighting inflation, unemployment, and the general health of the economy—preoccupied the electorate. But slowly the economic situation seemed to improve, and by election day the outlook was good. The electorate, though still wary, had become generally optimistic about the future, and the economic issues had declined in saliency accordingly. What is important is that no other issue replaced the economy as an area of high concern to the electorate. "The stability of the pension" rose from 2 percent to 6 percent in the most-important-issue polls between January and October, but this was hardly a striking development (see Table 5–10).

The electorate may not have noticed, but in 1976 the Federal Republic confronted high unemployment that was likely to continue for a decade (3 to 4 percent, compared with less than 1 percent from the mid-sixties to 1974). This was a consequence of low economic growth in 1974 and 1975 and of demographic trends. In particular, in the next ten years many more people will join the labor force than will retire. This situation is becoming increasingly dramatic for young people. The most desirable jobs are held by middle-aged workers (the average age of a German full professor is forty-three, that of a highly skilled worker in a big modern factory thirty-eight) who might well remain in their jobs for the next twenty-five years and thereby reduce economic opportunities for the young generation. In addition, the expansion of higher education during the last ten years has created a glut, leaving many highly trained people unable to find jobs that match their qualifications.[36]

Issues like these were raised cautiously by a few politicians, but one of the effects of the all-pervasive "Freedom instead of Socialism" slogan was that it tended to drown out any sophisticated discussion of the hard problems. It is interesting that when the delegates at the Hannover convention cheered the slogan, it was Kurt Biedenkopf who tried to explain its meaning. His speech satisfied the delegates who were more eager to get on with the campaign than to ponder ideological subtleties.[37] When Biedenkopf took up the problem a few weeks later in a lighter vein, showing that distributing beer free of

---

[36] Science Council, "Empfehlungen zu Umfang und Struktur des tertiaeren Bereiches" [Recommendations for the extent and structure of the tertiary area], Bonn, June 21, 1976.

[37] See Biedenkopf's speech at the Twenty-fourth National Party Convention, May 24–26, 1976, published by the National Headquarters of the CDU, Bonn, 1976.

TABLE 5–10

VOTERS' PERCEPTION OF MOST IMPORTANT ISSUE, BY PARTY IDENTIFICATION, JANUARY-OCTOBER 1976

(in percentages of responses)

Issues	All Respondents						CDU/CSU Identifiers				
	Jan.	Feb.	Apr.	Jun.	Sept.	Oct.	Jan.	Feb.	Jun.	Sept.	Oct.
Unemployment	26.9	25.9	25.7	24.9	19.4	22.0	24.8	25.1	23.3	18.9	20.1
Inflation	15.8	14.9	15.1	14.8	12.6	13.7	19.6	16.7	16.1	12.6	14.1
Internal security	7.7	6.2	7.4	9.4	7.5	8.8	11.6	7.8	11.2	8.0	11.0
Economic policy	9.3	7.7	7.2	8.0	6.7	6.5	10.3	7.9	8.7	7.6	6.2
Pensions	2.0	3.0	2.4	2.8	4.8	6.4					
Détente	3.4	3.6	2.1	2.8	4.0	3.6					
Social justice	3.0	2.6	3.1	3.4	3.2	3.4					
Youth unemployment	3.2	3.5	4.8	3.4	3.0	4.2					
Ostpolitik	—	2.6	2.1	—	2.6	2.8					

Issues	SPD Identifiers						Nonidentifiers				
	Jan.	Feb.	Apr.	Jun.	Sept.	Oct.	Jan.	Feb.	Jun.	Sept.	Oct.
Unemployment	30.0	27.6		27.3	23.2	21.5	29.5	27.0	26.1	19.2	25.5
Inflation	17.1	13.8		14.2	11.7	12.8	14.5	14.5	13.6	13.4	15.6
Internal security	6.7	5.1		8.3	6.6	6.5	5.7	5.3	8.4	6.5	8.8
Economic policy	8.8	6.7		7.2	5.9	6.2	9.6	8.3	7.3	7.5	7.0

NOTE: The survey question was open-ended: What do you think is the most important problem in the Federal Republic of Germany today?

SOURCE: See Table 5–2.

charge leads to state-owned breweries and finally to the absence of all beer, people smiled and missed the point.[38]

This was the background for a very provocative campaign. Immediately after the summer break a procedural issue entered the campaign. Helmut Kohl invited Helmut Schmidt to encounter him in a television debate of the kind Ford and Carter had recently announced. Schmidt rejected this invitation, pointing out that there were four party leaders and that it would be unfair to his coalition partner and the leader of the FDP, Hans-Dietrich Genscher, if he were to debate Kohl alone. On the other hand, he proposed twelve hours of television debate involving all four party chairmen.[39] Finally, three days before election day, a four-way debate was arranged. It lasted for almost four hours, starting just after eight and ending at midnight. More than 20 million viewers—over 50 percent of the electorate—tuned in, and towards the end the audience was still more than 10 million. It is extremely difficult to evaluate the impact of this discussion.[40] The likelihood that it was negligible is extremely high; votes are rarely swung by a single decisive event at the very end of a campaign. Nevertheless, the debate gave the voters a unique opportunity to see all four leaders in action. Genscher's sympathetic presence increased the appeal of the government side, while Strauss's presence was a burden to the CDU—as Schmidt had assumed it would be. By insisting on Strauss's participation in any televised debate, Schmidt underlined the belief that Strauss was the real power within the opposition.

One particular feature of the CDU campaign that deserves mention is the attempt made by Kurt Biedenkopf to challenge the SPD strongholds in the Ruhr region by accusing trade union officials of using their union positions for party ends. In the Federal Republic the unions are, according to their constitutions, neutral in party politics, but in fact they have close relations with the SPD. Biedenkopf's efforts gained a lot of attention—in particular, the unions were indignant—but the electoral result for the CDU was rather poor. Biedenkopf had touched on an important issue, but he had overlooked the fact that only a steady flow of information over a period of years will change

---

[38] Johannes Gross, "Freiheit statt Sozialismus" [Freedom instead of socialism], *Frankfurter Allgemeine Zeitung*, July 7, 1976, and Hans Heigert, "Ein Schlagwort auf der Reise" [A slogan en route], *Sueddeutsche Zeitung*, July 24, 1976.

[39] Wilm Herlyn, "Bisher stellte sich kein Kanzler dem Duell" [No chancellor has yet accepted the challenge], *Die Welt*, September 4, 1976.

[40] See Manfred Schell, "20 Millionen Buerger sassen um den Ring" [20 million citizens sat around the ring], and W. Hertz-Eichenrode, "Wahltag der Werte" [Election day of values], both in *Die Welt*, October 2, 1976.

party preferences. If the CDU hammers away at this issue steadily for the next four years, it may be decisive for 1980.[41]

The Outcome

The CDU/CSU won 48.6 percent of the total vote and again became the strongest party in Parliament.[42] Shortly after election day Helmut Kohl became leader of the parliamentary party. An analysis of the election returns shows three important elements for the future development of the CDU/CSU.

(1) In all the state elections between 1974 and 1976, the CDU/CSU had won, on average, 51.4 percent of the total vote. In the federal election the party showed a gain of 3.8 percentage points over its 1972 vote but a loss of 2.8 percentage points compared to the state elections. This can be explained first by the fact that the most important factor pushing voters to support the opposition, a negative perception of the economic situation, had vanished by election day. Second, Helmut Schmidt, as acting chancellor, had a much higher level of personal support than Helmut Kohl: just before election day, surveys showed that 49 percent supported Schmidt and only 38 percent Kohl. That the CDU/CSU vote was higher than Kohl's personal rating was a result of the fact that during the long period of economic difficulties the party had built up a fairly stable base which was able to resist the attractiveness of the acting chancellor.

(2) Overall, the outcome reflected a north-south asymmetry similar to that of 1972. The gains of the CDU increased from north to south. In Schleswig-Holstein the party gained just 2.1 percentage points, in Hamburg 2.4 percentage points, in Bremen 2.9 percentage points, in Lower Saxony 3.0 percentage points, in North Rhine-Westphalia 3.5 percentage points, in Rhineland-Palatinate 4.0 percentage points, and in Hesse 4.5 percentage points; two deviations followed— 2.8 percentage points in the Saar and 3.5 percentage points in Baden-Württemberg—before the CSU scored the Union's highest gain, 4.9 percentage points, in Bavaria. The picture is simply inverted for the Social Democratic party, which registered its worst results in Bavaria and its best results in the north.

This pattern reflects a structural asymmetry in the German elec-

---

[41] See, for example, L. Bewerunge, "Der geheimnisvolle 'Faktor Ruhrgebiet' " [The unpredictable 'Ruhr area factor'], *Frankfurter Allgemeine Zeitung*, August 31, 1976.

[42] Werner Kaltefleiter, "Der Gewinner hat nicht gesiegt," *Aus Politik und Zeitgeschichte*, December 11, 1976.

torate (see Table 5–11). The identifiers with the CDU/CSU are characterized by ties with the church, especially the Catholic church. In the north only 18 percent attend church at least once a month, but in the south 38 percent go to church regularly. In central Germany 28 percent belong to the "church culture" according to this criterion. On the other hand the identifiers with the SPD are associated with the "trade union culture." This culture is overrepresented in central Germany, where about 39 percent of the electorate are affiliated with the trade unions; the north is rated lowest with just 30 percent, and in the south 33 percent show union affiliation. The implication is that only 48 percent of the electorate in the north, but 71 percent of the electorate in the south, have a stable party identification—or that voter mobility in the north is potentially much higher than it is in the south. This is confirmed by a comparison of electoral results since the Hohenzollern Empire.[43]

(3) The higher the instability of party identification the more important are some variables determining the actual vote, especially the candidates' general popularity ratings. Schmidt's lead over Kohl was much larger in the north, where the electorate shows high mobility, than in other regions. In addition, the general support Schmidt got in the north was above average and the support for Kohl was above average in the south. This can easily be explained by the fact that Schmidt comes from the north, is a Protestant, and speaks the language of the north, while Kohl is a Catholic and speaks a dialect closer to that spoken in the south.

The gap between Kohl and Schmidt was enlarged by the voters' perception of Strauss. Strauss was considered nearly as important as Kohl among the leaders of the CDU/CSU, but his image was ambiguous in the south and negative in the north: Tables 5–12 and 5–13 show that new leadership had made the CDU more attractive in 1973 and that the lack of new leadership inside the CSU was a major burden for the opposition.

The CDU/CSU gained a significant victory in the south, receiving

---

[43] The most striking example is the fact that the northernmost state, Schleswig-Holstein, which voted SDP in 1919, produced the first Nazi majority in 1933. See: Rudolf Heberle, *From Democracy to Nazism. A regional case study on political parties in Germany* (New York: Fertig, 1970). Schleswig-Holstein experienced large fluctuations in the support for individual parties during the Hohenzollern Empire as well. The conservative party, for example, dropped from 21.6 percent to 9.3 percent of the votes between 1881 and 1884. Between 1887 and 1890, the Social Democrats were able to increase their share of votes from 21.5 percent to 32.2 percent. In recent times the CDU won 52 percent in the state elections of 1971, 42 percent in the federal elections of 1972, 53.5 percent in the municipal elections of 1974, and 51 percent in the state elections of 1975.

TABLE 5–11

DISTRIBUTION OF SOCIAL INDICATORS, BY REGION, SEPTEMBER 1976

Indicator	All Respondents	North	Central	South
Church Attendance				
More than once weekly	3.8	2.1	2.3	5.9
Once weekly	14.4	7.9	11.7	20.2
Once a month	12.0	7.8	14.5	11.6
More than once yearly	20.0	22.0	18.5	20.4
Once a year	14.2	16.6	12.8	14.3
Less than once a year	13.3	16.6	13.7	11.2
Never	14.8	18.4	16.1	11.8
Union Member in Respondent's Household				
Self	17.7	16.9	19.6	16.5
Self and others	3.5	2.3	3.8	3.8
Only others	11.5	9.9	14.1	9.9
No one	65.4	69.0	61.1	67.4
Social Class[a]				
Working class	39.4	30.1	38.1	45.1
Middle class	49.7	52.7	50.8	47.3
Upper class	7.4	12.4	5.9	6.2

[a] Respondent's self-identification.
SOURCE: See Table 5–2.

TABLE 5–12

VOTERS' RATINGS OF KEY CDU/CSU CANDIDATES, OCTOBER 1976
(in percentages)

Candidate	Named Candidate	Rating		
		Positive	Negative	Don't know
Kohl	90.4	64.8	17.7	17.5
Strauss	80.8	40.0	46.5	13.5
Stoltenberg	34.5	74.2	13.4	12.4
Biedenkopf	24.6	58.6	23.4	18.0
Carstens	24.2	50.8	34.4	14.7
Dregger	14.7	39.7	47.9	12.3
Barzel	13.5	64.5	24.0	11.5

NOTE: Respondents were asked to name the most important CDU/CSU candidates and to rate each either "positive" or "negative."
SOURCE: See Table 5–2.

TABLE 5–13

Voters' Ratings of Key cdu/csu Candidates, by Region, October 1976
(in percentages)

	North				Center				South			
	Named Candidate	Rating			Named Candidate	Rating			Named Candidate	Rating		
Candidate		Posi-tive	Nega-tive	Don't know		Posi-tive	Nega-tive	Don't know		Posi-tive	Nega-tive	Don't know
Kohl	88.9	60.5	19.6	16.4	88.2	59.4	19.6	21.0	92.8	70.4	14.7	14.9
Strauss	80.0	36.7	49.2	13.9	73.4	32.5	52.4	15.1	88.1	47.1	40.7	12.2
Stoltenberg	41.6	72.4	16.5	11.0	25.0	73.2	16.9	9.9	39.7	75.3	10.1	14.6
Biedenkopf	21.3	61.5	29.2	9.2	24.5	48.9	33.1	18.0	26.4	65.2	12.8	22.0
Carstens	26.6	54.3	29.6	16.0	20.5	44.8	42.2	12.9	26.2	53.4	31.3	15.3
Dregger	15.7	33.3	45.8	20.8	14.3	35.7	52.4	8.3	14.5	45.6	43.3	11.1
Barzel	13.5	51.2	29.3	19.3	13.1	66.2	24.3	9.5	13.5	69.0	20.2	10.7

NOTE: Respondents were asked to name the most important cdu/csu candidates and to rate each either "positive" or "negative."
SOURCE: See Table 5–2.

60 percent of the total vote in Bavaria. But it failed to gain a majority in the country as a whole. Clearly the cdu/csu must improve its position in the north. The fact that the party can win majorities in these regions as well has been demonstrated in the recent state elections between 1970 and 1975. The implication is that the cdu/csu will win a majority in the whole country only through a northern strategy, where "northern" includes the central regions. The question for the future development of the party is: given the overwhelming importance of the Catholic south to the party, will the internal decision-making process permit such a northern strategy? If not, the cdu/csu may win a few more state elections but never a national victory.

Epilogue

Just after the election, the cdu/csu was confronted with a new challenge. On November 19, the csu members of Parliament announced that they would not join the cdu in a common parliamentary party, as they always had since 1949.[44] It was obvious that their intention was to begin building up a nationwide csu. Strauss had often expressed the belief that a nationwide csu and a nationwide cdu would have better chances of together winning more than 50 percent of the total vote than did the cdu/csu partnership.[45] What Strauss overlooked was that a conservative nationwide csu had no realistic chance of expanding to the right: in the 1976 election only 0.4 percent of the total vote had gone to right-wing parties. On the other hand, theoretically, if the cdu were to move slightly to the left it might attract more of the floating vote than it had in 1976. The catch here was that the more different the two parties became—the more definitely the csu were identified with conservative policies and the cdu with relatively liberal ones— the harder it would be for them together to offer a viable alternative to the government.[46]

The decision of the csu parliamentary group, led by Franz Josef

---

[44] See, for example, "Chronik einer 27 jaehrigen Fraktionsgemeinschaft" [Chronicle of twenty-seven years in a united parliamentary group], *Süddeutsche Zeitung,* November 20, 1976, and Georg Schroeder, "csu: Ausbruch aus dem Turm des Zentrums" [csu: escape from the prison of centrist politics], *Die Welt,* November 22, 1976.

[45] See P. Diehl-Thiele, "Das schwierige Buendnis der Unions-Glieder" [The difficult alliance of Union elements], *Süddeutsche Zeitung,* November 24, 1976, and H. Riehl-Heyse, "Auf der Suche nach einem klaren Profil" [In search of a clear profile], *Süddeutsche Zeitung,* March 12, 1976.

[46] See Werner Kaltefleiter, "Verbal-Umarmung nach Spaltung" [Verbal embrace after splitting], *Wirtschaftswoche* (November 26, 1976), p. 24.

Strauss, was strongly opposed in Bavaria.[47] Moreover, the CDU announced that it would found a Bavarian CDU immediately if the CSU organized a separate parliamentary party, and the prospects of a successful CDU in Bavaria were much higher than those of a successful CSU in the rest of the country. Taking this into consideration, the decision finally was revoked and the deputies of both parties joined a united parliamentary group.[48]

The first important effect of these events was that the previously unchallenged power of Franz Josef Strauss was questioned. Whatever his future holds—either in Munich or in Bonn—Strauss will never regain his old position. As a result, the process of innovation among the CSU leadership may now be initiated. The second implication of this development is that the distance between the CDU/CSU and the FDP has decreased since, from the early sixties on, the leadership of Strauss was one of the main reasons for the Free Democrats' unwillingness to form a coalition with the CDU/CSU.

Shortly after this event another critical situation arose inside the CDU. In the last three years, Kurt Biedenkopf has risen to a position of rivalry with Kohl that has strained relations between the two foremost CDU leaders.[49] After the election Biedenkopf, criticized for some errors of judgment during the campaign and his inability to effectively reorganize the CDU, resigned as general secretary. He is now trying to find a new position inside the CDU. Whether he aims for the leadership of the CDU in North Rhine-Westphalia and eventually becomes minister-president of this important state or for one of the key positions in the Bundestag, perhaps in the hope of challenging Helmut Kohl, the implication will be internal power struggles that will damage the unity and the public image of the CDU/CSU. It is difficult to predict Biedenkopf's further career, but in the present situation he faces important rivals inside his own party.

For his part, Helmut Kohl has had difficulties in giving the parliamentary party and the party as a whole the leadership they now

---

[47] See R. Jaeger, "Was nuetzt uns ein Bruderkrieg. Ein Plaedoyer für die Einheit der Union" [What use is fratricide: a plea for the unity of the Union], *Die Zeit*, n. 49 (November 26, 1976).

[48] See "CDU und CSU bilden im Bundestag wieder eine gemeinsame Fraktion" [The CDU and CSU again form a common parliamentary group in the Bundestag], *Sueddeutsche Zeitung*, December 13, 1976, and Karl Feldmeyer, "Einigung unter Opfern" [Union with sacrifice], *Frankfurter Allgemeine Zeitung*, December 14, 1976.

[49] See W. Hertz-Eichenrode, "Kohl vor der Bewährungsprobe" [Kohl on probation], *Die Welt*, April 2, 1975, and Ludolf Herrmann, "Der Streit um den Kopf" [The fight for the lead], *Deutsche Zeitung*, May 31, 1974.

want.[50] Before the party convention of March 1977 the number of deputy chairmen was enlarged from five to seven to avoid another struggle for power; Kohl went along with this appeasement measure, and the main governing board of his party was weakened.[51] In the lobby of the Bundestag and among the press, speculation about Kohl's competence has increased, and the likelihood seems high that his position will be challenged during the next two or three years. Thus, despite its impressive showing at the polls, the CDU/CSU has behaved like a loser since the election. Though it was in one sense the winner, it clearly fell short of victory.

---

[50] See Hermann Rudolph, "Gedrückte Stimmung allenthalben" [General mood of depression], *Frankfurter Allgemeine Zeitung*, February 1, 1977.

[51] See "Kohl schlägt Geissler als CDU-Generalsekretär vor" [Kohl recommends Geissler as general secretary], *Die Welt*, January 28, 1977.

6

The CSU Campaign

Paul Noack

Any study of the CSU campaign must address the question first raised by the Bavarian Landtag election of 1974: Was the triumph of a conservative party a special case or part of an electoral trend?[1] Although the election returns in Bavaria in 1976 did not deviate from the national trend in absolute terms—both the CDU and CSU gained votes—the gains of the CSU were so large that one is again tempted to speak of a special case. Contrary to all long-term trends in the Federal Republic a party long dedicated to conservatism has been able to gain a position in this southernmost state of the country, where it has the status of a "government" party.[2] What is the explanation for this deviant tendency of the CSU?

This chapter cannot give a complete answer since it is limited to an analysis of the 1976 election and its results. Nevertheless the outlines of an answer can and should be given. They would run as follows: not all parties in the Federal Republic are "catch-all" parties, the negative German label for popular mass parties that seek to appeal to as wide a spectrum of the electorate as possible.[3] The CSU has never been such a party. Since 1945, as Alf Mintzel has pointed out, the CSU has emphasized and even cultivated its Christian *Weltanschauung*. It

---

[1] Alf Mintzel, "Die bayerische Landtagswahl vom 27. Oktober 1974. Triumph einer konservativen Partei: ein wahlsoziologischer Sonderfall?" [The Bavarian Landtag election of October 27, 1974: triumph of a conservative party—a deviant election?] *Zeitschrift für Parlamentsfragen*, vol. 6, December 1975, pp. 429–46.

[2] Admittedly, the adverse long-term trends in the Federal Republic have shifted with the growth of a conservative mood in the country since about 1972.

[3] The label can be found in Otto Kirchheimer, "Der Weg zur Allerweltspartei" [The way to the catch-all party], in Kurt Lenk and Franz Neumann, eds., *Theorie und Soziologie der politischen Parteien* [Theory and sociology of the political parties] (Neuwied am Rhein and Berlin: Luchterhand, 1968), p. 349.

has consistently done so despite some attenuation of its Catholic social conservatism and despite the pragmatism with which it has adapted its conservative program to the requirements of modern German society.[4]

The CSU Tradition

In many ways the Christian Social Union is unique in the German party landscape. For one thing it is the last survivor of the regional parties formed since 1945. While parties like the Bavarian party and the German party have died out, the csu has resisted even the inroads of the cdu in Bavaria.[5] Alone among the parties represented in the Bundestag since the 1950s, it has not attempted to organize or to campaign in the entire area of the Federal Republic.

The tradition of a Christian Bavarian party goes back to 1918.[6] At that time the Bavarian People's party (Bayerische Volkspartei, BVP) split off from the Bavarian branch of the Center party (Zentrum), the nationwide Catholic party of the Hohenzollern Empire and the Weimar Republic. The program of the new BVP sought to appeal to Bavarian Catholic voters and stressed federal and anti-Socialist goals; it was also designed to attract support from monarchist circles in Bavaria. During the Weimar Republic the BVP was primarily supported by church-related, peasant, and in later years industrial groups. In the Landtag elections from 1919 to 1932 it was the strongest party. Until 1920 it had a parliamentary alliance on the national level with the Center party. This association then broke up because of the far-reaching federalist constitutional proposals of the BVP.

The continuity of the BVP and the csu was primarily evident in the person of the last chairman of the BVP, Fritz Schäffer, who was

---

[4] Alf Mintzel, Die CSU: Anatomie einer konservativen Partei, 1945–1972 [The csu: Anatomy of a conservative party, 1945–1972] (Opladen: Westdeutscher Verlag, 1975), p. 517. This book is the comprehensive standard text on the history and sociology of the csu.

[5] Editor's note: The Bavarian party was a minor states'-rights party that stressed Bavarian particularism, supported rural interests, and advocated an anticlerical policy. The German party was a minor conservative party that traced its ideological origins back to the Hanoverian party of the Hohenzollern Empire and that had its major electoral base in Lower Saxony, especially in the rural areas. The Bavarian party was unable to win seats in the Bundestag after the 1949 election; the German party, after the 1957 election.

[6] See Karl Schwend, "Die BVP" [The BVP], in Erich Matthias and Rudolf Morsey, eds., Das Ende der Parteien, 1933 [The end of the parties, 1933] (Düsseldorf: Droste Verlag, 1960), pp. 457–519. Also see Karl Schwend, Bayern zwischen Monarchie und Diktatur [Bavaria between monarchy and dictatorship] (Munich: R. Pflaum, 1954).

also a charter member of the CSU and later served as finance minister under Konrad Adenauer.[7] The first chairman of the newly organized CSU was Joseph Müller, a recognized liberal and a defender of German unity. He remained chairman until 1949 when he attempted to incorporate the CSU into the national organization of the CDU. The attempt failed largely because the CSU wanted stronger protection for the states in the Basic Law (Grundgesetz) of the Federal Republic. For the same reason Bavaria was the only state to reject adoption of the Basic Law.

Since the elimination of the anticlerical Bavarian party in 1962, the CSU has continuously had an absolute majority of the seats in the Bavarian Landtag. Since 1961, when Franz Josef Strauss was elected state party chairman, the CSU's conservative philosophy has taken more definite shape. The CSU and CDU formed a united parliamentary group after 1949 in the Bundestag, but the Bavarian CSU delegates steadily retained their own state party group with a separate press and executive headquarters. In the period up to 1962 the major goal of the CSU state party group was to look after the interests of its members in the distribution of Bundestag positions, especially the composition of the top executive officials, the legislative committees, and their chairmen. By 1962, however, when Franz Josef Strauss was forced to abandon his post as a result of the Spiegel affair,[8] "it was obvious that under his ambitious leadership the CSU parliamentary group would formulate its own position on policy issues, even in the area of foreign policy."[9] Since 1969 this has been particularly true in foreign policy. Franz Josef Strauss, the undisputed leader whose title as chairman is inadequate to describe his power within the party, became one of the most important opponents of the Socialist-Liberal coalition government's foreign and financial policies. He even helped undermine the leadership of Rainer Barzel, the CDU/CSU candidate for chancellor in 1972, who had sought to fashion a limited understanding with the SPD-FDP coalition on the policy of *Ostpolitik*.

Ever since he entered politics Strauss has been one of the dominant political leaders of the Federal Republic. Born in 1915 in Munich, he was district officer in Upper Bavaria as early as 1945–1949 and

---

[7] For the early history of the CSU see Mintzel, *Die CSU*, pp. 90–120.

[8] The Spiegel affair involved highly questionable attempts by the Adenauer government to engage in summary arrests and seizures on the grounds that the weekly had illegally published military secrets. In the ensuing controversy Adenauer was forced to replace Franz Josef Strauss, the defense minister, who was implicated in the actions undertaken by the government.

[9] Gerhard Loewenberg, *Parlamentarismus im politischen System der Bundesrepublik* [original English title: Parliament in the German Political System] (Tübingen: Wunderlich, 1969), p. 201.

became general secretary of the party in 1948. Originally he belonged to the liberal wing of the csu led by Joseph Müller. Since the 1960s, however, he has increasingly played a leading role in shaping the conservative image of his party. His impact on the Federal Republic has been so far-reaching that outside of his home state Strauss is considered to be the very personification of Bavaria.

The controversies which have broken out between the cdu and csu since the close election defeat of 1976 can be traced not only to Strauss's conviction that the cdu did not wage a sufficiently hard-hitting campaign, but also to a sense of personal frustration caused by thwarted ambition. Strauss has never been able to become federal chancellor, although he has headed several ministries since 1953, most recently the Ministry of Finance from 1966 to 1969 in the grand coalition under Kurt Georg Kiesinger. One of the most brilliant political leaders of the Federal Republic (if also the most controversial), Strauss has represented the smaller party in the cdu/csu combination and thus has had to defer to the cdu's choice of cdu/csu candidate for chancellor. Under the circumstances his influence has been limited to preventing the cdu from making personnel appointments and adopting campaign policy stands that he finds unacceptable. Given the more liberal posture of the cdu, Strauss's influence has appeared to be mostly obstructive. Late in 1977 Strauss announced his hope of becoming minister-president of Bavaria after the 1978 Landtag elections —hardly his most cherished goal, but the best available after his reluctant withdrawal from national politics.

The CSU on the Eve of the 1976 Election

As previously noted, the csu has had an absolute majority of the seats in the Landtag since 1962, although it was not until 1970 that it gained a majority of the popular votes cast. In 1974 the party broke the 60 percent barrier, winning 62.1 percent in the state elections.[10] This is the result by which the 1976 election must be measured, since political circumstances had not changed: Helmut Schmidt was still federal chancellor and the csu could still point to the state of affairs in Munich when waging its fight against socialism. In Munich the spd was engaged in a suicidal internal dispute in which the left wing had gained the upper hand even though the city's population was undergoing a social transformation that seemingly made it ever less dis-

---

[10] Gerold Tandler, *Anhang zum Rechenschaftsbericht des Generalsekretärs der CSU* [Postscript to the report of the general secretary of the csu], Munich, June 25–26, 1976.

TABLE 6-1

RESULTS OF BAVARIAN LANDTAG ELECTIONS, 1946–1974
(in percentages)

Party	1946	1950	1954	1958	1962	1966	1970	1974
CSU	52.3	27.4	38.0	45.6	47.5	48.1	56.4	62.1
SPD	28.6	28.0	28.1	30.8	35.3	35.8	33.3	30.2
FDP	5.6	7.1	7.2	5.6	5.9	5.1	5.5	5.2

SOURCE: Central Institute for Social Scientific Research, Free University of Berlin.

posed to support Socialist experiments. The left wing of the SPD was nevertheless able to force the retreat of Hans-Jochen Vogel, previously a long-time mayor of Munich and now the federal minister of justice in the Socialist-Liberal cabinet. These constant internal party disputes in Munich were undermining the reputation of the entire Bavarian SPD organization.

While continuing to cultivate its primarily Catholic electorate, the CSU was able in 1974 to win a foothold in the Protestant part of Franconia. It is important to note that the Bavarian electorate is nowhere near as homogeneous as it appears from the outside. One must distinguish not only between the agrarian areas and the middle-sized and large cities, particularly Munich, Nuremberg, and Augsburg, but also between the historic Bavarian regions of Old Bavaria, Swabia, and Franconia. The special characteristics of each of these regions often fail to emerge in a general analysis but they are an important consideration in the election strategy of the CSU. Thus in 1970 the CSU was already able to capture a large percentage of the voters of the radical right party, the National Democratic party (NPD). (In 1966, the NPD won 7.4 percent in Bavaria; in 1970, 2.9 percent.) In 1970, as in 1976, the heavy accent on nationalism in the CSU campaign undoubtedly appealed to the traditionally Liberal party-oriented population of Middle and Upper Franconia. (These areas had supported the old nationalistic National Liberal party during the Hohenzollern Empire and the FDP during the Adenauer-Erhard years of the Federal Republic.) When the FDP entered the Socialist-Liberal coalition, it lost its appeal for nationalist-oriented liberals in Bavaria.

Outside the traditional strongholds of the party, such as the Upper Palatinate, Lower Bavaria, and Upper Bavaria (except Munich), there are considerable variations in the level of CSU membership. These are reflected in voter turnout, since the size of a party organization

FIGURE 6–1

ADMINISTRATIVE DISTRICTS AND BUNDESTAG REPRESENTATION IN BAVARIA

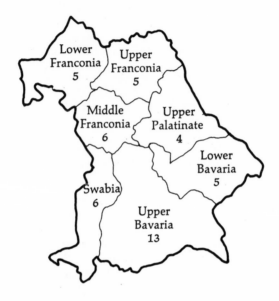

NOTE: The figures indicate the number of Bundestag candidates directly elected in each district.
SOURCE: Report of the Election Administrator of the Free State of Bavaria, October 1976.

can affect its potential voter turnout. For example, in Upper Franconia and Middle Franconia, party membership is only 1.46 percent and 1.57 percent respectively of the potential electorate. By contrast in Lower Bavaria and the Upper Palatinate, the figures rise to 2.53 percent and 2.94 percent respectively, double the level in Franconia.[11] Quite clearly in these "developing areas" the CSU still has possibilities for growth.

The membership structure of the CSU also reveals considerable underrepresentation of wage earners. Although election results indicate some lack of worker support, they hide the degree of the imbalance in party membership. No separate data are available on the worker component of the CSU electorate, but analysis of the 1976

---

[11] Ibid.

TABLE 6–2

EVOLUTION OF CSU MEMBERSHIP, BY ADMINISTRATIVE DISTRICT,
1972–1976

District Organizations	Membership, 1976	Membership Increase (in percentages of eligible electorate)	
		1972–74	1974–76
Upper Bavaria	30,741	1.74	2.14
Lower Bavaria	17,211	2.33	2.53
Upper Palatinate	19,221	2.64	2.94
Upper Franconia	10,273	1.08	1.46
Middle Franconia	8,458	1.31	1.57
Lower Franconia	15,772	1.74	2.03
Swabia	16,966	1.91	2.03

SOURCE: Gerold Tandler, *Anhang zum Rechenschaftsbericht des Generalsekretärs der CSU* [Postscript to the report of the general secretary of the csu], Munich, June 25–26, 1976.

Bundestag election shows that considerable differences exist between the southern, central, and northern areas of Germany. Thus in the worker strongholds of the north, the CDU gained 41.5 percent; in the center of Germany, only 37.4 percent; whereas in the south, 52.2 percent (comprising Hesse, Rhineland-Palatinate, Baden-Württemberg, and Bavaria). The result might even be higher for Bavaria alone.[12]

Even so it was the polarization after 1969 that first gave the csu the chance to move beyond its original agrarian and small-town, middle-class clientele. "It was only in the struggle between the Socialist-Liberal and Union camps over a clear parliamentary majority in the German Bundestag, and the formation of the first Socialist-Liberal coalition, that the csu was able not just to absorb almost completely the right splinter groups in the Protestant parts of Franconia, but also to make inroads into the urban electorate and the groups which heretofore had traditionally voted Liberal and Social Democratic."[13] The 1976 election campaign of the csu can best be understood therefore if it is remembered that in the past the party has significantly increased

[12] Figures from Social Science Research Institute, Konrad Adenauer Foundation, *Bundestagswahl vom 3. Oktober 1976: Tabellenband* [Bundestag election of October 3, 1976, volume of statistical tables], mimeographed.
[13] Mintzel, "Die bayerische Landtagswahl," 1974, p. 434.

TABLE 6–3

csu Members, by Occupation, 1976

Occupation	Percentage of CSU Members
Blue-collar workers	17.8
White-collar workers	24.9
Civil servants	15.6
Farmers	19.4
Professionals	17.3
Self-employed	3.2
Housekeepers	1.8
Total	100.0

Source: Same as for Table 6–2.

its electorate when there has been a sharp polarization between the cdu/csu and the spd-fdp coalition.

A Two-Front Campaign

The Campaign against the CDU. The csu election campaign proceeded on two fronts. First, the csu vehemently opposed the spd and the fdp. Second, however, except during the final "hot" phase of the campaign after August 1976, the csu squabbled interminably with the cdu over how the attack on the government parties should be conducted. The ups and downs of the dispute cannot be gone into here. They can best be summarized in a quotation from a German weekly magazine: "If the comparison were not macabre, one could almost liken the sequence of peace treaties between the Union parties to events in Lebanon, where Christians and Muslims alternately shoot, embrace, and then open fire again."[14]

The chronological and substantive phases of the dispute, which to a degree overlapped, can be characterized as follows: First, Strauss continued to indicate during 1975 his availability as a candidate for the chancellorship; in June 1976, his own party endorsed him as the most capable candidate. Second, the csu threatened to run as a "fourth party" that would campaign throughout the entire country. Only in November 1975 did it reluctantly decide to give up its plans. But the

---

[14] "Eine Rechnung die nicht aufging" [An equation that did not balance], *Die Zeit*, no. 48 (November 21, 1975).

decision was provisional and the party could always, for purposes of blackmail, renew its threat to run as a fourth party. Third, the csu insisted on exercising substantial influence on the elaboration of the campaign platform. While two-thirds of the text which was presented in May 1976 came from the cdu program, about a third came from the csu program. Fourth, the csu fought for weeks over whether the "core team" of party leaders would be small or large; if it were small—three or four key figures—Strauss would win considerable clout. But here too the csu lost: it was finally agreed that the core team would have ten members.

The first dispute came to a head on June 19, 1975, when the csu granted only conditional acceptance to the candidacy of Helmut Kohl, cdu chairman and minister-president of Rhineland-Palatinate. The csu acknowledged that the cdu, as the larger national party, should carry more weight in naming the candidate and agreed to support Kohl in the interest of the unity of the Union parties. But it also stated that, in the opinion of the party, Strauss was the better candidate. It was evident from this point on that personal reservations and substantive differences would continue to plague the cdu and the csu during the campaign.

The cdu sought to promote itself early in the campaign as the party that would really deal with increasing social dissatisfaction in contemporary society. The csu, by contrast, presented itself from the very beginning as a consciously conservative party with an anti-Socialist program.[15] Its influence on the campaign platform of the cdu lay mainly in the elimination of social policies that Strauss considered excessive.[16] Thus, in accordance with the wishes of the csu, sections were cut out of the final text of the campaign platform which advocated compensation payments for child rearing (as reimbursement to mothers during the time that they cannot be employed) and investment wages (a portion of wages paid in the form of shares of stock in the corporation).

Differences between the two parties were not revealed to the

---

[15] The basis of the campaign negotiations for the 1976 election are described in the position paper of the csu in the following terms: "A federal government supported by the cdu and csu will be grounded in Christian moral law and Western humanism and committed to the best German tradition; it will ensure that progress be pursued with the knowledge that there can be no transformation—no historical and social progress—without tradition, the indissoluble link between initiative and achievement, progress and freedom, law and order in our society." *Bayernkurier*, June 14, 1975.

[16] "Strauss streicht im Wahlprogramm" [Strauss strikes at the election platform], *Süddeutsche Zeitung*, May 21, 1976.

wider public when the csu held its party convention in mid-September 1975 and adopted the motto "Work for Germany." Strauss and Kohl had concurred in emphasizing that the next Bundestag election would chart the course of political party development until the year 2000; both parties were already focusing on freedom as the theme of the campaign.[17] It was only at the preelection convention of the csu on May 8, 1976, that the "Freedom or Socialism" slogan which would dominate the campaign emerged. Strauss repeatedly named the eminent economist Friedrich A. von Hayek as the originator of the slogan, in his *Der Weg zu Knechtschaft* [The road to serfdom] published at the end of World War II.

The general themes of the election campaign were set in a speech entitled "Socialism in Bonn—Practice since 1969," delivered by Richard Stücklen, the csu parliamentary leader. The subheadings of the speech are revealing: Special Favors for Radicals, The Red School, Socialist and Communist Action Groups, The Undermining of the Economy, Inflationary Policy, The Threat to Social Welfare, Socialist Foreign Policy, A European Popular Front, and so on. The csu general secretary, Gerold Tandler, wrote in the preface to a brochure prepared for the convention: "Either the Socialist experiments and bureaucratic dirigisme of the spd will progress further . . . or the Union will again be able to pursue the policy that delivered our country from desperation and hopelessness."[18]

The cdu hesitated before adopting the csu slogan, but finally agreed to use the allegedly weaker formulation: "Freedom instead of Socialism." In doing so, it demonstrated that in cdu/csu negotiations the csu united behind Franz Josef Strauss outweighed the much larger cdu when its ranks were divided. Moreover, several leading cdu politicians (including Karl Carstens, Alfred Dregger, and Hans Filbinger) openly supported Strauss's hard line.[19] The fact was, as one observer wrote before the election: "There has long existed a csu outside of Bavaria in the ranks of the cdu itself. . . . Particularly in the lower echelons of the party there is today obvious support for rigid confrontation and for mobilization based on partisan emotions and a

---

[17] csu state central committee, "Arbeit für Deutschland—Parteitag der Christlich Sozialen Union" [Work for Germany: party convention of the Christian Socialist Union], September 12–13, 1975, Munich.

[18] See csu state central committee, *Freiheit oder Sozialismus—Dokumentation* [Freedom or socialism—documentation], Munich, 1976.

[19] Professor Carstens was chairman of the cdu/csu group in the Bundestag at the time, Dregger chairman of the cdu in Hesse, Filbinger minister-president and chairman of the cdu in Baden-Württemberg.

desire to avenge the defeats of 1969 and 1972."[20] Here it must be remembered that the cdu/csu has always set more store by personality (Adenauer, Erhard) than by policy issues. It asks its leaders not to discuss issues but to personify them.

The anti-Socialist line had in no way changed by the time of the preelection convention of the csu in mid-September 1976; on the contrary it had been reinforced and reaffirmed. In his public speeches Strauss repeatedly used the slogan "Freedom or Socialism" and warned that the futures of Germany and Europe were at stake. The strategic purpose of the slogan was to get the cdu/csu to adopt a principled anti-Socialist position under the leadership of Strauss. As one observer has noted: "In Strauss's view socialism is a system of thought which claims to find the ultimate destiny of mankind in the progress of history. Such a system of thought is incompatible with the democratic principle that all political decisions are reversible by the electorate."[21] Another aspect of socialism to which Strauss objects is the collective organization of society, exemplified by the Soviet Union, in which "the freedom of the individual is but a function of societal freedom, not the result of individual right."[22]

The slogan "Freedom or Socialism" also had a tactical purpose: on virtually every issue it posited a pair of opposite solutions, permitting the cdu/csu to attack the implications of the coalition parties' stand even on issues where they had refrained from formulating concrete proposals of their own. The cdu/csu warned not that socialism was imminent but that if the coalition were elected socialism would continue to expand, acquiring a dynamism of its own which men like Helmut Schmidt would be powerless to impede.

The csu headquarters argued that if equating democratic socialism with unfreedom were felt to be harsh or unfair in the north, it certainly was not perceived this way in Bavaria. This was undoubtedly true. The csu had never had an "Ahlen Program," the platform adopted by the cdu in 1947 advocating the socialization of basic industries.

[20] Hermann Rudolph, "Auf der Gegendünung nach oben [Backlash against the lost election], *Frankfurter Allgemeine Zeitung*, August 7, 1976.
[21] Friedrich Karl Fromme, "Wahlkampf ist auch Friedenszeit" [An election campaign is also a time of peace], *Frankfurter Allgemeine Zeitung*, August 18, 1976.
[22] "Eine Partei des irdischen Lebensglücks—Eberhard Pickart befragt Franz Josef Strauss" [A party of peace on earth—Eberhard Pickart questions Franz Josef Strauss], in *Zur Wahl gestellt—Ansichten, Absichten, Befürchtungen und Versprechungen von Hans-Dietrich Genscher, Helmut Kohl, Helmut Schmidt und Franz Josef Strauss* [Put to the choice—views, intentions, fears, and promises of Hans-Dietrich Genscher, Helmut Kohl, Helmut Schmidt and Franz Josef Strauss] (Stuttgart, Zurich: Belser, 1976), p. 96.

Unlike the cdu's, the csu's working-class members remained relatively uninfluential. Moreover, for decades the csu had presented itself as a consistently anti-Socialist party. Already in the 1974 Landtag election campaign it had successfully used slogans similar to the one adopted in 1976. Thus, in Bavaria the slogan confirmed the electorate's perception of the csu and was intended less to defame the opponent than to mobilize sympathizers to support the csu.

The Campaign against the SPD-FDP. The csu could assume in its campaign that it was in fact a popular mass party. Although its electorate included a disproportionate number of professionals, it also had the backing of half of the workers. The result was a campaign without a narrowly defined target group.

The csu campaign was centralized in two respects. First, it was obviously designed to make the most of the personality of Franz Josef Strauss. There was practically no csu publicity in which Strauss's photograph or at least his signature did not appear. Helmut Kohl, by contrast, got short shrift. It must be admitted, however, that Kohl did at least appear in the csu campaign publicity, whereas the csu would accuse the cdu of preventing any mention of Strauss in the campaign publicity for the northern part of the Federal Republic. In any case Strauss was clearly the most sought-after speaker and appeared at rallies more often than any other opposition spokesman (140 times).

Second, the management of the csu campaign was centralized. Each of the leading politicians, for example, was required to donate ten campaign appearances which were to be used in whatever way the state party central committee saw fit. This centralized control, introduced by General Secretary Tandler in 1972, made the csu without a doubt the most modern and effective party organization in the entire Federal Republic.[23] One of the party's strengths is the system of managers or chairmen, one for each Bundestag electoral district, who are appointed and supervised by the party leadership. In the 1976 campaign the electoral district chairmen, acting on instructions from the party leadership, orchestrated the choice of campaign issues as well as speaker schedules at the local party level, thereby allowing for great efficiency and flexibility in the direction of the campaign.

The media campaign too was highly centralized. Between December 1975 and July 1976 a series of twenty-one campaign advertisements—"arguments," as they were called—touching on various campaign themes were published in Bavarian newspapers. The first began

---

[23] Mintzel, *Die CSU*, pp. 327–37.

with the reminder, "Only twenty-eight weeks to the election," the last with "Only four days to the election." Even the usual German campaign brochures presenting personal messages from the individual candidates were centrally planned in May and June, as were the so-called candidate flyers which combined central party propaganda with publicity for individual candidates. The csu published a "vacation magazine" for the summer vacation period (August in Bavaria) which discussed the themes of the election in a humorous and satirical vein. Almost none of the csu leaflets were initiated by individuals and those few that were tended to be taken for party publicity. There was no publicity in the national media, with the exception of television where the csu, like the other parties, was allocated time on the basis of the number of seats it had in the Bundestag.

In interviews after the election csu spokesmen explained that the 1976 campaign—on which the party had spent about DM8 million—had run much more smoothly than the 1972 campaign, for several reasons. It had been more carefully planned in advance,[24] for one thing, and Helmut Schmidt had been a less charismatic opponent than Willy Brandt. In addition, the 1976 campaign slogans had focused on fundamental issues that had emerged spontaneously out of the sharply diverging goals of the competing parties; by contrast, the slogans in the 1972 campaign had exaggerated the importance of trivial issues. Finally, in 1976, in contrast to 1972, the party had been convinced it could win the election. csu party leaders believed that the cdu and csu complemented each other in the sense that many voters in Bavaria voted csu although their political views were closer to those of the more liberal cdu. Conversely in the rest of Germany voters who voted cdu might in fact be closer to the more conservative csu. In this fashion, according to csu estimates—which would appear to be quite exaggerated—the cdu/csu electorate comprises 60 percent who share the more liberal views of the cdu and 40 percent who share the more conservative views of the csu. In any case, since the csu leaders continued to believe even after the elections that the 1976 election could and should have been won, the bitter postelection dispute with the cdu should not be surprising. According to csu leaders a major contributing cause of the electoral defeat was the ratification of the Polish treaties by the cdu/csu-governed states in the Bundesrat on March 12, 1976. In the judgment of csu General Secretary Tandler, "The ratifica-

---

[24] Author's interview with the general secretary of the csu, Gerold Tandler, December 10, 1976, and interviews with personnel of the csu state central committee.

tion of the Polish treaties cost us on the average at least 1 percent of the national vote."[25]

The Election Results

The election results of October 3 exceeded the expectations even of the CSU leaders. As compared with the Bundestag elections of 1972, the CSU improved its position by 4.9 percentage points, to 60.0 percent of the vote in Bavaria. By contrast, the CDU's best statewide result— 53.3 percent in Baden-Württemberg—was 6.7 percentage points less. From 1961 to 1972 the CSU had always remained in the neighborhood of 55 percent of the vote in Bavaria. Its gains in 1976 were all the more significant in that they were not the result of the absorption of a smaller party but instead were gains at the expense of the established parties. (The SPD lost 5 percentage points in Bavaria, declining to 32.8 percent; the FDP gained only 0.1 percentage point, to 6.2 percent.)[26]

It is interesting to note that the gains were distributed throughout the state. This serves to reinforce our previous analysis to the effect that the CSU has achieved a uniform "penetration level" both geographically and sociologically in Bavaria. Future electoral gains will at best be quite limited. But in 1976 the CSU registered gains in each of the forty-four Bavarian electoral districts, whereas the SPD lost votes in each. Of forty-four representatives elected directly by the single-member majority system, the CSU won forty. Above all, it was able to wrest from the SPD four of the five electoral districts in Munich. Only in the Munich-North district—where the former mayor and incumbent federal minister of justice, Hans-Jochen Vogel, was running—could the SPD maintain even a weakened position. For the

---

[25] Author's interview with Tandler, November 22, 1976. The Polish treaties were negotiated in 1975 and provided for the return to the Federal Republic of ethnic Germans from Polish territory, extension of long-term credits by the Federal Republic to Poland, and a lump-sum payment to Poland to settle pension claims stemming from the wartime occupation of Poland by Nazi Germany. Ratification of the treaties was highly controversial, particularly in the Bundesrat because the CDU/CSU had the votes, if they so decided, to reject the treaties. Although some last minute maneuvering produced a unanimous vote in support of the treaties, Strauss criticized Kohl's leadership and implied that *he* would have demanded more concessions from Poland.

[26] The figures are taken from *Mitteilungen und Bekanntmachungen des Landeswahlleiters des Freistaates Bayern* [Announcements of the state election chairman of Bavaria] and also *Statistischer Bericht B VII* [Statistical report B VII], January-May 1976; *Wahl zum 8. Deutschen Bundestag 1976 in Bayern* [The election of the eighth German Bundestag in Bavaria 1976], issue 6, Final Results, published in October 1976.

TABLE 6–4

Bundestag Election Results in Bavaria, 1969–1976
(in percentages)

Party	1969	1972	1976
CSU	54.4	55.1	60.0
SPD	34.6	37.8	32.8
FDP	4.1	6.1	6.2

SOURCE: Same as for Figure 6–1.

state as a whole, the SPD's contingent of directly elected representatives shrank from thirteen to four. In total the CSU won fifty-three seats in the Bundestag (compared with forty-eight in 1972) and the Bavarian SPD only twenty-nine, as against thirty-three in 1972.

The election results in the administrative districts and big cities of Bavaria also demonstrate that the CSU has definitely outgrown its original farmer/Catholic/lower-middle-class electoral clientele. Although the gap between the CSU's best showing in an administrative district (Lower Bavaria, with 69.7 percent) and its worst (Middle Franconia, with 51.2 percent) was 18.5 percentage points, increases were registered in all administrative districts. The increases in the two strongest districts (Lower Bavaria and Upper Palatinate) were only 3.5 and 4.2 percentage points respectively, but those in the CSU's two weakest districts (Middle Franconia and Upper Bavaria) were 5.3 and 5.9 percentage points. This shows that the CSU tapped its voter reserves more effectively in the areas where it was weakest than in its strongholds.

This was true as well in the three largest Bavarian cities, where the CSU normally does rather poorly. Outside of Munich, the CSU won 64.2 percent in Upper Bavaria; 55.1 percent in Middle Franconia without Nuremberg; and 66.1 percent in Swabia without Augsburg, compared with 63.7 percent including Augsburg. Nevertheless, in all three of these cities, the CSU's gains were above average: in Munich from 40.6 to 47.2 percent, making the CSU for the first time the strongest party in the Bavarian state capital; in Nuremberg—another city where the SPD lost its absolute majority—from 37.5 to 47.2 percent; and in Augsburg from 45.5 to 51.4 percent. Apart from an absolute increase in CSU votes throughout the state, the striking sociological result of the 1976 election was the party's success in increasing its support among all segments of Bavaria's social structure. This is

161

TABLE 6–5

BUNDESTAG ELECTION RETURNS IN BAVARIA, BY ADMINISTRATIVE DISTRICT,
1972 AND 1976

(in percentages)

District	1972	1976
Upper Bavaria		
CSU	52.7	58.6
SPD	38.7	32.0
Lower Bavaria		
CSU	66.2	69.7
SPD	30.0	26.0
Upper Palatinate		
CSU	61.2	65.4
SPD	34.4	29.9
Upper Franconia		
CSU	50.9	55.5
SPD	43.2	39.2
Middle Franconia		
CSU	45.9	51.2
SPD	44.6	40.2
Lower Franconia		
CSU	58.5	62.3
SPD	35.1	31.6
Swabia		
CSU	59.0	63.7
SPD	34.5	29.6

SOURCE: Same as for Figure 6–1.

of particular interest because it points out that despite Bavaria's increasing industrialization the SPD was unable to garner the votes that it traditionally attracts from this type of developing social structure.

Given the generally leftist mood that prevailed after 1969, and especially after 1972, the reorientation of party voting within the various age cohorts of the Bavarian electorate has been dramatic.[27] Before 1976 it was taken for granted that (1) the older the age cohort, the higher the CSU vote, and (2) women consistently vote more conservatively than men. Neither was true in 1976. Although the younger age cohorts still voted SPD more frequently than the older ones, the margin was minimal, as the following statistics show:

---

[27] Bavarian Office of Statistics, "Die Bundestagswahl 1976 in Bayern—Stimmengewinne der CSU besonders bei den jungen Männern" [The 1976 Bundestag election in Bavaria: gains in votes among young men], December 7, 1976, Munich.

Age Cohort, Bavarian Electorate	Percentage of Vote for CSU, 1976*
18–24	57.3
25–34	57.8
35–44	60.2

* Bavarian Office of Statistics, Munich.

Furthermore, the rate of growth of the CSU vote was much higher in the eighteen to forty-four age cohort than in the older cohorts. And for the first time the eighteen to twenty-four-year-old men voted CSU more frequently than did women (men, 57.7 percent; women, 56.9 percent). The question which these data suggest cannot yet be answered: is the rise in the CSU vote—especially among the young—the result of a genuine increase in conservatism, or is the younger generation holding the governing coalition accountable for its job insecurity? The most that can be said is that the majority of the youth no longer seek radical changes in the existing social and political system.

The Aftermath

Even before the election there were indications that in the event of an electoral defeat the CSU would no longer be willing to accept the

TABLE 6–6

CHANGE IN VOTE BETWEEN BUNDESTAG ELECTIONS OF 1972 AND 1976
IN BAVARIA, BY AGE AND SEX OF VOTER
(in percentage-point gains and losses)

	Age of Voter					
Party	18–24	25–34	35–44	45–59	60 and over	All Voters
All voters						
CSU	+6.8	+6.2	+7.8	+3.9	+1.7	+4.9
SPD	−7.6	−6.0	−8.3	−3.0	−0.8	−4.6
Male voters						
CSU	+8.2	+6.8	+8.4	+5.0	+1.8	+5.8
SPD	−8.3	−6.0	−8.8	−3.8	−0.7	−5.2
Female voters						
CSU	+5.3	+5.8	+7.3	+3.1	+1.3	+4.2
SPD	−6.7	−6.2	−7.7	−2.4	−0.7	−4.1

SOURCE: Bavarian Office of Statistics.

fact that its own electoral success compensated for the weaker electoral outcome of the CDU. As the CSU chief had pointed out, a change in political party alignments would be necessary after a CDU/CSU electoral defeat. This conclusion was justified by the preelection argument that the FDP was subjected to a form of "Babylonian captivity" by the SPD. Thus coalition possibilities between the CDU/CSU and the FDP no longer existed; to form a new government the CDU/CSU could not compensate for its loss of an electoral majority by seeking a coalition agreement with the FDP.[28]

Most newspapers covered the CDU and CSU returns under the rubric "CDU/CSU." Yet even on election night, this no longer rang true. On October 3, Strauss had declared, "if the electoral system prevents the CDU/CSU from winning, then something must surely be changed." One journalist interpreted the statement thus: "Since the CSU chairman Strauss cannot bring about a change in the electoral system (in favor of a single-member plurality system for the entire Bundestag, for example) he must have been referring to the kind of change in the party system that has always been associated with the extension of the CSU's party activities from a strictly Bavarian to a nationwide level."[29] The fact is, of course, that the CSU's position in the CDU/CSU joint national parliamentary group was stronger after the election than before.

In mid-October it became evident that Strauss thought the time had come to end the association of the two parties in Parliament which dated from 1949.[30] His decision was heavily influenced by CDU coalition negotiations with the FDP in Lower Saxony and the Saar which led to an agreement between the two parties in December. Strauss feared that this would make it impossible for the CDU/CSU to function as a vigorous opposition at the federal level, especially in the Bundesrat where the CDU/CSU state governments had a majority. Despite these early signs of Strauss's intentions, the actual decision of the CSU parliamentary group on November 19 in Kreuth, Bavaria, to dissolve the joint CDU/CSU parliamentary group came as a surprise in German political circles. The initial negotiations between Kohl and

---

[28] Among others, *Zur Wahl gestellt*, p. 105: "If the FDP continues to put the governmental transition mechanism out of commission the question of reexamining the political party landscape will naturally come to the fore again."

[29] Herbert Riehl-Heyse, "Zornige Kurfürsten, verstörte Genossen" [Stubborn counts, disturbed comrades], *Süddeutsche Zeitung*, October 5, 1976.

[30] For the views of the CSU leader see "Gemeinsame Unionsfraktion noch nicht sicher: Strauss stellt seine Bedingungen" [The Union group is still not certain: Strauss sets conditions], *Frankfurter Allgemeine Zeitung*, October 12, 1976.

Strauss seemed to promise favorable results. Moreover, the possibility that the CSU would expand northward as a fourth national party would have incalculable consequences for the entire party system.

The underlying rationale for the CSU's becoming a fourth national party was that a more liberal CDU and an uncompromisingly conservative CSU might attract more voters than the CDU/CSU one-party coalition. At first, however, the CSU based its decision on tactical parliamentary considerations: as an independent parliamentary party, the CSU would be allotted more time for debate in Parliament, which would mean that CDU/CSU policies could be presented in greater depth; the CSU would also receive more funds and its own chamber for caucus deliberations. At the same time the CSU would continue to cooperate with the CDU under some common arrangement yet to be determined.

Despite the rationale, the decision of the CSU to break with the CDU/CSU joint parliamentary group triggered rather more discontent among CSU rank and file supporters—especially in Franconia and Swabia—than the Bundestag party representatives and the party central committee had expected. While the party membership did not rise in revolt, they passed resolutions in several places declaring their unequivocal opposition to any expansion of the CSU as a fourth national party.

Meanwhile on November 22, the CDU asked the CSU to declare its commitment to the continued unity of the Union parties. Concurrently the CDU was preparing to establish its own state party organization in Bavaria. Given the fact that opinion polls estimated the CDU potential in Bavaria at between 15 and 30 percent, a separate CDU party organization in Bavaria could not possibly meet with the approval of Strauss, for it would jeopardize the absolute majority of the CSU—for example, in the 1978 Landtag elections. Undoubtedly the CSU had underestimated the vehemence and firm determination of the CDU's reaction. While it could not have expected the CDU to endorse CSU expansion, it had probably hoped for help from the more conservative members of the CDU central committee. Certainly a degree of moderation in the CDU's reaction would have gained time for the CSU.

On the other hand, by late November it was also clear that to retract the resolution of November 19 would amount to a serious, hardly acceptable defeat for Strauss and his friends. Unmistakable evidence came on November 24 when the future chairman of the CSU group in the Bundestag, Fritz Zimmermann, met with Carstens, the previous chairman of the joint CDU/CSU group. Their talks and also those that proceeded between Strauss and Kohl showed above all how irreconcilable were their opinions, particularly since Strauss's remarks branding Kohl as intellectually and personally incapable had become public.

Because of the surprisingly strong resistance of the CDU, both parties agreed—after several unsuccessful rounds of talks which had seemed to make the separation of the parties inevitable—to continue their association in Parliament. Facilitated by a surprising offer made by the CSU state central committee on December 9, the new agreement, reached on December 12, Strauss said, was to guarantee greater efficiency along with greater independence. According to the agreement, the CSU would retain its right to vote independently of the CDU on important questions in the Bundestag. For its part, the CDU conceded that coalitions with the FDP at the state level should not impede joint CDU/CSU policies at the national level. Finally, the CSU formally renounced any intent to expand the party nationally.

The subsequent year demonstrated that the far-reaching differences of opinion among the leaders of the two parties had not been resolved. To be sure, the terms of the controversy had shifted. Whereas *Ostpolitik* had been the major focus of earlier CDU/CSU quarrels, the issue in 1977 was above all policy toward the FDP. In effect the two parties were already skirmishing in preparation for the 1980 Bundestag election. Helmut Kohl, the CDU leader of the opposition, advocated a cautious policy, since he saw the FDP as his future coalition partner in 1980. Franz Josef Strauss, on the other hand, repeatedly demanded a policy of outright opposition to the FDP, since in his view the hope for future coalitions with the FDP was delusive. The CDU/CSU's goal should rather be to eliminate the FDP in 1980 by reducing its electorate below 5 percent of the popular vote and thereby preventing it from receiving proportional-representation seats in the Bundestag.

Still another conflict between the two parties was prompted by the weak performance of Helmut Kohl as opposition leader. Already during the course of 1977 there was talk about the future CDU/CSU candidate for chancellor. And the CSU made it quite clear that circumstances had not changed at all since 1975–1976. Thus the floor leader of the CSU parliamentary group in the Bundestag, Fritz Zimmermann, announced at the end of November 1977 that, as far as the CSU was concerned, Franz Josef Strauss was every bit as much a potential candidate for chancellor as Helmut Kohl. Moreover he indicated that the CSU had not renounced its pretension to national party status and would be ready at any time to seek to achieve it.

Quite obviously, the near breakup of the two parties shortly after the election of 1976 had not been caused by short-lived differences of opinion over momentary issues. Rather it reflected fundamental dissension over the future role of both parties in the ideological arena. The question that must be raised is whether it is possible to settle the basic differences between the CDU and CSU which have surfaced. It is still not clear, for example, whether the general future strategy of the CDU/CSU will be to move toward a conservative or a Christian-liberal policy emphasizing social reform. In this context, the attempt of the CSU to separate itself from the CDU can be seen as an attempt by conservatives of *both* parties to impose their policy line. At the time of writing they had not (yet) succeeded.

Conclusion. Although the CSU has not entirely eliminated differences of interest among its electoral supporters, it has gone far toward minimizing them. This was shown by the 1976 campaign and election results. Whether this development will continue in years to come is difficult to predict since the party's success in 1976 depended on specific political and personal variables. The most important of these was the party chairman, Franz Josef Strauss, a political leader who in the national arena has a polarizing effect and in the state arena personifies Bavarian self-reliance vis-à-vis north German pretensions of cultural superiority. Second, as a state party, the CSU represents a special (and, since the last election, self-conscious) development of German conservatism. Third, the party has been able to convert traditional Bavarian particularism into a Bavarian version of anti-socialism. These three points are related. Even the simple resignation of the present chairman could cause considerable losses in party affiliation. And even though the two Union parties have agreed once again to coordinate their parliamentary policies, the compromise is not a firm one and it is still possible that they might develop along separate lines. The extent to which competition will overshadow cooperation cannot be foreseen. If the CSU were to develop into a national party, however, it would face the thorny question of the extent to which it would be able to retain the specific Bavarian peculiarities on which a major portion of its success has rested.

7

Election Themes and the Prestige Newspapers

Klaus Schönbach and Rudolf Wildenmann

Overview

Did the mass media decide the 1976 Bundestag election? Since October 3, 1976, the issue of whether the press or radio, and even more television, aided the SPD-FDP coalition to their victory has been discussed in the Federal Republic of Germany.[1] The SPD under Chancellor Helmut Schmidt and the FDP under Hans-Dietrich Genscher together won only 300,000 more votes than their opponents. With an electorate of some 42 million voters, this was more than a close race. On the basis of the Landtag elections between 1974 and the spring of 1976, it could be forecast that the Union parties would achieve roughly 52 percent of the votes. At least this is true on the basis of the results of the Landtag elections—and even if one takes into consideration the divergent voter behavior in Landtag as opposed to Bundestag elections.

The debate over the influence of the mass media on the election outcome has had to do with some peculiarities of the West German media system. There are but two national television networks in the Federal Republic, both of which are considered to be *"öffentlich-rechtlich"* institutions (legally regulated public bodies). Representatives of

---

[1] See Karl-Otto Saur, "Beschwörungsformeln vor dem Bildschirm" [Incantations before the television screen], *Süddeutsche Zeitung*, May 28/29/30, 1977; Kurt Reumann, "Hat das Fernsehen die letzte Bundestagswahl entschieden?" [Did television decide the last Bundestag election?], *Frankfurter Allgemeine Zeitung*, April 23, 1977; Elisabeth Noelle-Neumann, "Das doppelte Meinungsklima. Der Einfluss des Fernsehens im Wahlkampf 1976" [The twofold climate of opinion: the influence of television in the 1976 election], *Politische Vierteljahresschrift* (special election issue, "Wahlsoziologie heute," Max Kaase, ed., 1977); "Rundfunkjournalisten als Wahlhelfer? Zur Diskussion über die Wahlniederlage von CDU/CSU und ihre möglichen Ursachen" [Television journalists as election workers? A discussion of the defeat of the CDU/CSU and possible explanations], *Media Perspektiven*, no. 1 (1977), pp. 1–10.

all of the important groups in society (parties, unions, churches, organizations, and so on) sit on the board of controls of each network which oversees the programming and personnel policy of the networks. One of the national networks, the Arbeitsgemeinschaft öffentlich-rechtlicher Rundfunkanstalten der Bundesrepublik Deutschland (ARD), constituted in 1954, broadcasts a consolidated program produced by nine of the twelve state broadcasting stations located in the Federal Republic, including West Berlin. The other, the Zweites Deutsches Fernsehen (ZDF, Second German Television Network), was founded in 1961. Beyond these two national networks, the television viewer in the Federal Republic can receive one of five regional television stations, whose programs tend to be aimed at highly educated audiences. Consequently, any given viewer can choose among three programs at most.

Thus, the overwhelming importance of television during a political campaign is not surprising. Television seems to be better suited than any other medium to change opinions since the viewer's opportunity for selective exposure to political arguments is limited by the small choice among different networks and by spatial and temporal limitations which apply to the reception of television. Furthermore, television has a strong reputation for accuracy and thus a high degree of credibility in the Federal Republic.[2] Finally, television has become truly omnipresent. There was at least one television set in 96 percent of German households in 1976, and an average of 78.7 percent of the population turned their television on at least once a day. While the number of households with radios was slightly higher (97 percent), the daily audience figure for television exceeded that of radio (75.5 percent) by more than three percentage points.[3]

---

[2] Elisabeth Noelle-Neumann, "Der getarnte Elefant. Über die Wirkung des Fernsehens" [The masked elephant: on the effects of television], in *Öffentlichkeit als Bedrohung. Beiträge zur empirischen Kommunikationsforschung* [The threat of publicity: contributions to empirical communications research], Alber Broschur Kommunikation, vol. 6 (Freiburg-München: Verlag Karl Alber, 1977), pp. 115–26. Cf. Winfried Schulz, *Medienwirkung und Medienselektion. Methoden und Ergebnisse der Forschung zum Inter-Media-Vergleich von Fernsehen, Radio, Zeitung, Zeitschrift* [The effects of media and media selection: methods and results of research on the inter-media comparison of television, radio, newspapers, and periodicals], G+J Schriftenreihe (Hamburg: Kindler & Schiermeyer, Gruner + Jahr, 1971), pp. 104–11.

[3] "Funkmedien-Analyse 1976—Basisdaten vorgelegt" [Broadcast analysis for 1976: basic data], *Media Perspektiven*, no. 6 (June 1976), pp. 277–84. Although the use of radio has steadily increased in recent years as a result of the rise in the number of journal-type shows, radio is still less important as a source of information than as a source of "background" entertainment (music while working, and so on).

Nevertheless, one must not underestimate the influence of the printed media. A study by Erwin Scheuch and Rudolf Wildenmann in 1960–1961 already pointed to a direct correlation between an increase in television audiences and an increase in readership. Television, they concluded, stimulates a demand for information which is then satisfied by increased reading.[4] It is likely, however, that the effect of newspapers and magazines is different from that of television since the printed media allow for much greater selectivity on the part of the consumer than do broadcast media. There are three major reasons for this.

(1) Newspapers and magazines as a rule can be read anywhere, at any time; their entire content is at the reader's disposal, and he is free to block out dissonant information.

(2) The range of choice is significantly higher among newspapers and magazines in the Federal Republic than among television programs, particularly in the area of national news reporting. In 1976 there were 121 daily newspapers in West Germany (including West Berlin) which had sections devoted to politics,[5] and 218 magazines, of which at least four—the illustrated news magazines *Stern, Quick, Neue Revue*, and *Bunte*—cover a practically unlimited variety of subjects including political events.[6] Finally, there were thirteen weekly newspapers, three Sunday newspapers, and two news magazines— *Spiegel* and *Capital*—from which to gain political information in 1976.[7] The high population density of the Federal Republic increases the cir-

<hr>

[4] Erwin K. Scheuch and Rudolf Wildenmann, "Das Forschungs-programm der 'Wahlstudie 1961'" [The research program of 'Election Study 1961'], in Erwin K. Scheuch and Rudolf Wildenmann, eds., *Zur Soziologie der Wahl* [Electoral sociology] (Köln-Opladen: Westdeutscher Verlag, 1965), pp. 9–38.

[5] Walter J. Schütz, "Publizistische Konzentration der deutschen Tagespresse. Zur Entwicklung der publizistischen Einheiten seit 1945" [Journalistic concentration in the German daily press: Development of journalistic enterprises since 1945], *Media Perspektiven*, n. 5 (1976), pp. 189–90.

[6] Helmut H. Diedrichs, "Ökonomische und publizistische Konzentration der Pressemedien in der Bundesrepublik 1975/76" [Economic and journalistic concentration of the print media in the Federal Republic 1975–76], *Media Perspektiven*, May 1976, pp. 200–16.

[7] Horst Decker, Wolfgang R. Langenbucher, and Günther Nahr, *Die Massenmedien in der postindustriellen Gesellschaft. Konsequenzen neuer technischer und wirtschaftlicher Entwicklungen für Aufgaben und Strukturen der Massenmedien in der Bundesrepublik Deutschland* [The mass media in postindustrial society: the effects of new technical and economic developments on the tasks and structures of the mass media in the Federal Republic of Germany], Kommission für wirtschaftlichen und sozialen Wandel, vol. 111 (Göttingen: Schwartz, 1976), pp. 52–54.

culation of these publications and thus, at least in principle, promotes the reader's freedom of choice.[8]

(3) The extremely varied—and often quite low—credibility of the printed media limits their ability to persuade.

But regardless of their ability to change opinions, the mass media share one important function: the press and television define the issues that will enter the public debate. In a complex society where citizens have few sources of primary information, the media determine what will be perceived as political reality by the average person.[9] This area of influence, known as the agenda-setting function of the mass media, has only recently begun to be systematically investigated by mass communications researchers.[10] Its technical characteristics and credibility give television an advantage in this area, but there are printed media, too, which are able to influence the public agenda.

Along with the weekly newspapers such as *Zeit* and magazines such as *Spiegel*, the four prestige newspapers—*Frankfurter Allgemeine Zeitung (FAZ), Die Welt, Süddeutsche Zeitung (SZ),* and *Frankfurter Rundschau (FR)*—form a sort of hybrid between the press and the broadcast media. On the one hand the four quality papers facilitate selective assimilation by their readers, as do all printed media, which makes it unrealistic to expect that they will change voters' opinions. On the contrary, surveys and content analyses have shown that the political positions of the *FAZ, Welt, Süddeutsche Zeitung,* and *Frankfurter Rundschau* can be quite clearly identified and are well

[8] One must add to the foregoing one peculiar characteristic of the German information system: the concentration of reporting in the national capital. Not only news agencies such as *Deutsche Presse Agentur* (DPA) but also many daily newspapers have qualified journalists in Bonn. This medium-sized city, thus, is the seat not only of the Bundestag and the parties but also of a news and opinion market that transmits information to the entire Federal Republic. During the campaign the Bonn representatives of the media usually accompanied the candidates on their election trips and reported on them, a practice that began during Konrad Adenauer's campaign in 1957. Special trains of the "Bundesbahn" [Federal Railroad Company], airplanes, and processions of cars filled with party activists and journalists were part of every candidate's retinue.

[9] See Winfried Schulz, *Die Konstruktion von Realität in den Nachrichtenmeldungen. Analyse der aktuellen Berichterstattung* [The construction of reality in newscasts: analysis of news reporting], Alber Broschur Kommunikation, vol. 4 (Freiburg-München: Verlag Karl Alber, 1976); Hans Mathias Kepplinger, *Realkultur und Medienkultur. Literarische Karrieren in der Bundesrepublik* [Real culture and media culture: literary careers in the Federal Republic], Alber Broschur Kommunikation, vol. 1 (Freiburg-München: Verlag Karl Alber, 1975).

[10] See Jack M. McLeod, Lee B. Becker, and James E. Byrnes, "Another Look at the Agenda-Setting Function of the Press," *Communication Research,* vol. 1 (1974), pp. 131–66; Niklas Luhmann, "Öffentliche Meinung" [Public opinion], *Politische Vierteljahresschrift,* vol. 11 (1970), pp. 2–28; Scheuch and Wildenmann, "Das Forschungs-programm der Wahlstudie 1961," pp. 32–34.

known.[11] In other words, the reader knows which editorial line to expect and adjusts his selection accordingly. On the other hand, the detailed and informed reporting of these four newspapers gives them a reputation for accuracy that closely approaches that of television.[12] It also makes them leaders for the other daily newspapers and political periodicals in the Federal Republic. Seventy percent of the daily newspaper editors interviewed in one survey replied that they used the reporting of the quality newspapers in their own editorial work.[13]

One other characteristic distinguishes the four major papers from the remainder of the press and gives them their special importance in setting the agenda: in the unanimous opinion of experts, these newspapers correspond almost perfectly with the "official" political spectrum of the Federal Republic. On the left-right scale, the *FR* is located halfway between "decidedly left" and "moderately left," the *SZ* between "moderately left" and "middle," the *FAZ* between "middle" and "moderately right," and the *Welt* between "moderately right" and "decidedly right."[14] Thus, by examining these four papers alone, one can survey a rather full range of problems dealt with by all of the mass media in the campaign.

Method

The Data Base. This chapter examines the role of the prestige newspapers during the campaign. Before any results are presented, a note on methodology is in order.

---

[11] Klaus Schönbach, *Trennung von Nachricht und Meinung. Empirische Untersuchung eines journalistischen Qualitätskriteriums* [The separation of news and opinion: empirical investigation of journalistic quality criteria], Alber Broschur Kommunikation, vol. 5 (Freiburg-München: Verlag Karl Alber, 1977), p. 62.

[12] See Emil Dovifat, *Handbuch der Publizistik* [Guide to journalism], vol. 1: *Allgemeine Publizistik* (Berlin: De Gruyter, 1968), p. 284; Ralf Zoll and Eike Hennig, *Massenmedien und Meinungsbildung. Angebot, Reichweite, Nutzung und Inhalt der Medien in der BRD* [Mass media and the formation of opinion: supply, range, use and content of the media in the Federal Republic of Germany] (Munich: Juventa Verlag, 1970), p. 186; Hermann Meyn, "Politische Tendenzen überregionaler Tageszeitungen in der Bundesrepublik Deutschland" [Political tendencies of national daily newspapers in the Federal Republic of Germany], *Publizistik*, vol. 10 (1965), pp. 412–23.

[13] Elisabeth Noelle-Neumann, *Die betriebliche Anpassung lokaler und regionaler Abonnementzeitungen an die durch intra- und intermediären Wettbewerb der Massenkommunikationsmittel ausgelösten Veränderungen der Leserbedürfnisse* [The corporate adjustment of local and regional subscription newspapers to the change in reader demand effected by intra- and intermedia competition in means of mass communication] (Allensbach: Institut für Demoskopie, 1971), p. 20.

[14] Schönbach, *Trennung von Nachricht und Meinung*, p. 62.

First, the period considered here runs from Monday, June 28, through Saturday, October 9, 1976. The investigation begins, then, one week after the last preelection party convention, that of the spd, held in Hanover on June 18 and 19. The goals of the three major parties, therefore, were known to all of the media by the time our study begins. An interval of one week was allowed after the spd convention since in the immediate aftermath of the convention the activities of the spd would have artificially dominated the media. Our span ends one week after the election so that the papers' immediate reactions to the outcome can also be studied.

Within this time span, six one-week periods were selected for special scrutiny:

Week 1: June 28–July 3
Week 2: August 2–August 7
Week 3: August 30–September 4
Week 4: September 13–September 18
Week 5: September 27–October 2
Week 6: October 4–October 9.

(Each week has only six days because none of the four papers appears on Sunday.) The choices were made on both substantive and practical grounds. During the vacation period, from the end of June to the beginning of September, the themes associated with the October 3 election had practically no importance in the newspapers. August 30 was a turning point, the day on which the parties' first television spots appeared, marking the beginning of the "hot phase." From here on the election campaign was front-page news. For this reason three weeks in September were chosen, including the last week before the election.

For each of these six weeks the content of the four newspapers was systematically reviewed and the material for detailed analysis selected in two steps:

(1) First, all articles related to the 1976 Bundestag election or, after October 3, to the results of the election were selected. Both of these categories are used by the press department of the German Bundestag in its following of the prestige newspapers.

(2) This comprehensive election coverage was then sorted and only commentaries, lead articles, and editorials were retained. Thus, the material chosen for this investigation is essentially opinion— opinion judged to be important and worthy of discussion by the editors of the four papers. While in the area of news reporting German editors and journalists are constrained by strong prevailing standards of objectivity, in their editorial pages and opinion columns they are

free to express their own assessment of the relative importance of the various themes and issues.[15] By focusing our examination on the latter, we increase our chances of accurately distilling the themes that the major newspapers themselves regarded as most worthy of discussion.

Content Analysis. Which themes did the four leading newspapers bring into the public discussion in their opinion pages? To answer this question empirically, we used a method which, since its introduction in 1969, has become a standard classification scheme, involving six main themes and fifty subthemes.[16] The six main categories are (1) ideology, (2) social groups, (3) domestic policy, (4) foreign policy, (5) performance of the government or opposition, and (6) politicians. The fifty subthemes are listed at the end of this chapter.

Beyond standardizing the rules of coding, this categorization system offered another even more important advantage: it provided a means of coding both the 1976 campaign platforms of the major parties and the findings of a representative opinion survey,[17] so that the themes considered important by the parties and by the population could be compared with those selected by the newspapers. For this reason we refrained from devising an original coding scheme more closely adapted to our material. Each of the selected articles was coded according to which of the fifty subthemes it addressed at least once. The coding unit and the unit of enumeration was the article.

---

[15] See Johan Galtung, Mari Holmboe Roge, "The Structure of Foreign News: The Presentation of the Congo, Cuba, and Cyprus Crises in Four Norwegian Newspapers," *Journal of Peace Research*, vol. 2, 1965, pp. 64–91. James D. Halloran, Philip Elliott, Graham Murdock, *Demonstrations and Communication: A Case Study* (Harmonsworth, Middlesex: Penguin, 1970). Schönbach, *Trennung von Nachricht und Meinung*, p. 81. Cf. for example Deutscher Presserat, "Publizistische Grundsätze (Presse-kodex)" [Journalistic principles (press code)], *Der Journalist*, no. 1 (1974), pp. 97–99.

[16] Hans D. Klingemann, *Standardcode zur Verschlüsselung der Einstellungen zu den politischen Parteien in der Bundesrepublik Deutschland* [The standard code for the codification of attitudes on the political parties in the Federal Republic of Germany], duplicated manuscript (Mannheim: ZUMA, 1976). Examples of application in Hans D. Klingemann, "Issue-Orientierung, Issue-Kompetenz und Wahlverhalten aus Kommunalpolitischer Perspektive" [Issue orientation, issue competence and voting behavior in the perspective of community policy], in *Kommunales Wahlverhalten* [Community voting behavior], Konrad-Adenauer Foundation (Bonn: Eichholz, 1976), pp. 199–240, and Klaus Schönbach, "Wahlprogramme und Wählermeinung 1976" [Election platforms and voter opinion 1976], *Politische Vierteljahresschrift*, Schwerpunktheft *Wahlsoziologie heute* [Electoral sociology today], Max Kaase, ed., 1977.

[17] Schönbach, "Wahlprogramme."

Results of the Analysis

A total of seventy-four commentaries were analyzed. Table 7–1 shows how they were distributed among the four newspapers over the six weeks studied. The most obviously opinionated among the newspapers was the *FAZ*. It ran almost a third more commentaries than the other three papers before the election as well as the most extensive coverage of the results. In all of the papers the number of opinion pieces increased sharply after August 30, as the hot phase of the campaign was beginning.

Campaign Themes in the Prestige Newspapers. Prior to October 3 the commentaries that appeared in the four newspapers followed two broad patterns of argumentation. The criterion for distinguishing between them is the numerical ratio of concrete factual statements to statements of principle or symbolic themes. On the one hand, the *FAZ* tended to direct its attention and the reader's to the factual problems connected with the election; the other three quality newspapers, on the other hand, tended to argue at the normative level, bringing ideological and moral considerations into the discussion.

Table 7–2 illustrates this finding. Each of the selected articles up to October 3 was examined and the occurrence of each of the six main themes totaled for each paper. A theme mentioned more than

TABLE 7–1

OCCURRENCE OF OPINION ARTICLES, BY WEEK AND NEWSPAPER
(in number of articles)

Week	Welt	FAZ	SZ	FR	Total, Major News- papers
June 28–July 3	3	—	2	1	6
August 2–August 7	—	1	1	2	4
August 30–September 4	3	6	6	4	19
September 13–September 18	3	4	2	3	12
September 27–October 2 ·	4	5	2	3	14
October 4–October 9	4	9	3	3	19
Campaign	17	25	16	16	74

SOURCE: Authors.

TABLE 7–2

OCCURRENCE OF MAIN CAMPAIGN THEMES IN PRESTIGE-NEWSPAPER
COMMENTARIES, JUNE 28–OCTOBER 3, 1976
(in percentages)

Main Themes	Welt	FAZ	SZ	FR	Average, Major Newspapers
Ideology	15.5	5.2	15.0	7.4	10.5
Social groups	5.2	12.1	2.5	3.7	6.2
Domestic policy	13.8	31.0	12.5	9.3	17.1
Foreign policy	5.2	—	7.5	9.3	5.2
Performance of the government or opposition	25.8	34.5	45.0	38.0	34.8
Politicians	34.5	17.2	17.5	33.3	26.2
Total	100.0	100.0	100.0	100.0	100.0
N	(58)	(58)	(40)	(54)	(210)

SOURCE: Authors.

once in the same article was listed only once, but where several themes were discussed in a single article each was listed.

Three of the main themes were considered evidence of argument from principle, namely, ideology, performance of the government or opposition, and politicians. The first of these covers concepts such as Marxism, the left, freedom, liberalism, democracy, and conservatism. In our coding scheme "ideological-normative" themes are those themes which discuss ideologies or social norms. (This does not, however, mean that other problems dealt with by the newspapers need be unrelated to ideology. Some of the following quotations substantiate this suspicion.) The second, performance of the government or opposition, covers general statements about the ability or inability of the government or opposition, their role concepts, their manner of self-presentation, and campaign style. The third theme, politicians, covers discussion of the ability and image of the candidates. In these three areas, our content analysis rates the FAZ at 56.9 percent, but the other three papers all over 75 percent (75.8 percent in the Welt, 77.5 percent in the SZ, and 78.7 percent in the FR).

The Welt and SZ placed particular emphasis on ideological-normative content. With respect, for example, to the CDU/CSU election slogan "Freedom instead of/or Socialism," the two newspapers offered different assessments. The Welt wrote: "The slogan Freedom or

177

Socialism, which has been decried as asinine and misleading, was not artificially attached to the election . . . but articulates a discussion that erupted long before the 1976 election over the general problem of 'value and norm consciousness.' "[18] The *SZ* rejected this approach: "The slogan Freedom or/instead of Socialism, which was initially so strident, has now been softened and overused, with the consequence that this misdirected ideological crutch has become useless."[19]

The three main themes taken as suggestive of argument from fact were social groups, domestic policy, and foreign policy. The themes relevant to social groups—such as young people, the elderly, the lower class, the middle class, or the upper class—and their respective organizations took up little space in the 1976 campaign. Neither the media nor the parties placed any stress on the social stratification of German society, although analyses of the election results would show the strong influence of class or group identification on voting behavior. The *FAZ* addressed this subject most directly, criticizing, in particular, the unions:

> With its position on the . . . "Radikalenerlass" [a 1972 decree which prevents radicals from entering public service] this union [the railroad union] has shown that it demands a part in the discussion of all general political questions. And the idea was once again introduced to at least begin the practice of letting only union members receive the fringe benefits of collective bargaining contracts, and thus to set in motion a process which would result in 100 percent union membership.[20]

Domestic policy, too, seems to have been the domain of the *FAZ*. It was particularly concerned with measures to stabilize the economy, on the one hand, and with social policy on the other. The *FAZ* demanded of the future government a stronger emphasis on private investment and monetary stability: "Whoever views realistically the future of our economy must also recommend an economic policy which stimulates entrepreneurial activity."[21] "The strengthening of trust in the stability of our currency should be the primary task of any government."[22] In the area of social policy after the election, the *FAZ* sought above all a halt to the expansion of unjustified social

---

[18] *Welt*, October 2, 1977.
[19] *Süddeutsche Zeitung*, August 5.
[20] *Frankfurter Allgemeine Zeitung*, September 4.
[21] Ibid.
[22] *Frankfurter Allgemeine Zeitung*, September 17.

services: "First of all the hectic rise in social services is in fact the cause of the instability of the whole economy . . . those who want to ensure solidity in the long run must combat the hubris of a swollen welfare state."[23] Foreign policy, which had dominated the 1972 Bundestag campaign, played almost no role in the media coverage or in the statements of the parties in 1976.

Overall, the most important theme of the commentaries in the *FAZ, Welt, SZ,* and *FR* was the performance of the government and the opposition. All four publications were concerned about the style of the debate between the parties. The *FR* in particular complained of the oversimplification implicit in the Union's polemics: "CSU Chairman Strauss has even accused the chancellor before millions of television viewers of being too small for the job and having to compensate by wearing platform soles."[24] "CDU politicians used to refer to the GDR as Communist. Now because the SPD cannot be hit with 'Communist,' the GDR itself is being referred to as 'Socialist' in CDU advertisements."[25] The *Welt* on the other hand compared Helmut Schmidt's campaign and campaign style to an amateur theatrical production.[26] "The heat excuses a lot, but not the SPD's attempt to convert the opposition into a party of big capitalists and right-wing radicals."[27] By contrast the *SZ* and *FAZ* gave bad marks to all: "In the general scuffle for the best place on the television screen, rational arguments cannot penetrate."[28] "One party leader finds the opposition 'piggish,' another calls his opponent a 'rascal,' and a long debate ensues. The campaign is revolving around itself. And we should write about it?"[29]

Finally, we must examine the debate over the characteristics of the politicians in the newspapers. The campaign was highly personalized —particularly in the *Welt* and the *FR*. The *Welt* mentioned Schmidt twice as often as Kohl, but almost exclusively in negative contexts. The *FR* dealt similarly with Helmut Kohl, but did so less overtly: Kohl was the subject of five commentaries, Schmidt four. In all of the newspapers the only other candidates to play even a minor role were

---

[23] *Frankfurter Allgemeine Zeitung,* September 4. In the weeks immediately after the election, the question of safeguarding the social welfare system in a period of declining growth rates led to a serious crisis in the new governing coalition.

[24] *Frankfurter Rundschau,* September 13.

[25] *Frankfurter Rundschau,* June 30.

[26] *Welt,* September 3. The comparison referred specifically to the Hamburg Ohnsorg Theater.

[27] *Welt,* June 29.

[28] *Süddeutsche Zeitung,* September 3.

[29] *Frankfurter Allgemeine Zeitung,* September 15.

Genscher and Strauss. Thus, the symbolic value of the leading candidates in determining voting behavior was underscored by the newspapers.

After the election, there were three main lines in the thematic structure of the commentaries (see Table 7–3).

(1) The emphasis on the politicians decreased (radically so in the *Welt* and the *FR*), and substantive problems of domestic policy gained in significance. The confrontation between the two candidates was largely forgotten.[30] Now the solution of difficult problems was at issue: "How are the national finances to be overhauled, how are social security payments to be assured? How do we get rid of unemployment?"[31]

(2) The performance of the government and the opposition remained an important subject area for all four newspapers. Everywhere coalition possibilities were discussed and commentators speculated on the strength of the SPD-FDP alliance. The *Welt* made no attempt to conceal its regret over the "false" coalition that had emerged: "[Genscher] now cannot govern as he did in 1972 with the strongest party against the second-strongest party, but instead must support a diminished SPD. Without him the chancellor could not see over the top of his plate. We are witnessing an exercise in government by pygmies [*Schrumpf-Germanen*]."[32] Only the *FR* attempted to sum up the campaign; it expressed the fear that the atmosphere of confrontation might continue after the election: "If everything that has so far transpired in the Bundesrat is allegedly the product of crystal clear rationality, then there is a lot in store for our country since the opposition politicians are no longer secretly threatening to use the club of the Bundesrat and do not even attempt to maintain the façade of alleged state interests."[33]

(3) Concern with ideology increased slightly in the *FAZ* and *SZ*. The *FAZ* demanded that leftist tendencies be countered in the new government and the *SZ* praised the voter for his democratic conduct: "Never before have so many voters gone to the polls as this Sunday, and never before have the extreme splinter parties received so few votes."[34]

---

[30] Only the *Welt* headlined two commentaries of October 4, "Victor Helmut Schmidt" and "Loser Helmut Kohl," but the articles made it apparent that the names should have been reversed.

[31] *Frankfurter Allgemeine Zeitung*, October 5.

[32] *Welt*, October 4.

[33] *Frankfurter Rundschau*, October 5.

[34] *Süddeutsche Zeitung*, October 4.

TABLE 7–3

OCCURRENCE OF MAIN CAMPAIGN THEMES IN PRESTIGE NEWSPAPER
COMMENTARIES, OCTOBER 4–9, 1976

(in percentages)

Main Themes	Welt	FAZ	SZ	FR	Average, Major Newspapers
Ideology	12.5	16.3	22.2	—	14.3
Social groups	4.2	2.3	—	7.7	3.1
Domestic policy	25.0	23.3	16.7	15.4	24.4
Foreign policy	—	2.3	—	—	1.0
Performance of the government or opposition	33.3	39.5	44.4	53.8	40.8
Politicians	25.0	16.3	16.7	23.1	19.4
Total	100.0	100.0	100.0	100.0	100.0
N	(24)	(43)	(18)	(13)	(98)

SOURCE: Authors.

Themes of Commentaries over Time

In order to shed some light on the evolution of the campaign, we analyzed the frequency with which the various themes were mentioned in the course of the campaign (disregarding the week of June 28 to July 3, which contained little relevant material). The results of this analysis are shown in Table 7–4 and Figures 7–1 and 7–2.

Figure 7-1 shows the development over time of the three main themes that were treated least often by the major papers: ideology, social groups, and foreign policy. All three fell from an already low point of departure in early August to an absolute trough in mid-September. During the campaign's hottest phase in the last weeks of September other themes became more important. Only for a short period just before election day did these three themes once again command attention: even the issue area we have called social groups—previously much neglected—was dug out in the final flurry of campaign activity.

Figure 7–2, which charts the development of the three most discussed themes, shows a different trend. Specific domestic policy problems steadily gained in significance. From an initial position of only 5.9 percent, they rose to 24.3 percent of all the issues discussed in major-newspaper commentaries. The reverse was true for the char-

TABLE 7–4

OCCURRENCE OF MAIN CAMPAIGN THEMES IN PRESTIGE NEWSPAPER COMMENTARIES, BY WEEK

(in percentages)

Main Themes	June 28–July 3	July 2–July 7	August 30–September 4	September 13–September 18	September 27–October 2	October 4–October 9
Ideology	16.7	11.8	7.7	5.3	14.1	14.3
Social groups	—	5.9	6.2	2.6	9.0	3.1
Domestic policy	—	5.9	18.5	18.4	20.6	24.4
Foreign policy	—	11.8	4.6	—	7.7	1.0
Performance of the government or opposition	66.6	47.0	30.8	47.5	24.3	40.8
Politicians	16.7	17.6	32.2	26.2	24.3	19.4
Total	100.0	100.0	100.0	100.0	100.0	100.0
N	(12)	(17)	(65)	(38)	(78)	(98)

SOURCE: Authors.

FIGURE 7-1

IMPORTANCE OF IDEOLOGY, SOCIAL GROUPS, AND FOREIGN POLICY IN
CAMPAIGN COMMENTARY OF THE FOUR PRESTIGE NEWSPAPERS

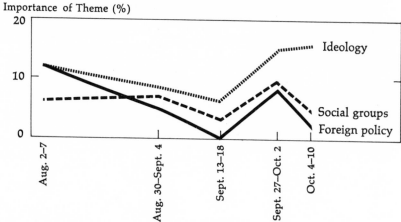

SOURCE: Authors.

acteristics of the politicians. The period of greatest significance came
at the beginning of the hot phase when almost a third (32.2 percent)
of all of the arguments we coded dealt with the personalities of the
politicians. Subsequently the attention given to this subject consistently declined. Clearly, as the campaign advanced the debate
became increasingly objective: the difficulties confronting a future
government emerged as the major focus of interest and the leading
personalities receded into the background.

Finally the curve obtained for the performance of the government
and the opposition is quite peculiar. Widely covered in the beginning,
this theme declined perceptibly in late August, rose very steeply in
mid-September, was only sparingly documented in election week, and
rose to prominence again immediately after the election. What was the
reason for this uneven pattern?

Most of the discussion falling under this broad theme early in the
summer focused on the campaign styles of the candidates and parties.
By mid-summer the sensitivity of all newspapers to the wild claims of
campaign advertising would be heightened. In addition, the slogans
and advertising methods that would shape the campaign were apparent and newspaper commentators were eager to size them up. But
their initial sensitivity was already blunted by the beginning of the

FIGURE 7–2

IMPORTANCE OF DOMESTIC POLICY, POLITICIANS, AND PERFORMANCE OF
GOVERNMENT OR OPPOSITION IN CAMPAIGN COMMENTARY OF THE
FOUR PRESTIGE NEWSPAPERS

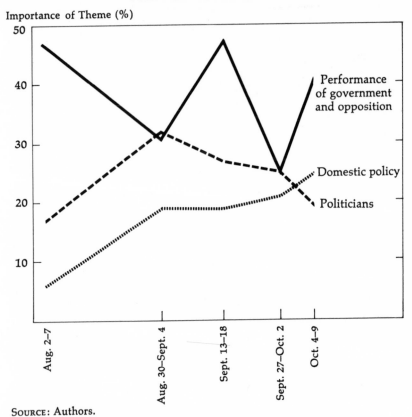

SOURCE: Authors.

hot phase, which would explain the disappearance of this subject at
the beginning of September. During the last four weeks before the
election, however, when the contest was particularly bitter, the subject
of campaign style was again debated widely, subsiding shortly before
election day as substantive issues took over center stage. After October 3, a further dimension was added when the coalition question
rose to the fore.

Prestige Newspapers and Election Platforms. Parties have a legitimate
interest in seeing to it that areas in which they have shown competence

184

TABLE 7-5

OCCURRENCE OF MAIN CAMPAIGN THEMES IN PRESTIGE NEWSPAPER
COMMENTARIES, JUNE 28–OCTOBER 3, 1976

Main Themes	Welt	FAZ	SZ	FR	Average, Prestige Newspapers
Ideology	17.6	6.0	18.8	9.5	12.6
Social groups	5.9	14.0	3.1	4.8	7.4
Domestic policy	15.7	36.0	15.6	11.9	20.6
Foreign policy	5.9	—	9.4	11.9	6.3
Performance of the government or opposition	15.7	24.0	31.2	19.0	21.7
Politicians	39.2	20.0	21.9	42.9	31.4
Total	100.0	100.0	100.0	100.0	100.0
N	(51)	(50)	(32)	(42)	(175)

NOTE: Category 55, "self-preservation," is excluded.
SOURCE: Authors.

and initiative are covered by the mass media. How well did they suc-
ceed in the 1976 Bundestag campaign? To answer this question we
have drawn up a rough comparison between the campaign platforms
and the commentaries that appeared in the prestige newspapers. For
obvious reasons we considered only the period before the election and
can refer to Table 7–2, with one minor modification: category 55,
"self-presentation," is excluded from the analysis since it is not dealt
with in the party platforms although it often commanded considerable
space in the newspapers. With the elimination of this subtheme, we
obtain the thematic breakdown for the four newspapers shown in
Table 7–5.

Table 7–6 shows the results of a content analysis of the election
platforms of the SPD, CDU/CSU, and FDP, using the same categorization
scheme applied to the newspaper commentaries.[35] It shows which
themes were considered important for the campaign by the parties
themselves.

To compare the thematic structures of the newspaper commentaries and the campaign platforms, we have used a simple dissimilarity
coefficient which corresponds to the structure of the data and the level

[35] Schönbach, "Wahlprogramme."

TABLE 7-6

OCCURRENCE OF MAIN CAMPAIGN THEMES IN THE PLATFORMS OF THE
SPD, CDU/CSU, AND FDP
(in percentages)

Main Themes	SPD	CDU/CSU	FDP
Ideology	7.7	16.9	13.6
Social groups	10.9	8.2	4.8
Domestic policy	50.8	52.4	61.2
Foreign policy	15.7	17.2	13.3
Performance of the government or opposition	8.9	5.3	2.5
Politicians	6.0	—	4.6
Total	100.0	100.0	100.0
N	(728)	(343)	(353)

SOURCE: Authors.

of the measurement:[36] the lower the coefficient, the more similar the distribution of themes. Table 7–7, which gives the results of this calculation, clearly shows that the thematic emphasis of the FAZ was closest to that of the three election platforms. If we turn back to Tables 7–5 and 7–6, the main differences between the parties and the Welt, SZ, and FR become clear. All of the platforms dealt with domestic policy problems in a much more concrete fashion than did these newspapers and placed far less stress on the personalities of the politicians. The FAZ, with its decidedly problem-oriented reporting, reflected this tendency toward rationality and concreteness; the other three papers more frequently discussed basic questions of an ideological or moral nature.

This finding can be further substantiated by including a second source of official campaign statements, the policy speeches of party chairmen Brandt, Kohl, and Genscher at the respective conventions. Table 7–8 shows the thematic structure of these texts,[37] and in Table

---

[36] To obtain the dissimilarity coefficient, the differences between the percentages of a main theme in the two texts to be compared are added as amounts and then divided by two. See the "index of dissimilarity" in Otis Dudley Duncan, Ray P. Cuzzort, Beverly Duncan, *Statistical Geography* (Glencoe: The Free Press, 1961), p. 83. The lower this value is the more similar are the texts compared to the main groups examined.

[37] Schönbach, "Wahlprogramme."

TABLE 7-7

COMPARISON BETWEEN THEMATIC STRUCTURE OF PRESTIGE NEWSPAPER
COMMENTARIES AND OF THE CAMPAIGN PLATFORMS OF THE
SPD, CDU/CSU, AND FDP
(dissimilarity coefficients in percentage points)

Campaign Platforms	Welt	FAZ	SZ	FR	All Prestige Newspapers
SPD	49.9	32.2	54.3	48.8	43.1
CDU/CSU	50.3	44.5	49.7	56.6	47.8
FDP	52.9	46.1	51.2	54.8	48.6

NOTE: For an explanation of method, see footnote 36.
SOURCE: Authors.

TABLE 7-8

OCCURRENCE OF MAIN CAMPAIGN THEMES IN POLICY SPEECHES OF
BRANDT, KOHL, AND GENSCHER
(in percentages)

Main Themes	Brandt	Kohl	Genscher
Ideology	36.4	28.0	31.0
Social groups	5.8	9.1	2.4
Domestic policy	12.7	19.8	9.5
Foreign policy	11.6	14.2	12.5
Performance of the government or opposition	27.1	19.4	35.7
Politicians	6.4	9.5	8.9
Total	100.0	100.0	100.0
N	(173)	(211)	(168)

NOTE: Only the passages of the policy speeches dealing with each chairman's own party were analyzed.
SOURCE: The speeches analyzed were Willy Brandt, Dortmund, June 18-19, 1976; Helmut Kohl, Cologne, May 1976; and Hans-Dietrich Genscher, Freiburg, May 30, 1976.

7-9 we can see the corresponding dissimilarity coefficients that emerge from a comparison with the newspaper commentaries.

The policy speeches of the chairmen are more general, less specific, than the campaign platforms. They provide the ideological background for the parties' concrete policy proposals.[38] This ideological emphasis

---

[38] Ibid.

TABLE 7–9

COMPARISON BETWEEN THE THEMATIC STRUCTURE OF PRESTIGE NEWSPAPER
COMMENTARIES AND OF POLICY SPEECHES OF BRANDT, KOHL, AND GENSCHER
(dissimilarity coefficients in percentage points)

Convention Policy Speeches	Welt	FAZ	SZ	FR	All Prestige Newspapers
Brandt	35.7	45.1	22.5	36.8	35.6
Kohl	29.7	31.2	24.2	33.4	25.0
Genscher	40.0	49.2	19.7	38.8	38.6

SOURCE: Authors.

accounts for the low dissimilarity ratings of the *Welt*, the *FR*, and particularly the *SZ*. Their shallow coverage of domestic policy, which forced up their dissimilarity coefficients with respect to the platforms, does not have the same effect here since the policy speeches dealt with few problems of domestic policy. Instead the greatest differences arise in the area of ideology. Here the party chairmen outdid even the ideology-oriented *Welt* and *SZ*. Overall, the thematic structure of the newspaper commentaries corresponded more closely to that of the speeches, especially Helmut Kohl's, than to that of the campaign platforms.

It is clear from these findings that the quality newspapers perceive their roles differently. The *FAZ* sees itself as something of an intermediary between the various social groups; it attempts to articulate problems of national policy and to transmit an understanding of these to its readers.[39] The other three papers are more clearly partisan and commit themselves to the "right" alternative. Here another of our findings is important: while the policy stands of these papers are different from "official" policy in the party platforms they are remarkably similar in their thematic structure to the concerns of the electorate. Overall the media reacted in much the same way as the voters to the campaign statements of the parties.

A study by Klaus Schönbach, comparing the contents of platforms and speeches with the answers in a representative opinion survey taken in May and June 1976, showed that Kohl hit upon the themes that concerned the voter more often than did his two com-

---

[39] Rudolf Wildenmann and Werner Kaltefleiter, *Funktionen der Massenmedien, Demokratische Existenz heute* [Function of the mass media, democratic existence today], Schriften des Forschungsinstitut für politische Wissenschaft der Universität Köln, no. 12 (Frankfurt-Bonn: Athenäum Verlag, 1965).

TABLE 7–10

MAIN THEMES CITED BY THE ELECTORATE IN EVALUATING THE SPD,
THE CDU/CSU, AND THE FDP, MAY–JUNE 1976

Major Themes	Percentage of Responses
Ideology	10.0
Social groups	11.2
Domestic policy	18.8
Foreign policy	8.1
Performance of the government or opposition	37.1
Politicians	14.8
Total	100.0
N	(15,014)

SOURCE: Authors.

petitors, but that the electoral *platform* of the SPD corresponded more closely to public opinion than did that of the CDU/CSU or the FDP.[40] The respondents were asked to name the good and the bad points of the three party groups represented in the Bundestag. Their answers were categorized by the same coding scheme used here for the four prestige newspapers.

If we now look at all of the responses of those questioned in the aforementioned poll, we arrive at something of a theme profile of the electorate. It discloses which policy areas the voter considered sufficiently important to use as criteria for the evaluation of the parties at the beginning of the 1976 election. Table 7–10 shows the results of this consolidation.

Table 7–11 shows the dissimilarity coefficients calculated for the views of the electorate and the prestige newspaper commentaries. All are lower than those calculated for the party platforms and the policy speeches. The *Welt, FR,* and *FAZ*—but particularly the *SZ*— more frequently addressed the themes mentioned as important by the voters in May–June 1976 than they did those found to be important in the platforms and policy speeches. A comparison of the results of Table 7–5 and Table 7–10 shows that there are slight differences in the extent to which the voters and the newspapers were concerned with the personalization of politics: the newspapers paid more attention to

---

[40] Schönbach, "Wahlprogramme."

TABLE 7–11

COMPARISON BETWEEN THEMATIC STRUCTURE OF PRESTIGE NEWSPAPER
COMMENTARIES AND ELECTORATE'S EVALUATION OF THE SPD, CDU/CSU,
AND FDP, MAY–JUNE 1976
(dissimilarity coefficients in percentage points)

	Welt	FAZ	SZ	FR	All Newspapers
Electorate	29.0	25.2	17.2	31.9	21.0

NOTE: All themes mentioned by the electorate, whether in a positive or negative light, were included in this calculation.
SOURCE: Authors.

politicians. On the other hand, the voters more frequently mentioned government and opposition achievements. But all the indications are that the four prestige newspapers attuned their agendas more to the perceptions of the electorate (their audience) than to the policy speeches of Brandt, Kohl, and Genscher or to the party platforms. Overall, the party platforms were reflected least in the commentaries of the prestige newspapers.

The Influence of the Press

"The press is significantly more than a purveyor of information. It may not be successful much of the time in telling people what to think, but it is stunningly successful in telling its readers what to think *about*."[41] If Cohen's thesis is correct—and more recent results of communications research tend to corroborate it[42]—then the voters continued to discuss issues during the 1976 campaign that they already considered important before the campaign began. The prestige newspapers clearly did not single out any themes that were significantly different from those mentioned by the respondents in the May–June survey. The debate in the press coincided more closely with the preoccupations of the voters than with those of the candidates or parties. Within this framework, the papers examined differed somewhat from one another. The *FAZ* focused its attention on the substantive issues

[41] B. C. Cohen, *The Press, the Public, and Foreign Policy* (Princeton: Princeton University Press, 1963), quoted by McLeod, Becker, and Byrnes, *Another Look*, p. 134.
[42] Hans Mathias Kepplinger, Elisabeth Noelle-Neumann, *Community and Communication*, ongoing UNESCO research program at the University of Mainz.

addressed in the campaign, thus most clearly defining itself as an intermediary between policy makers and population; the other papers concerned themselves more closely with the ideological and moral issues of the campaign.

Whether the media were cause or effect—reflecting the opinions of the population or reinforcing a public discussion that had begun before the campaign—could only be determined with certainty by further analysis. Considering what we know about the restricted effects of printed media, the *FAZ*, *Welt*, *SZ*, and *FR* do not seem to have snatched the voter out of the clutches of the cdu/csu despite a preexistent trend.[43] Moreover, our study shows that the preconditions for such an effect, as far as the contents of the newspapers are concerned, were absent. We certainly do not find the same distribution of political themes in the editorials of the four prestige papers and in the parties' platforms. On the contrary, the themes exploited by the cdu/csu—particularly those centered around the slogan "Freedom or/instead of Socialism"—had little appeal either to the newspapers or to the public.[44] Only the *Welt* endorsed the slogan. The *SZ* and the *FR* were negatively disposed toward it, and the *FAZ* hardly gave it any recognition at all.[45] On this point and throughout the campaign, instead of governing the shape of the debate, the German prestige newspapers merely confirmed it.

Coding Scheme

1 *Ideology*

11 left
12 progressive
13 democratic
14 liberal

---

[43] Noelle-Neumann, "Das doppelte Meinungsklima."

[44] A pilot study showed how frequently this slogan precipitated a negative association with its originators. Cf. Zentrum für Umfragen, Methoden und Analysen, *Konservativismus-Liberalismus-Sozialismus. Explorationsstudie über das Verständnis von drei politischen Begriffen in der Bevölkerung* [Conservatism, liberalism, socialism: an exploratory study of the perception of three political concepts by the population] (Mannheim: zuma, 1976).

[45] Another poll prepared by a research seminar in Mannheim in 1975–1976 already indicated in May–June 1976 that the cdu/csu would not win this election: Cf. the report by Rudolf Wildenmann, "Wie die Deutschen wählen" [How the Germans vote], *Capital*, vol. 15, no. 8 (1976), pp. 35–40; Rudolf Wildenmann, "Brot und keine Spiele" [Bread and no games], *Capital*, vol. 15, no. 9 (1976), pp. 93–104.

191

15 conservative
16 radical
17 Christian
10 other ideological-normative themes

2   *Social Groups*

21 churches
22 the upper class
23 the middle class
24 the lower class
25 the people
26 the elderly
27 youth
20 other social groups

3   *Domestic Policy*

31 economic policy
32 salary and price policy
33 employment policy
34 social policy
35 tax policy
36 educational policy
37 national security, law and order, legal policy
38 armed forces
39 general domestic policy
30 other domestic policy themes

4   *Foreign Policy*

41 German policy
42 *Ostpolitik*
43 relations with the West
44 individual European states
45 the Third World
46 general foreign policy
40 other foreign policy themes

5   *Performance of the Government or Opposition*

51 government and opposition achievements
52 coalition behavior
53 political morality

8

Public Opinion Polling in the Federal Republic of Germany

Max Kaase

Thirty-three years after the end of World War II, the techniques of empirical social research, in particular the public opinion survey, have become standard tools of analysis in the social sciences, economics, and journalism in the Federal Republic of Germany. It is certainly no accident, then, that public opinion polling for political purposes and on behalf of political patrons has been a highly controversial subject among both the public at large and members of the social science community.[1]

In the 1950s and early 1960s controversy within the German social science community flared up over the possible implications of public opinion polling for some of the central problems of democratic theory, such as the realization in practice of direct democracy.[2]

---

[1] The criticism that has been directed against political public opinion research does not necessarily entail a general rejection of the techniques of empirical social science. A much more fundamental debate is going on in the social sciences, however, over the worth of all empirical social science research. See: Erwin K. Scheuch, "Sozialer Wandel und Sozialforschung" [Social change and social research], *Kölner Zeitschrift für Soziologie und Sozialpsychologie*, vol. 17, no. 1 (Cologne & Opladen: Westdeutscher Verlag, 1965), pp. 1–48.

[2] A comprehensive overview of the controversy and a good summary of the literature are provided by Edgar Traugott, *Die Herrschaft der Meinung* [The power of public opinion] (Düsseldorf: Bertelsmann Universitäts Verlag, 1970). A firsthand impression of the diverging points of view can be obtained from: Theodor W. Adorno, "Zur gegenwärtigen Stellung der empirischen Sozialforschung in Deutschland" [The present status of empirical social research in Germany], in *Empirische Sozialforschung* [Empirical social research] (Frankfurt: Institut zur Förderung öffentlicher Angelegenheiten, 1952), pp. 27–39; Wilhelm Hennis, *Meinungsforschung und repräsentative Demokratie* [Public opinion research and representative democracy] (Tübingen: J. C. B. Mohr, 1957); Kurt Sontheimer, "Meinungsforschung und Politik" [Public opinion research and politics], *Der Monat*, vol. 16, no. 188 (1964), pp. 41–46; Gerhard Schmidtchen and Elisabeth Noelle-Neumann, "Die Bedeutung repräsentativer Bevölkerungsumfragen für die offene Gesellschaft" [The importance of public opinion polling for an open society], *Politische Vierteljahresschrift*, vol. 4, no. 2 (Cologne & Opladen: Westdeutscher Verlag, 1963), pp. 168–95; Elisabeth Noelle, *Die Politiker und die Demoskopie* [Politicians and public opinion research], Allensbacher Schriften [Allensbach papers] no. 9 (Allensbach-Bonn: Verlag für Demoskopie, 1968).

Among the public at large, attention focused on the strengths and weaknesses of public opinion polling during election campaigns, especially with respect to forecasting election outcomes for political candidates and parties.

Not only the ritualistic aspect of elections and election campaigns,[3] but also their significance as instruments for determining governments in Western democratic societies help explain the vital interest of the elites as well as the public in everything associated with elections. But there are other reasons for the fascination with public opinion polling. Citizens, politicians, political parties, and interest groups are curious to find out "what gives." There is the exaggerated if mistaken fear of manipulating public opinion through the use of opinion polls. And there is anxiety over the possible impact of publishing the results of political opinion polls. All of these have helped bring political opinion polling down from its scientific ivory tower into the real world of everyday politics. This observation is, to be sure, neither original nor limited to the Federal Republic.

In his introduction to the second edition of one of the earliest publications in postwar Germany on the methodology of empirical social research, René König pointed to problems which continue to be of special concern in public discussions of this discipline.[4] In particular, König mentioned two instances where polls had become highly controversial: the wrong prediction by a majority of American public opinion pollsters of the outcome of the 1948 American presidential election; and the discussion of a report by the *New York Times* correspondent in Bonn of an opinion survey undertaken by the U.S. high commissioner for Germany (HICOG) of attitudes among the West German population toward National Socialism in 1952. Using these two examples, König showed, first of all, that the public presentation of poll findings systematically fails to reveal their probabilistic and time-bound nature. An awareness of these limitations can significantly qualify the interpretation of poll evidence. Moreover, in the reporting of opinion poll findings by the mass media there is a further danger. Constraints of time and space, fear of placing excessive intellectual demands on the reader, as well as the frequent lack of intellectual qualification among the journalists themselves can produce distorted reporting and distorted interpretation of the evidence.

---

[3] Murray Edelman, *The Symbolic Uses of Politics* (Chicago: University of Illinois Press, 1970), pp. 16–21. Although somewhat cynical, Edelman's characterization of campaigns would appear to be quite appropriate.

[4] René König, ed., *Das Interview, Praktische Sozialforschung I* [Practical social research I], 2d ed. (Cologne: Verlag für Politik und Wirtschaft, 1957), pp. 13–33.

A second problem mentioned by König is the threat that lies in the free availability of public opinion data in Western liberal democracies. In particular, he discusses the misuse of such data to support the vested interests of significant social and political elites. Since these elites have high stakes in the political decision-making process, there is a natural tendency for them to counteract "unfavorable" published findings by questioning their quality and reliability, if not the whole repertory of empirical social science research. A special version of this criticism is deeply rooted in any elitist political philosophy that basically challenges the wisdom and judgment of mass publics in social and political matters.[5]

A third problem can be traced to the uneven quality of empirical research. Just a few studies of poor quality can very easily lead to a general rejection of the technique of public opinion polling since those prejudiced against polling will seek to publicize its failures. A final problem deals with the tendency to consider public opinion polling the only, or the most important, research technique of social science. The assumption, however, that polling can answer all conceivable questions is preposterous and dangerous.

The Development of Public Opinion Research in Postwar Germany

In the late 1930s when Americans and European emigrants like Paul F. Lazarsfeld were at work on the development and application of modern social science research techniques in the United States, the political leaders of the Third Reich were regularly receiving reports from informants of the security services on the climate of German public opinion.[6] The experience from those days that giving information away very frequently had fatal consequences, but also the anxiety of many former Nazis to avoid being "found out" after the war had ended, both make it understandable that there was apprehension over the improper use of public opinion polling methods in early postwar Germany.[7]

Despite these reservations and the absence of a suitable infrastructure for opinion polling in postwar Germany, the technique of

[5] See Elisabeth Noelle, *Umfragen in der Massengesellschaft* [Surveys in mass society], Rowohlts deutsche Enzyklopädie [Rowohlts German encyclopedia], 7th ed., vol. 177 (Reinbek at Hamburg: Rowohlt Taschenbuch Verlag, 1976), pp. 11–31.

[6] Volker R. Berkhan, "Meinungsforschung im 'Dritten Reich'," [Public opinion research in the 'Third Reich'], *Militärgeschichtliche Mitteilungen*, no. 1 (1967), pp. 83–119.

[7] Leo D. Crespi, "America's Interest in German Survey Research," in *Empirische Sozialforschung*, p. 216.

public opinion polling was adopted relatively quickly and successfully. This can clearly be attributed to the support of public opinion research by the British, French, and especially the American occupation authorities. Although the Allies were undoubtedly impressed by the democratic potential of polling methods, it can be assumed that they were above all interested in finding out about the development of German public opinion on key political issues.[8]

This interest is documented in the collection of seventy-two large-scale opinion surveys conducted between October 1945 and September 1949 under the auspices of the Office of the Military Government, United States (OMGUS), in the American occupation zone.[9] After the establishment of the Federal Republic in 1949, the OMGUS Opinion Survey Section became the Reactions Analysis Staff of the Office of the U.S. High Commissioner for Germany. Until 1955 it was responsible for many comprehensive public opinion surveys of the entire Federal Republic. To complete this part of the picture it should be noted that since 1952 public opinion surveys have regularly been conducted in the Federal Republic of Germany, as well as in other countries of the Western world, at the behest of the United States Information Agency (USIA).[10]

In many different and special ways, the American occupation forces supported the adoption in Germany of the latest and most highly developed techniques of interviewing, sampling, and evaluation. Scholarships were made available to German social scientists for research trips to the United States. German co-workers were trained in the sections of OMGUS and HICOG responsible for public opinion research.[11] German social scientists received support to exchange opinions and scientific know-how among themselves.[12] Unquestionably, other factors also encouraged the adoption of the new techniques.

---

[8] According to the information available, the American occupation forces made far and away the most important contribution to the development of German market and public opinion research.

[9] Anna J. Merritt and Richard L. Merritt, *Public Opinion in Occupied Germany* (Urbana: University of Illinois Press, 1970), pp. 3–9.

[10] Results of such studies are to be found in: Richard L. Merritt and Donald J. Puchala, eds., *Western European Perspectives on International Affairs* (New York: Frederick A. Praeger, 1968).

[11] Founded in 1951, the DIVO Institute (Deutsches Institut für Volksumfragen, German institute for public opinion surveys) was one of the best and most renowned institutes during the 1950s and 1960s. Its first five associates had been interviewers on the HICOG Reactions Analysis Staff. The foundation of DIVO was only made possible by an ongoing contract with HICOG to undertake a series of research studies.

[12] Crespi, "America's Interest," pp. 215–17.

The full history of this fascinating development has not yet been written, nor can it be written within the limits of this chapter. A date nevertheless to keep in mind is May 8, 1947, when Elisabeth Noelle-Neumann and Erich Peter Neumann established the Institut für Demoskopie (IfD, Institute for public opinion research) in Allensbach am Bodensee. The first large market as well as public opinion research institute of West Germany, the IfD is still in operation.[13] There are now more than 100 professional institutes of market and public opinion research in the Federal Republic, many of which are using opinion polling techniques and are conducting large-scale cross-sectional national surveys. Only a few of these institutes, however, have gained significance as agencies of political opinion research for political parties, the mass media, or other political institutions.

The Development of Research on the Sociology of Elections

As pointed out in the preceding section, the former occupation authorities were highly interested in the investigation of public opinion in postwar Germany. From their perspective of reeducation or political monitoring (to use the current term), the central question was whether democratic principles could successfully be implanted, not just in political institutions, but also in the citizens of the new Republic.

During the period of social and political normalization in the Federal Republic, especially after the successful consolidation of the political party system following the 1953 Bundestag election, more and more political public opinion research was undertaken on behalf of the political parties and the government—just as it was in other democratic countries. Slowly these groups began to explore the potential of these research techniques to help them maintain or acquire political power. This type of research was carried out largely in the professional commercial institutes which had been established since 1947. It is noteworthy, however, that initially the increased reliance of the federal government and of the parties on opinion research did not boost the quality of empirical social science research either in the professional institutes or in the universities.

---

[13] The institute owed its establishment not only to the assistance of the French occupation forces but certainly also to the fact that Elisabeth Noelle had been an exchange student in the United States in the late 1930s. There for the first time she was brought into contact with modern techniques of empirical social research. This experience found its way into her doctoral dissertation at Berlin: "Meinungs- und Massenforschung in den USA" [Public opinion and mass research in the United States], which was published in 1940.

199

There are many reasons why this research had such a slow start in the Federal Republic. The major tasks of the commercial public opinion and market research institutes were to establish themselves economically, earn credibility for their products, and overcome the initial phase of improvisation. Another important factor was that universities at that time had not yet established full-fledged social science curricula so that well-trained young professionals were almost impossible to find.

With respect to the universities, other factors have to be taken into account. In the United States there are at least two major social science research centers with nationwide interviewing teams: the Institute for Social Research (ISR) at the University of Michigan in Ann Arbor, and the National Opinion Research Center (NORC) at the University of Chicago. There is as yet no comparable research center in the Federal Republic.[14] The lack of such a center, however, can only partially account for the dearth of German university-based empirical research in the field of electoral behavior in the fifties.

At that time government agencies and scientific research foundations were heavily supporting the natural sciences, and it was virtually impossible to obtain research money for the social sciences. Thus, the studies of the 1953 and 1957 elections could not, because of inadequate financial support, be based on the findings of national opinion surveys.[15] A second reason for the relative scarcity of electoral studies in the Federal Republic in the 1950s is that Germany had fallen behind during the war and was struggling to catch up with scientific developments in other countries. In this respect, it is important to note that the limited financial resources of the universities did not allow for necessary institutional growth. Finally, the way in which German universities are typically organized, with one or only a very few professors representing an entire scientific discipline, has also contributed to delay.

The Cologne election study of 1961 was the first significant breakthrough in the study of electoral sociology in the Federal Republic. For

---

[14] The closest to the two American institutions is the Zentrum für Umfragen, Methoden und Analysen [Center for surveys, methods, and analyses] which was founded in Mannheim in 1974 and is fully financed by the Deutsche Forschungsgemeinschaft (DFG, German research association). ZUMA does not have, however, its own staff of interviewers but rather relies by means of cooperative agreements on the staffs of GETAS and INFRATEST.

[15] The studies are: Wolfgang Hirsch-Weber and Klaus Schütz, Wähler und Gewählte [The voters and the elected officials], 2d ed. (Cologne & Opladen: Westdeutscher Verlag, 1967) and Dolf Sternberger, Friedrich Erbe, Peter Molt, Erwin Faul, Wahlen und Wähler in Westdeutschland [Elections and voters in West Germany] (Villingen: Ring Verlag, 1960).

the first time survey research was extensively used: three national opinion surveys and three waves of panel interviews in four localities were conducted.[16] Since 1961, the study of electoral behavior in German universities has regularly used public opinion surveys. This has been possible, however, only because individual scholars have undertaken research projects for the national and state governments, the mass media, and political parties. In their contracts these scholars have ensured that their right to publish their findings and to freely disseminate the data will be unrestricted.[17]

The quality of the contributions of the professional market and public opinion research institutes to the national and international literature on electoral sociology varied. Before the 1961 Bundestag election, a few studies appeared in the publication series of the Institut für Demoskopie. These, however, are of little avail since no serious effort was made to integrate new theoretical developments and empirical findings reported in the American and German literature on electoral sociology. Also worthy of mention is a three-wave panel investigation conducted by the Deutsches Institut für Volksumfragen (DIVO) during the 1957 Bundestag election. Unfortunately this study has been available only in the form of a preliminary report and has never been published.[18]

The 1961 Bundestag election was the subject of the first detailed book-length analysis of an election to be published by a professional institute in Germany.[19] Moreover, since 1969 associates of the Institut für Demoskopie in Allensbach, particularly Elisabeth Noelle-Neumann,

---

[16] The research design and first results of the Cologne study of the 1961 election are summarized in Erwin K. Scheuch and Rudolf Wildenmann, eds., *Zur Soziologie der Wahl* [The sociology of elections], special issue 9 of the Kölner *Zeitschrift für Soziologie und Sozialpsychologie* (Cologne & Opladen: Westdeutscher Verlag, 1965).

[17] The fact that there were few studies of the early Bundestag elections either by universities or by commercial institutes is best demonstrated by the so-called German Electoral Data Project, a joint project of the Inter-University Consortium for Political and Social Research (ICPSR) in Ann Arbor, the Zentralarchiv für Empirische Sozialforschung (ZA, Central archives for empirical social research) at the University of Cologne and the Zentrum für Umfragen, Methoden und Analysen (ZUMA) in Mannheim. The goal of the project was to make freely available to all interested scholars at least one, eventually several, machine-readable data sets—standard format OSIRIS—for each Bundestag election since 1949. It was impossible to find a single commercial or scholarly data set for the elections of 1949 and 1957 which would meet minimal standards. However, data for all other Bundestag elections through the 1976 election are freely available.

[18] The original key punch cards of this quite sophisticated study have still not been found despite intensive searching.

[19] Viggo Graf Blücher et al., *Der Prozess der Meinungsbildung* [The process of opinion formation] (Bielefeld: EMNID, 1962).

have taken an increasingly active part in scholarly discussions.[20] But above all, the Institut für angewandte Sozialwissenschaft (INFAS, Institute for applied social science), which was established in 1959, has contributed significantly to the theoretical development of the study of electoral sociology through its publications and its participation in scholarly conferences.[21]

Despite the involvement of several professional market and public opinion research agencies in scholarly activities, critics point to these agencies' quasi-monopolization of political research. Furthermore, the critics are completely agreed that several features of these institutes are incompatible with an optimal scientific use of the data. In order to remain in the market they have to make a profit, a legitimate motive but not one necessarily conducive to innovative research and high quality standards; the concentration of research in only a few institutes strengthens their position vis-à-vis the scientific community; and they depend on clients who understandably have not the slightest interest in making research data publicly accessible.[22] Precisely because of the politically controversial nature of electoral research and the public debates which arise in every election over the quality and reliability of publicly disseminated findings from electoral studies, it would seem to be urgently necessary that the original data along with full documentation be made publicly available. This step would help to make the public debate more objective and would permit the testing of published reports and findings about the elections. Research data might be entrusted to such institutions as the Inter-University Consortium for Political and Social Research (ICPSR) at Ann Arbor or the Zentralarchiv at the University of Cologne, which could make them accessible to the public. Yet, as the documentation from the Zentralarchiv about the development of its electoral data bank indicates, the principle that electoral research findings should be made publicly

---

[20] Elisabeth Noelle-Neumann has had especially great influence on the scholarly development of communication studies.

[21] See Klaus Liepelt and Alexander Mitscherlich, eds., *Thesen zur Wählerfluktuation* [Theses to explain voter fluctuation] (Frankfurt: Europäische Verlagsanstalt, 1968) as well as several essays by Klaus Liepelt published in the *Politische Vierteljahresschrift* which is the official journal of the German Association for Political Science and is published by the Westdeutscher Verlag in Opladen. Furthermore, an edition of the journal *TRANSFER* is worth mentioning; it treats questions dealing with the sociology of elections and includes articles by several associates of the INFAS institute: "Wahlforschung: Sonden im politischen Markt" [Electoral research: Polling the political marketplace], *TRANSFER*, no. 2 (1976).

[22] Traugott, *Die Herrschaft der Meinung*, pp. 39, 42, 52–53; Kurt Koszyk, "Wirkungen der Massenkommunikation" [Effects of mass communication], *Aus Politik und Zeitgeschichte*, no. B 39 (Bonn: Bundeszentrale für Politische Bildung, September 23, 1972), p. 9.

available has obviously not yet been accepted in the Federal Republic (see Table 8–1).

Seventy-six percent of the fifty-two survey studies on electoral behavior which the Zentralarchiv had obtained by 1975 and which have consequently been made available to interested scholars were provided by independent scholars, all of them from Mannheim or Cologne. The majority of survey studies stemming from political parties were supplied by the Free Democratic party although some also came from the CDU-affiliated Sozialwissenschaftliches Forschungsinstitut der Konrad-Adenauer-Stiftung (Social science research institute of the Konrad Adenauer foundation). Practically none of the everincreasing number of survey studies by the mass media, the national government, and the state governments was opened to public use (with the exception of the data generated by the Second German Television Network—ZDF—which financed a whole series of studies listed in column 2 of Table 8–1). Especially noteworthy is the very sharp drop in the number of survey studies released to the Zentralarchiv since 1973. Fortunately, it has been ascertained that the 1976 Mannheim election study, a three-wave panel funded by ZDF, will be made available to all interested individuals and groups through the ICPSR and the Zentralarchiv in 1978.

The Organization of Political Public Opinion Research

It is well known that most of the political research presently conducted in the Federal Republic by the market and public opinion research institutes is concentrated in only 7 of the more than 100 institutes.[23] These 7 institutes are alphabetically listed with their estimated gross business volume in 1975 and some additional information in Table 8–2.

There are no reliable up-to-date statistics on the amount of money spent for political research in the Federal Republic since 1975 by market and public opinion research institutes on behalf of their clients. Of course, the institutes themselves do not volunteer such information and it may well be that these figures are not known even to them. At least four of the seven institutes heavily engaged in political research have recently provided estimates regarding the present volume of political research: INFRATEST and MARPLAN estimate that 5 percent of their gross annual *income* stems from political re-

---

[23] The total of forty-nine institutes for which this information is available reflects—because of its voluntary nature—a little less than half of the market and public opinion research institutes presently operating in the Federal Republic. However, among those forty-nine are all of the institutes which are of particular interest for this study.

TABLE 8-1

ELECTION DATA HELD AT THE CENTRAL ARCHIVE FOR EMPIRICAL
SOCIAL RESEARCH AT COLOGNE UNIVERSITY, 1975

Year Data Collected	Data from Independent Scholars		Mass media	Data from Organizations			Total Investigations
	Research funds	Contract research[b]		Political parties	Research institutes[c]	National, state govts.	
1953[a]	1N						1
1960				1N			1
1961[a]	3N 3R						6
1962		1S 1R		1S		1S	4
1963		2R					2
1964		1N		1N			2
1965[a]		3N 2R		1N			6
1966		4S		2S 1R	1S		8
1967		1N 1S					2
1968		1N 1S					2
1969[a]		6N 1S		2N			9
1970		3S		1S			4
1971							
1972[a]		6N	1N				7
1973							
1974							
1975							
Total	4N 3R	18N 11S 5R	1N	5N 4S 1R	1S	1S	54

[a] Year of a Bundestag election.   [b] Research contracted for media, parties, and national and state governments.

[c] Includes market and public opinion research institutes.

NOTE: The abbreviations refer to the universe of the investigation. Key: N = national; S = state; R = regional (electoral district or comparable unit). SOURCE: Compilation of data from the Zentralarchiv für Empirische Sozialforschung kindly prepared by Erwin Rose.

TABLE 8–2

GROWTH AND BUSINESS VOLUME OF SELECTED GERMAN MARKET AND
PUBLIC OPINION RESEARCH INSTITUTES, 1975

Institute	Year Established	Average Yearly Business Volume, 1971–75 (in millions of DM)	Business Volume, 1975 (in millions of DM)	Number of Full-Time Employees
EMNID	1948[a]	3.3	3.7	46
GETAS	1959[b]	3.7	3.6	37
IfD	1947	4.0	4.3	82
INFAS	1959	—	5.7	67
INFRATEST	1955[c]	30.5	33.5	364
MARPLAN	1959	4.6	4.7	36
WICKERT	1951	3.9	4.1	37
Total	—	—	59.6	669

[a] EMNID was established in 1945 but did not come into full operation until 1948.
[b] GETAS grew out of the Institut für Motivforschung (Institute for motivation research) which was established in 1956 and did not conduct any cross-section national sample surveys until 1966.
[c] INFRATEST grew out of the Fachinstitut für Media- und Kommunikationswissenschaft (Technical institute of media and communications science) which was established in 1947.
NOTE: The institutes listed here are those most heavily engaged in political survey research. The remaining forty-four institutes included in this study had a total business volume of DM121.9 million in 1975 and a total of 1,397 full-time employees.
SOURCE: With the permission of the publisher, these data are drawn from the confidential "Informationsdienst zu Fragen der Kommunikation in der Wirtschaft" [Information service for communication problems in the domestic economy], CONTEXT, no. 267 (Düsseldorf: M. Marcoty, 1975), pp. 5–6, and have been tabulated in somewhat modified form.

search; the respective figures for EMNID (the German affiliate of the Gallup organization) is 10 percent and for the Institut für Demoskopie 25 percent.

Of the seven institutes engaged in political and sociological research only the Institut für angewandte Sozialwissenschaft (INFAS) is clearly affiliated with a political party, the SPD. This, of course, does not mean that parties and governmental agencies do not prefer to work with particular institutes. In 1976, the strongest ties between research institutes and political organizations were as follows:[24]

[24] "Politik mit falschen Zahlen" [Politics with the wrong numbers], Der Spiegel, vol. 30, no. 37 (1976), pp. 76–77.

EMNID	Press and Information Agency of the federal government
GETAS	CDU/CSU
IfD	CDU/CSU; Press and Information Agency of the federal government
INFRATEST	SPD; Office of the Chancellor; Press and Information Agency of the federal government

The methods of financing political and sociological studies for political parties are especially interesting. Besides the income they receive from membership dues, contributions from wealthy supporters, and other intraparty sources, political parties can count on regular public support from the national government. They are in a position, therefore, to support their own individual research foundations.[25] To be sure, these foundations have been established not only to conduct or support survey research but also to foster political education, to study party history, and to pursue other general goals.

There is no reliable published information as to when the parties (national and state branches), government agencies (especially the Office of the Chancellor and the Press and Information Agency of the national government), interest groups, mass media, and other organizations began to use public opinion polling for the purpose of supporting their political goals. In an article published in 1955 Elisabeth Noelle-Neumann revealed that, as far as she was aware, the FDP was the first party to commission a political opinion poll, in 1950.[26] Between that year and 1955 the FDP and the CDU/CSU, Noelle-Neumann said, had regularly used opinion polling, especially before elections. It is also known that after the 1957 Bundestag election EMNID was commissioned to undertake a basic research project for the CDU/CSU in preparation for the 1961 Bundestag elections.[27] Apparently the SPD

---

[25] The four major party foundations are the Friedrich-Ebert-Stiftung of the SPD, the Konrad-Adenauer-Stiftung of the CDU, the Hanns-Seidel-Stiftung of the CSU, and the Friedrich-Naumann-Stiftung of the FDP. Of these, only the Konrad-Adenauer-Stiftung has a social science research institute conducting independent research in cooperation with public opinion research institutes.

[26] Elisabeth Noelle, *Auskunft über die Parteien* [Information on political parties], Allensbacher Schriften No. 2 (Allensbach and Bonn: Verlag für Demoskopie, 1955), p. 30.

[27] Karl-Georg von Stackelberg, *Souffleur auf politischer Bühne* [Prompter on the political stage] (Munich: Verlag Moderne Industrie, 1975).

started to use public opinion research somewhat later than the other parties; the establishment of the INFAS institute in 1959 would appear to be directly related to this development. In any case, Traugott points to the very considerable influence that was exerted by findings of political opinion research on the formulation of the Godesberg Program (a revised statement of the SPD's ideological and political principles) in 1959. In turn the program has played a decisive role in defining the current governmental policies of the SPD.[28]

It should also be noted that, of all the German market and public opinion research institutes the Institut für Demoskopie, thanks to its regular work on behalf of the Press and Information Agency of the national government, possesses the most complete and comprehensive collection of political polling data. Moreover, many of the findings of these opinion polls have been published in the series *Jahrbuch der Öffentlichen Meinung* and since 1976 in the series *Allensbacher Jahrbuch der Demoskopie.*[29] Thus, on topics such as the party preferences of the German public, time series data beginning in 1950 are available for inspection.

With few exceptions opinion research studies for political parties and various governmental agencies which were not carried out by independent scholars have not been published.[30] As a result the findings and interpretations of these studies cannot be subjected to outside scientific evaluation. This shortcoming, which could not be sufficiently compensated by independent, university-based research because of inadequate research infrastructure and research funds, has been increasingly met during the last twelve years by the mass media. The media have prevented the rise of a dangerous political monopoly over electoral data controlled by the political parties and the government.

---

[28] Traugott, *Die Herrschaft der Meinung*, pp. 109–22; see also Scheuch, "Sozialer Wandel und Sozialforschung," p. 16.

[29] Elisabeth Noelle and Erich Peter Neumann, eds., *Jahrbuch der Öffentlichen Meinung* [Yearbook of public opinion] (Allensbach and Bonn: Verlag für Demoskopie, 1947–55; 1958–64; 1965–67; 1968–73); Elisabeth Noelle-Neumann, ed., *Allensbacher Jahrbuch der Demoskopie 1974–1976* [Allensbach yearbook of public opinion research 1974–1976], vol. VI, (Munich-Vienna-Zürich: Verlag Fritz Molden, 1976).

[30] Only the Social Science Research Institute of the Konrad-Adenauer-Stiftung has transferred several data sets of studies to the ICPSR and the ZA for registration, storage, and free distribution among interested scholars. From time to time the Institut für Demoskopie has made available some original data sets of its own surveys to the Roper Center in Williamstown and to selected American social scientists. In addition, since 1973 the IFD has transferred all materials collected since 1947 to the Bundesarchiv, Koblenz. These materials will be available to the general public at the end of a thirty-year imposed time limit.

Undoubtedly, this is a favorable development. Nevertheless, it must be stressed again that in the long term the only effective means of scientific evaluation and control is the unconditional release and availability of all data. So far many clients, even those outside the strictly political arena, have not wanted, or have not been aware of the necessity, to agree to opening data to the public.

Problems of Political Public Opinion Polling

One of the fascinations of elections for the social scientist is the almost unique opportunity they offer him to test and improve his techniques of empirical research by referring to an absolutely reliable datum: the official outcome of a given election. Deviations between sample estimates and the real outcome are statistically preprogrammed and give no cause for alarm as long as they do not systematically overstep the limits set by statistical theory. If two political parties or coalitions enjoy rather equal electoral support, it is quite possible that the public opinion pollster will declare the wrong party or coalition the winner. Though this should not be regarded as an indictment of the pollster's craft—the risks of sampling procedures are well known—a wrong election prediction invariably causes a public outcry. Commentators deplore the weaknesses of public opinion research and demand that in the future the publication of polling results not be permitted, at least not before elections.

That such criticism often comes from journalists and other members of the intellectual elite may well reflect disenchantment with a world where everything seems to become quantifiable; also a tendency to equate public opinion research with the loss of individuality in contemporary society. From this perspective a wrong electoral prediction can easily be interpreted as the triumph of man's invincible individuality. But such an interpretation clearly cannot suffice to explain why public opinion reacts with such sensitivity to errors in election projections. Rather, the essence of the problem, the real reason for opposition to the publication of polling results before election day, is to be found in the still unanswered question of how such publications affect subsequent electoral behavior.

The two effects that are invariably mentioned in this context are the bandwagon effect and the underdog effect. The former is the proposition that an individual votes for the anticipated winner because he likes to join with the strong; the latter is the proposition that the individual votes for the expected loser out of sympathy. Until now neither of these two propositions has been reliably proved in any scientific study.[31] Moreover, it would be wrong to state that the two propositions have ever been properly operationalized and then tested with appropriate research techniques. It is precisely this ambiguity that leads to constant controversy over the publication of polling results before elections.[32]

During the last few years, an additional important consideration of special concern for political parties with committed memberships is whether the publication of poll results before elections has an effect on the readiness of party members to campaign actively for the party (encouragement versus frustration). In addition, the effect on voter turnout—the willingness to accept "the costs" of participation—is not to be ignored. Here again, there are no reliable research findings.

The publication of survey data on election outcomes before elections has been standard practice in the United States since 1948.[33] By contrast, results of public opinion polls on the outcome of elections were hardly publicized in the Federal Republic before 1965. According to available information no polling data at all were published before the elections of 1949 and 1953. In 1957 and 1961 an election forecast by the Institut für Demoskopie was published in the *Frankfurter Allgemeine Zeitung* one day before the election.[34] Finally, for the first

---

[31] One of the reasons for the inconclusiveness of findings certainly is that the theoretical propositions underlying both hypotheses have not been properly spelled out. A new perspective on this problem has been offered by Elisabeth Noelle-Neumann with her theory of the spiral of silence (*Schweigespirale*) as one building block for a more general theory of public opinion. This theoretical perspective may well prove useful for new empirical studies in this field. For a recent account of her work, see Elisabeth Noelle-Neumann, *Öffentlichkeit als Bedrohung* [The threat of publicity], Beiträge zu empirischen Kommunikationsforschung [Essays on empirical communications research], vol. 6 (Freiburg: Verlag Karl Alber, 1977).

[32] A completely different question is whether one should welcome or deplore the possibility of influencing potential voters by the publication of the current electoral strength of political parties. This is discussed by Klaus Hartenstein, one of the co-owners of the INFAS institute, in his article "Vom Nutzen und Schaden veröffentlichter Umfrageergebnisse" [The advantages and disadvantages of published survey results], *TRANSFER*, vol. 2 (1976), pp. 13–18. If one agrees on normative grounds with the proposition that there should be the fullest publicity of polling results, then one must above all stress the need to establish professional controls in order to prevent the manipulation and falsification of data for political advantage.

[33] This practice has not gone unchallenged in the United States any more than in the Federal Republic. In 1964 a congressional hearing was held to determine the potential harmful effects of such publications and, in particular, of the early election night projections by the three major television networks.

[34] Noelle, *Umfragen in der Massengesellschaft*, p. 10. Moreover, in just a few cases the Institut für Demoskopie published forecasts for state legislative elections of 1954 and 1955. See Elisabeth Noelle and Erich Peter Neumann, eds., *Jahrbuch der Öffentlichen Meinung 1947–1955*, p. 308.

time in 1965 there were a number of election forecasts which not only began to appear as much as several months before the election but also predicted quite different results.

The first serious controversy over the role of public opinion polling arose when Elisabeth Noelle-Neumann of the IfD and Karl-Georg von Stackelberg of the EMNID institute broadcast election forecasts on national television the evening of election day in 1965. The forecasts that led to the controversy are worth noting (see Table 8–3).

Interesting though they are, the negative long-term economic consequences for the EMNID institute of its wrong election forecast cannot be discussed here. The public controversy was sparked by something else. Although the IfD's forecast on the evening of the election was quite accurate, its forecast four weeks earlier had predicted a much more favorable outcome for the SPD. The divergence between the two forecasts led to the charge that the institute had manipulated the poll results in order to favor the CDU/CSU.

In the end, this particular controversy remained (as one might have anticipated) unresolved. It led, however, to a nonsensical—since unenforceable—decision on the part of the research institutes belonging to the Arbeitskreis deutscher Marktforschungsinstitute (ADM, association of German market research institutes): namely, not to publish any findings on the current popular strength of the political parties during the last two months before the 1969 election. As a matter of fact this regulation, although somewhat modified, is still in effect. An explicit distinction is now made between election forecasts—in other words, predictions of the election outcome—which

TABLE 8–3

ELECTION FORECASTS AND OFFICIAL RESULTS, BUNDESTAG ELECTION
OF 1965
(in percentages)

	Forecasts			
	August	Election Night		Official Result
Party	IfD	IfD	EMNID	(second ballot)
CDU/CSU	45.5	49.5	45.0	47.6
SPD	43.5	38.5	45.0	39.3
FDP	Not provided	8.0	Not provided	9.5

SOURCE: Siegfried Weischenberg, "Pannen der Wahlprognostik" [Failures in election forecasting], Das Parlament, vol. 26, no. 38 (September 18, 1976).

may not be published, and findings about the current popular strength of the political parties, which may be published. It need hardly be emphasized that this subtle distinction has escaped the general public, and that the research institutes themselves have always been interested in using the concept of forecast or prediction in presenting their data to the public. Thus far it can confidently be stated that the publication of findings about the current popular strength of political parties before elections has become a familiar and unchallenged practice.

Until the contrary is proven, the influence of election forecasts on electoral behavior must be considered a real possibility. Therefore, in addition to the social scientists themselves, the mass media have become particularly interested in examining the factors that can influence the findings of public opinion surveys. These factors will be briefly discussed in the following subsections.[35]

The Quality of the Market and Public Opinion Research Institutes. The differing quality of the research institutes is a matter that usually is not systematically discussed in public. Yet with one exception, none of the polling organizations has been seriously challenged in this respect.

The notable role of the mass media in promoting critical discussion of political opinion research is best illustrated by *Der Spiegel*, the leading political weekly magazine of the Federal Republic (comparable to *Time* or *Newsweek* in the United States). Just before the national election of 1976 *Der Spiegel* published the findings of a quality test of six leading public opinion research institutes. These institutes had declared themselves willing to include a question on the CDU/CSU campaign slogan "*Freiheit statt Sozialismus*" (freedom instead of socialism) in their omnibus surveys and had also agreed to the publication of their findings in *Der Spiegel*.[36] GETAS could not participate in this test because at the time the institute was not conducting an omnibus survey. The only pollster who refused to participate was the Wickert Institutes. In its report, *Der Spiegel* pointed to a whole series of earlier findings which may well call into serious question the quality of the work of the Wickert Institutes.[37]

Apart from the issue of evaluating the general performance of the research institutes, there has been some discussion of the particular

---

[35] See also Siegfried Weischenberg, "Pannen der Wahlprognostik" [Failures in election forecasting], *Das Parlament*, vol. 26, no. 38 (September 13, 1976), p. 13.

[36] "Politik mit falschen Zahlen," pp. 84, 90–91.

[37] Ibid., pp. 79, 86, 90–91.

sampling method chosen by an institute. While GETAS, INFAS, INFRATEST, and MARPLAN use multistage probability samples, EMNID and the Institut für Demoskopie chiefly rely on quota samples.[38] The Wickert Institutes often use telephone samples for their so-called *Blitzumfragen* (instant surveys), a practice that is problematic and error-prone because of the unrepresentative social status of German telephone owners.

The Calculation of Election Forecasts. All of the institutes have their own procedures for determining the probable electoral strength of the political parties at a particular time before the election. In arriving at their forecasts, however, all of the institutes face the following common problems:

(1) *Distribution of the undecided.* On average some 15 to 25 percent of respondents refuse to answer questions about their party preference or voting intentions. Since the voter turnout in the Federal Republic has been more than 90 percent for the last two elections and it is therefore known that most of these respondents will actually vote, the undecideds must be distributed among the parties according to some definite formula in order to produce a sufficiently accurate prediction.[39]

(2) *Estimation of voter turnout.* Experience with public opinion polling has shown that it is more difficult to find out the size of voter turnout than the distribution of party preferences.[40] Institutes usually avoid this difficulty by not publishing any information at all about voter turnout or the formula for distributing undecided voters among the parties and the nonvoters in their election forecasts.

(3) *Distorting effects of recall questions.* Answers to recall questions about voting decisions at any past election always deviate significantly from the official returns for that election. Although the patterns of influence that may explain such deviations have

---

[38] Some not entirely unbiased remarks on this controversy can be found in: Noelle, *Umfragen in der Massengesellschaft*, pp. 137–46. See also Erwin K. Scheuch, "Auswahlverfahren in der Sozialforschung" [Selection methods in social research], *Handbuch der empirischen Sozialforschung* [Handbook of empirical social research], René König, ed., vol. 3a, 3rd rev. ed. (Stuttgart: Ferdinand Enke Verlag, 1974), pp. 16–21.

[39] For a general description of the methods used by the Institut für Demoskopie, see Jürgen R. Hofmann, "Geheime Wahl ohne Geheimnis" [Secret election without secrets], *Das Parlament*, vol. 18 (September 1976), p. 6.

[40] Jürg Steiner, *Bürger und Politik* [Citizens and politics], *Politik und Wähler*, vol. 4 (Meisenheim/Glan: Anton Hain Verlag, 1969), pp. 12–15.

not been adequately explored, institutes use these deviations in varying ways to adjust (that is, to correct) predictions from newly gathered data.[41]

Distinction between the First Ballot and the Second Ballot. In a Bundestag election every citizen has two ballots. The first ballot is cast for a candidate in a single-member electoral district, and the candidate who wins a plurality is directly elected; the second ballot is cast for a party list. In distributing the total number of Bundestag seats, only the second ballot outcomes are used; in essence, strict rules of proportional representation are followed. Accordingly, election forecasts are usually based on second-ballot preferences. Nevertheless, since 1972 the Institut für Demoskopie has been referring to first-ballot preferences in most of its election forecasts. The reasons advanced for this new procedure have not been very convincing, and it has received vigorous public criticism.[42]

The Bundestag Election of October 3, 1976

Role of the Mass Media in the Preelection Period. The campaign that ended at 6 P.M. on Sunday, October 3, 1976, when the polls closed, had been, in the eyes of many observers, dull. On the other hand, it had informed citizens as never before about the party preferences of the voters and changes in party strength from the beginning of the year right up to election day. In addition to a multitude of brief reports in newspapers, weeklies, and magazines, several periodicals devoted whole series of articles to reporting the findings of their own empirical studies of the parties' electoral prospects. Among these were the following: (1) the weekly *Der Spiegel* in a series of articles by Werner Kaltefleiter beginning in February 1976; (2) the monthly *Capital* in two articles by Rudolf Wildenmann in August and Sep-

---

[41] The problem is identified and explained in Max Kaase, "Die Bundestagswahl 1972: Probleme und Analysen" [The Bundestag election of 1972: problems and analyses], *Politische Vierteljahresschrift*, vol. 14, no. 2 (June 1973), pp. 145–50, and Peter Hoschka and Hermann Schunck, "Schätzung von Wählerwanderungen" [Estimation of voter changes], *Politische Vierteljahresschrift*, vol. 16, no. 4 (December 1975), pp. 502–505. Elisabeth Noelle-Neumann justifies methods of adjustment in "Wahlentscheidung in der Fernsehdemokratie" [Electoral decision in TV-democracy], in *Auf der Suche nach dem mündigen Wähler* [In search of the mature voter], Dieter Just and Lothar Romain, eds., Schriftenreihe der Bundeszentrale für Politische Bildung [Monograph series of the federal center for political education], vol. 101 (Bonn: Bundeszentrale für Politische Bildung, 1974), pp. 161–205, especially p. 165.

[42] Klaus Dreher, "Hexeneinmaleins der Demoskopie" [The witchcraft of public opinion research], *Süddeutsche Zeitung*, September 22, 1976, p. 5.

tember 1976; (3) the illustrated weekly *Stern* in reports by the Institut für Demoskopie in every issue published during the last six weeks before the election (a practice already begun in the 1972 election campaign); and (4) the illustrated weekly *Quick* in reports based on surveys conducted by the *Quick*-owned Kehrmann Market Research Institute in every issue published during the last eight weeks before the election.

Furthermore, a great number of essays, reports, and other types of information on the electoral prospects of the parties or on other questions relating to the election appeared in daily newspapers, scientific journals, and popular magazines as well as on radio and television. Moreover, newspapers partially previewed election reports that had been released to press agencies by *Quick* or *Stern*. And radio and television stations financed their own surveys; the Second Television Network, for example, sponsored a three-wave panel study of a representative cross-section of the West German voting-age population.

A single public opinion survey, depending on the size of the sample and the methods used, costs between $30,000 and $75,000; the enormous costs incurred by the mass media give a ready indication of the importance they attributed to the publication of polling data. The free availability of information made the campaign decidedly different from previous ones. It was no longer possible for political parties and politicians to gain free publicity by leaking favorable polling results to the mass media.

Taken by itself, the increasing role that the mass media assume during election campaigns in providing a broad base of information including findings from public opinion surveys may cause no particular concern.[43] In fact, it may well be argued that the media have stepped in to fulfill the important function of providing a diversity of views otherwise no longer available to the individual citizen because of the cost of producing this information. On the other hand, the demonstrable impact the media have on the political process in Western democracies raises difficult problems regarding the legitimacy of the media. According to article 21 of the federal constitution, political parties are assigned a central role in West German politics, which is reflected, for example, in their public financing. (Under a 1967 law which was later amended, the parties receive the equivalent of about $1.75 per citizen who voted for them at the election.) One of the

---

[43] At this point it should be mentioned in passing that no comparable control took place by social scientists. Independent scholars neither participated significantly in the studies commissioned by the mass media nor conducted their own studies of the 1976 Bundestag election.

important tasks of parties in a parliamentary system is to control the government, but another is to stimulate and sustain a high level of public trust in liberal democratic institutions.

It is exactly this responsibility that political parties—not only in the Federal Republic, but also in other Western democracies—have not lived up to. An overwhelming concern with their own well-being, too tight a relationship with the executive branch of government, and an underrating of moral integrity have created a vacuum which the media have, at least in part, filled. But the media are not a formal part of the political institutional structure, and the basis for their legitimacy as well as their modes of operation are unclear.

It is in this sense that the media's role in providing information about election campaigns and survey findings about the standing of the parties signals a structural problem of much wider significance. At present the media's attempts to provide extensive information and public control over governmental decision making are clearly welcome, even necessary. But it must not be forgotten that these tasks rightfully belong to the parliaments of Western democracies, parliaments that unfortunately, and partly through their own doing, have suffered an increasing defunctionalization.

Political Developments between the 1972 Bundestag Election and the Summer of 1976. In the 1972 Bundestag election, for the first time in the history of the Federal Republic, the SPD became the strongest political party. Yet it lost electoral support rather quickly as a consequence of increasing economic difficulties and the Guillaume scandal, which in April 1974 led to Willy Brandt's resignation as chancellor.[44] In three of the eleven state legislative elections between March 1974 and April 1976, the SPD lost more than 7 percentage points, between 3 and 5 percentage points in another three elections, and between 0.9 and 2.7 percentage points in four elections; only in the Saarland was the party able to increase its electoral strength by 1 percentage point. The FDP, the smaller coalition partner of the SPD, was not able to make up for the SPD's losses. As a result, the CDU/CSU registered heavy gains, especially in 1974. Even in 1975, in Schleswig-Holstein, the CDU/CSU scored further gains. These were far smaller, however, than had been expected, and the relatively better showing of the SPD was attributed to the prudent policies of the new chancellor, Helmut Schmidt. Quite early in the preelection maneuvering for 1976, therefore, the SPD and the FDP indicated their willingness, in the event of victory at the

---

[44] On the Guillaume scandal and Brandt's resignation, see Chapter 3 in this volume, p. 63.

upcoming election, to form another coalition under the leadership of Helmut Schmidt. As a result political discussions in the early stages of the 1976 election campaign focused on the question whether Helmut Kohl, the CDU/CSU candidate for chancellor, would be able to win an absolute majority in Parliament. The extent to which these developments were reflected in the public's preference for the political parties is shown in Table 8–4. These IFD data clearly indicate that —if sampling error is taken into account—from late 1973 on, government and opposition were never able to gain a comfortable lead over their respective opponents. This becomes even more apparent when survey projections of the parties' strength by other institutes are brought into the picture.

In its documentary report on political public opinion research in the Federal Republic, *Der Spiegel* provides a longitudinal survey of party preferences from January until August 1976. This survey is based on the monthly findings of IFD, EMNID, GETAS, and INFRATEST, which used approximately the same question to elicit voting intentions (How would you vote if there were Bundestag elections next Sunday?). Out of a total of thirty surveys (GETAS did not collect such data for two months), the SPD and the FDP together had a majority twenty times, the coalition and the opposition were tied three times, and the CDU/CSU had a majority only seven times (four of which were reported by the IFD).

The Election Campaign. Germans returning from their vacations in July and August found themselves in the midst of an election campaign conducted with considerable bitterness by the political leaders and parties. The emotions of the party leaders were especially aroused by the CDU/CSU campaign slogan, which reduced the electoral decision of October 3 to a simple alternative between "freedom" (the CDU/CSU) and "socialism" (the SPD-FDP).

Although political-party workers tried hard to spend all the campaign money at their disposal (the total amount spent on the campaign, including government contributions, is estimated at $125 to $150 million), they were unable to awaken the same degree of public interest in politics as in 1972 (see Table 8–5).

Empirical studies have repeatedly demonstrated that the population of the Federal Republic (and other countries as well) has mixed feelings about election campaigns. Hardly anyone considers campaigns to be harmful, but more than a third of the population regards them as superfluous. Only every sixth citizen of the Federal Republic considers an election campaign to be absolutely necessary. Of course

TABLE 8-4

DEVELOPMENT OF PARTY PREFERENCES, 1972–1976
(in percentages of respondents)

Political Parties	1972 Dec.	1973 Jun.	1973 Dec.	1974 Jun.	1974 Dec.	1975 Jun.	1975 Dec.	1976 Jan.	1976 Feb.	1976 Mar.	1976 May	1976 Jun.	1976 Jul.	1976 Aug.
							Date of Survey							
CDU/CSU	45	46	50	49	53	47	47	49	51	52	51	49	50	49
SPD	48	44	35	41	38	42	41	41	38	38	41	39	43	42
FDP	6	9	13	9	7	10	10	9	9	9	7	10	6	8
Other parties	1	1	2	1	2	1	2	1	2	1	1	2	1	1

NOTE: The survey question was: If there were a Bundestag election next Sunday, which party would you vote for?
SOURCE: Noelle and Neumann, *Jahrbuch der Öffentlichen Meinung 1968–1973*, p. 304; Noelle-Neumann, *Allensbacher Jahrbuch der Demoskopie 1974–1976*, pp. 118–19; the data for July and August also come from the Institut für Demoskopie and are to be found in *Der Spiegel*, "Politik mit falschen Zahlen," p. 78.

TABLE 8–5

FREQUENCY OF POLITICAL DISCUSSIONS IN THE FAMILY AND AT THE
WORK PLACE, 1969, 1972, AND 1976 CAMPAIGNS
(in percentages of respondents)

Discussions Occur	In the Family			At the Work Place		
	1969	1972	1976	1969	1972	1976
Frequently	14	38	12	12	38	14
Occasionally	27	35	34	24	31	33
Rarely	8	5	12	6	6	10
Never	50	22	42	58	25	43

SOURCE: Max Kaase, "Die Bundestagswahl 1972: Probleme und Analysen" [The Bundestag election of 1972: problems and analyses], *Politische Vierteljahresschrift*, vol. 14, no. 2 (June 1973), p. 158. The data for 1976 are drawn from a publication of the Forschungsgruppe Wahlen [Research group on elections], *Wahlstudie 1976, 2. Welle* [Election study 1976, 2nd wave], mimeographed, Mannheim, 1976, pp. 98, 101.

these figures reveal nothing about the possible effects of campaigns. Usually they are credited with mobilizing voters. They seem to have done so in 1976, according to data from a study published in *Stern*.[45]

Clearly, as far as the outcome of an election is concerned, it is more important to know whether the election campaign brought about changes in support for the parties than to know merely whether it persuaded people to go to the polls. Before an empirical answer can be given, one methodological point requires brief mention. Unless the social researcher uses panel studies—that is, requestions the same interviewees over time—he can only determine net changes in partisan preference. Panel studies with their more detailed results allow one to determine where changes in partisan preference among individuals cancel each other out. Aggregate statistics of normal survey polling cannot detect such movements. It is important therefore to note that the figures in Table 8–6 are aggregate estimates indicating only *net variations* of party strength during the election campaign.[46] The two

[45] "Muss Wahlkampf sein?" [Must there be an election campaign?], *Stern*, no. 41 (September 30, 1976), p. 32. Another objectively measurable effect of the election campaign is the size of voter turnout. The fact that the 1976 Bundestag election with a 90.7 percent turnout almost reached the peak registered in 1972 (91.1 percent) supports the thesis that the campaign of 1976 was indeed successful in mobilizing the voters.

[46] At this point the methodological reservations discussed above will not be taken up again since a change in the relative strength of the political parties is under consideration and one can presume that the methodology applied by the institutes had not been changed in the course of the studies.

illustrated weeklies *Quick* and *Stern* published the data shown in Table 8-6 for the period from August 8 to September 26, the last weeks before election day.

Setting aside the matter of the sampling error that is unavoidable in this kind of survey, one must conclude that the election campaign did not systematically influence the *net strength* of the political parties. If an adjustment for second ballots in the published *Stern* data is made, it is also possible to conclude that the predictions of the two major party leaders during the last stages of the campaign were unfounded. Contrary to the assertions of Helmut Schmidt, who predicted a clear majority for the coalition, and of Helmut Kohl, who

TABLE 8–6

DEVELOPMENT OF PARTY PREFERENCES IN THE LAST EIGHT WEEKS
BEFORE THE ELECTION, 1976
(in percentages of respondents)

Preferred Party	Approximate Date of Survey							
	Aug. 8	Aug. 15	Aug. 22	Aug. 29	Sep. 5	Sep. 12	Sep. 19	Sep. 26
Findings published in *Quick*								
CDU/CSU	47.0	47.0	49.0	48.1	47.6	47.8	47.4	47.7
SPD	44.0	45.0	42.0	42.6	42.9	42.5	43.2	43.3
FDP	8.0	7.0	8.0	8.3	8.7	8.6	8.3	8.2
Other parties	1.0	1.0	1.0	1.0	0.8	1.1	1.1	0.8
Findings published in *Stern*[a]								
CDU/CSU	No Survey	No Survey	49.5	49.2	49.7	50.4	49.3	48.6
SPD			42.4	41.5	41.6	39.5	43.7	43.1
FDP			7.3	8.0	7.8	9.1	6.2	6.6
Other parties			0.8	1.3	0.9	1.0	0.8	1.7

[a] The results in *Stern* provide a somewhat misleading picture since they are based on first-ballot preferences, whereas only second-ballot preferences determine the distribution of seats in the Bundestag. In the second-ballot surveys which were reported by *Stern* for not exactly comparable points in time, the CDU/CSU and the SPD received on the average 1.5 percentage points less, and the FDP 3 percentage points more, than they received in the *Stern* surveys shown here.

NOTE: The survey question was: Which party would you vote for if there were an election next Sunday?

SOURCE: *Quick*, nos. 34–41 (Munich: Heinrich Bauer Verlag, 1976); *Stern*, nos. 36–41 (1976).

foresaw a slight absolute majority for the CDU/CSU, we can see that (1) the CDU/CSU had no chance at any time to become the government party, and (2) the lead of the SPD and the FDP, although constant, was very small.

Against this background of steady electoral support for the political parties, it is nevertheless interesting to note the significant shifts in the general climate of public opinion which occurred during the weeks before the election. The concept of a "climate of public opinion," which crops up from time to time in the literature on elections, has gained new scholarly attention in recent years and has given rise to interesting theoretical speculations.[47] Without entering into that discussion, we should note that, though the strength of the political parties did not change, a significant change occurred in the popular expectation of which parties would win. In the course of the campaign the popular conviction that the CDU/CSU would win the election steadily gave way to the conviction that the SPD-FDP coalition would carry the day (see Table 8–7).

This finding is doubly interesting in that the CDU/CSU mounted a much more effective campaign in 1976 than it had in 1972. By means of provocative slogans, good advance preparation, and solid work at the grass roots, the party conveyed the impression of being firmly committed to victory (see Table 8–8).[48]

The Outcome of the 1976 Bundestag Election. Since the 1965 Bundestag election, the two German television networks (ARD and ZDF) have vied for the honor of being the first to correctly project the outcomes of elections on the basis of early returns from key precincts. Also since 1965, Elisabeth Noelle-Neumann, either alone or in conjunction with representatives of other institutes, has appeared on television shortly after the closing of the polling stations to announce her forecast of the results. This well-publicized forecast is usually based

---

[47] From the earlier literature see Bernard R. Berelson, Paul F. Lazarsfeld, William N. McPhee, *Voting* (Chicago: University of Chicago Press, 1954), pp. 100, 300–1; Erwin K. Scheuch, "Die Sichtbarkeit politischer Einstellungen im alltäglichen Verhalten" [The visibility of political attitudes in daily behavior], in *Zur Soziologie der Wahl*, Scheuch and Wildenmann, eds., pp. 169–214. Among the recent contributions see Elisabeth Noelle-Neumann, "Die Schweigespirale" [The spiral of silence], *Standorte im Zeitstrom* [Vantage points in time], Ernst Forsthoff and Reinhard Hörstel, eds., Festschrift in honor of Arnold Gehlen (Frankfurt: Athenäum-Verlag, 1974), pp. 299–330; Noelle-Neumann, "Wahlentscheidung in der Fernsehdemokratie," pp. 161–205; Elisabeth Noelle-Neumann, "Menschen unter Konformitätsdruck: Eine Theorie der öffentlichen Meinung" [The pressure to conform: a theory of public opinion], *TRANSFER*, vol. 2 (1976), pp. 211–20.

[48] *Stern*, no. 41 (1976), p. 33.

on the findings of a public opinion poll conducted by IFD during the last week before the election.

In 1976 Elisabeth Noelle-Neumann had signed a contract with ZDF, while the ARD had contracted with the INFAS institute (which was already lined up to do the network's election-night projections) to conduct a straw poll of voters as they emerged from the polls. This was

TABLE 8–7

EXPECTED WINNERS IN THE BUNDESTAG ELECTION, 1976
(in percentages of respondents)

Expected Winner	June	July	Early August	End of August	Early September	Mid-September	End of September
					Approximate Date of Survey		
CDU/CSU	42	36	39	37	35	35	34
SPD/FDP	28	32	33	38	34	37	40
Don't know	30	32	28	25	31	21	26

NOTE: The survey question was: Who do you think will win the Bundestag election?
SOURCE: *Stern*, no. 41 (1976), p. 17.

TABLE 8–8

PERCEPTION OF INVOLVEMENT BY PARTY MEMBERS, 1972 AND 1976
(in percentages)

Response	November 1972	September 1976
	Date of Survey	
CDU/CSU members	8	25
SPD members	44	17
FDP members	7	2
No difference	33	47
Undecided	9	11

NOTE: The survey question was: In your opinion, which party members are most active in the campaign and demonstrate the greatest degree of political commitment?
SOURCE: *Stern*, no. 41 (1976), p. 33.

the first time that this well-known U.S. technique had been used in a Bundestag election.[49] In Table 8–9, the forecasts of Noelle-Neumann and the INFAS institute are contrasted with the official outcome of the election.

The election outcome was a bitter disappointment for the CDU/CSU, for Helmut Kohl, and most especially for Franz Josef Strauss, the leader of the CSU. The Social Democratic-Liberal coalition was confirmed in office—and the quality and reliability of political public opinion polls in the Federal Republic were vindicated (at least until the next wrong forecast in a national or state election).

The political consequences of this election are as yet difficult to assess. The reduction of the coalition's parliamentary majority from 271 to 253 seats does not necessarily constitute a serious disadvantage, especially if it is assumed that internal party and coalition cohesion becomes greater when majorities are small rather than large. Above all, the outcome of the election could enable Chancellor Helmut Schmidt to control extreme left-wing groups within the SPD more effectively than in the past. The real problem facing the coalition is the role of the FDP. On the basis of the public opinion polls, the Liberals had counted on a much better electoral result. The poor showing of the FDP has—not unexpectedly—reopened intraparty debate over whether the FDP should continue to commit itself to a coalition with the SPD or whether an overture toward the CDU/CSU would be more appropriate.

The first significant results of this debate have been decisions by the regional FDP party organizations in Lower Saxony and the Saar to join CDU-controlled state governments. These decisions have been taken despite the danger of jeopardizing the party's unity. Undoubtedly, the FDP's rapprochement with the CDU/CSU can have a serious impact not only on the Bonn government coalition but also on the election chances of the FDP in the state elections coming up after 1977.

Public observers agreed that the Socialist-Liberal coalition in Bonn got off to an extremely bad start. Nevertheless, with the next Bundestag election planned for late 1980, it was clearly much too early to speculate about the future of the present government and its chances for reelection, assuming the SPD and FDP decided to remain allied. A major drawback for the CDU/CSU was the conflict between Helmut Kohl and Franz Josef Strauss and their respective parties. The initial decision of the CSU parliamentary group on November 18,

---

[49] At the time when this chapter was completed, information on the technical details of the study was not yet available.

TABLE 8–9

ELECTION FORECASTS AND THE ELECTION OUTCOME, 1976
(in percentages)

Turnout and Parties	Forecasts			Official Returns			
	IfD		INFAS	1976 Bundestag election		1972 Bundestag election	
	1st ballot	2d ballot	2d ballot	1st ballot	2d ballot	1st ballot	2d ballot
Voter turnout	92.0[a]	92.0	[b]	90.7	90.7	91.1	91.1
CDU/CSU	49.2	48.5	49.0	48.9	48.6	45.4	44.9
SPD	43.5	40.8	41.0	43.7	42.6	48.9	45.8
FDP	6.4	9.6	9.0	6.4	7.9	4.8	8.4
Other parties	0.9	1.1	1.0	1.0	0.9	0.9	0.9

[a] Voter turnout was merely estimated.
[b] No forecast of voter turnout was given.
SOURCE: Election night broadcasts of ZDF and ARD and Federal Statistical Office, Wiesbaden.

1976, to no longer formally enter a unified parliamentary group with the CDU was revoked after massive intervention by members of the CSU and CDU as well as the CDU leadership. Still, the possibility remained that the CSU would decide to establish itself as a national party, thereby cutting directly into the reservoir of CDU voters.

Those intraparty conflicts, poor government performance, continuing high rates of unemployment, and an unsatisfactory rate of economic growth all contributed to a feeling of gloom among West German elites as well as the public.[50] That responsibility for these shortcomings was primarily assigned to the governing SPD-FDP coalition is a normal phenomenon in democratic politics and not a cause for concern. What is extremely important, however, is that the public's dissatisfaction with those in office does not become generalized to the nonpartisan institutions of the political system at large in a way that would threaten identification with the democratic order. As survey data indicated, disenchantment of that kind was not imminent.[51]

Concluding Remarks

In this chapter an attempt has been made to describe the postwar development of public opinion research in Germany and to touch on several problems connected with political opinion polling.

Unquestionably the large number and variety of currently active market and public opinion research institutes guarantee that the findings of political opinion polling are being neither monopolized nor manipulated. Yet this variety will not necessarily safeguard the principle of pluralism of opinion and information. After all, only a few of the institutes are heavily engaged in electoral research, and they are to a certain extent dependent on their clients, who control the dissemination of the data collected. Little by little in Western democratic industrial societies, parliaments, which should exercise control over governments, have typically permitted the control of public opinion research—which because of its innate plebiscitary elements invites abuse anyway—to be shifted to the mass media. As for control by objective scholars, this possibility is not feasible as long as academic institutions and resources remain inadequate.

Both in theory and in practice, public opinion polling, a major technique of empirical research, is well developed in the Federal

---

[50] This climate of opinion is well described in the *New York Times*, July 3, 1977, p. 7.

[51] *Der Spiegel*, "Staatsverdrossenheit: Schon in Ordnung" [Political alienation: an accomplished fact], vol. 31, no. 27 (1977), pp. 25–28.

Republic. Its strengths and weaknesses are well known. Not surprisingly, given its importance for the maintenance and acquisition of political power, it has become on occasion the subject of public debate. This was true in the past and will continue to be true in the future, at the very least as long as scholars are unable to provide a convincing answer to the question of the impact of election forecasts on actual voting behavior.

APPENDIX

Recent Bundestag Election Statistics

Compiled by Richard M. Scammon

All of the data in the following tables are derived from the series *Wahl zum 8. Deutschen Bundestag 1976,* published by the Statistisches Bundesamt in Wiesbaden.

The party abbreviations used in these tables are:

SPD—Sozialdemokratische Partei Deutschlands
(Social Democratic party)

CDU/CSU—Christlich-Demokratische Union Deutschlands/
Christlich-Soziale Union
(Christian Democratic Union/Christian Social Union)

FDP—Freie Demokratische Partei
(Free Democratic party)

In the tables the phrase "party-list voting" refers to the *Zweitstimme,* the second of two votes each German elector casts in voting for the Bundestag. The *Zweitstimme* is a party-list vote as contrasted to the *Erststimme* or first ballot, which is cast directly for a local district member of the Bundestag.

Postwar Distribution of Seats in the Bundestag
(directly elected seats in parentheses)

Election	Total		SPD		CDU/CSU		FDP		Others	
1949	402	(242)	131	(96)	139	(115)	52	(12)	80	(19)
1953	487	(242)	151	(45)	243	(172)	48	(14)	45	(11)
1957	497	(247)	169	(46)	270	(194)	41	(1)	17	(6)
1961	499	(247)	190	(91)	242	(156)	67		—	
1965	496	(248)	202	(94)	245	(154)	49		—	
1969	496	(248)	224	(127)	242	(121)	30		—	
1972	496	(248)	230	(152)	225	(96)	41		—	
1976	496	(248)	214	(114)	243	(134)	39		—	

Popular Vote in the 1976 Bundestag Election (Party-List Voting), by State

State	Total Vote	SPD	CDU/CSU	FDP	Others
Schleswig-Holstein	1,680,086	779,599	740,927	147,622	11,938
Hamburg	1,168,087	614,284	418,994	118,969	15,840
Lower Saxony	4,658,978	2,129,502	2,129,143	369,526	30,807
Bremen	472,988	255,544	153,842	55,903	7,699
North Rhine-Westphalia	10,989,562	5,153,959	4,892,278	860,331	82,994
Hesse	3,558,002	1,626,365	1,593,695	300,864	37,078
Rhineland-Palatinate	2,429,253	1,013,574	1,211,208	183,575	20,896
Baden-Württemberg	5,405,534	1,980,313	2,882,365	489,661	53,195
Bavaria	6,713,695	2,201,692	4,027,499	419,335	65,169
Saar	746,315	344,187	344,850	49,299	7,979
Total, Federal Republic of Germany	37,822,500	16,099,019	18,394,801	2,995,085	333,595

NOTE: The CDU was on the ballot in all states save Bavaria as the CDU; in that state, as the CSU. Principal parties in the "others" category were the National Democratic party (NDP), with 122,661 votes, and the Communist party (DKP), with 118,581 votes. No other party list won as many as 25,000 votes.

DISTRIBUTION OF SEATS IN THE BUNDESTAG, BY STATE, 1976

State	Bundestag			SPD			CDU/CSU			FDP (all seats state list)
	Total	Direct	State	Total	Direct	State	Total	Direct	State	
Schleswig-Holstein	22	11	11	10	6	4	10	5	5	2
Hamburg	14	8	6	8	8	0	5	0	5	1
Lower Saxony	62	30	32	29	18	11	28	12	16	5
Bremen	5	3	2	3	3	0	2	0	2	0
North Rhine-Westphalia	148	73	75	70	45	25	66	28	38	12
Hesse	47	22	25	22	17	5	21	5	16	4
Rhineland-Palatinate	31	16	15	13	6	7	16	10	6	2
Baden-Württemberg	71	36	35	26	4	22	38	32	6	7
Bavaria	88	44	44	29	4	25	53	40	13	6
Saar	8	5	3	4	3	1	4	2	2	0
Total, Federal Republic of Germany	496	248	248	214	114	100	243	134	109	39

NOTE: The heading "Direct" indicates seats won on the first ballot in direct single-member contests. The heading "State" indicates seats won on the second ballot from the state party lists. The workings of the electoral system are described in detail in Chapter 2 in this volume.

Party-List Vote in Bundestag Elections, by State, 1961–1976

State	Election	Turnout	SPD	CDU/CSU	FDP	Others
Schleswig-Holstein	1961	88.0	36.4	41.8	13.8	8.1
	1965	85.9	38.8	48.2	9.4	3.6
	1969	86.0	43.5	46.2	5.2	5.1
	1972	90.5	48.6	42.0	8.6	.8
	1976	90.6	46.4	44.1	8.8	.7
Hamburg	1961	88.6	46.9	31.9	15.7	5.5
	1965	86.4	48.3	37.6	9.4	4.7
	1969	87.6	54.6	34.0	6.3	5.1
	1972	92.2	54.4	33.3	11.2	1.0
	1976	91.1	52.6	35.9	10.2	1.4
Lower Saxony	1961	88.5	38.7	39.0	13.2	9.1
	1965	87.3	39.8	45.8	10.9	3.5
	1969	87.5	43.8	45.2	5.6	5.4
	1972	91.4	48.1	42.7	8.5	.7
	1976	91.4	45.7	45.7	7.9	.7
Bremen	1961	88.2	49.7	27.0	15.2	8.2
	1965	86.1	48.5	34.0	11.7	5.8
	1969	86.3	52.0	32.3	9.3	6.4
	1972	91.0	58.1	29.6	11.1	1.2
	1976	90.0	54.0	32.5	11.8	1.6
North Rhine-Westphalia	1961	88.4	37.3	47.6	11.8	3.4
	1965	87.6	42.6	47.1	7.6	2.7
	1969	87.3	46.8	43.6	5.4	4.2
	1972	91.8	50.4	41.0	7.8	.8
	1976	91.3	46.9	44.5	7.8	.8
Hesse	1961	89.2	42.8	34.9	15.2	7.1
	1965	87.4	45.7	37.8	12.0	4.4
	1969	88.2	48.2	38.4	6.7	6.7
	1972	91.7	48.5	40.3	10.2	1.0
	1976	91.9	45.7	44.8	8.5	1.0

State	Election	Turnout	SPD	CDU/CSU	FDP	Others
Rhineland-Palatinate	1961	88.2	33.5	48.9	13.2	4.4
	1965	88.0	36.7	49.3	10.2	3.8
	1969	87.0	40.1	47.8	6.3	5.8
	1972	91.6	44.9	45.9	8.1	1.1
	1976	91.5	41.7	49.9	7.6	.9
Baden-Württemberg	1961	84.8	32.1	45.3	16.6	6.0
	1965	84.8	33.0	49.9	13.1	4.0
	1969	85.1	36.5	50.7	7.5	5.3
	1972	90.2	38.9	49.8	10.2	1.1
	1976	89.1	36.6	53.3	9.1	1.0
Bavaria	1961	87.2	30.1	54.9	8.7	6.2
	1965	85.9	33.1	55.6	7.3	3.9
	1969	85.2	34.6	54.4	4.1	7.0
	1972	89.8	37.8	55.1	6.1	1.0
	1976	89.6	32.8	60.0	6.2	1.0
Saar	1961	87.7	33.5	49.0	12.9	4.6
	1965	89.2	39.8	46.8	8.6	4.8
	1969	89.1	39.9	46.1	6.7	7.3
	1972	92.9	47.9	43.4	7.1	1.6
	1976	92.9	46.1	46.2	6.6	1.1
Total, Federal Republic of Germany	1961	87.7	36.2	45.3	12.8	5.7
	1965	86.8	39.3	47.6	9.5	3.6
	1969	86.7	42.7	46.1	5.8	5.5
	1972	91.1	45.8	44.9	8.4	.9
	1976	90.7	42.6	48.6	7.9	.9

District Vote in Bundestag Elections, 1972 and 1976
(in percentages)

State and District	October 1976				November 1972			
	SPD	CDU/CSU	FDP	Others	SPD	CDU/CSU	FDP	Others
Schleswig-Holstein								
001 Flensburg-Schleswig	47.6	43.2	8.6	.6	49.4	41.3	8.6	.8
002 Nordfriesland-Dithmarschen-Nord	42.2	48.1	9.0	.6	44.5	46.2	8.5	.9
003 Steinburg-Dithmarschen-Süd	44.5	47.4	7.3	.8	45.7	46.6	6.7	1.0
004 Rendsburg-Eckernförde	45.6	45.5	8.3	.6	46.9	44.5	7.9	.7
005 Kiel	54.6	36.1	8.4	.9	55.5	34.5	9.3	.7
006 Plön-Neumünster	48.2	43.5	7.6	.7	50.1	42.0	7.2	.7
007 Pinneberg	44.6	44.2	10.5	.8	47.0	41.9	10.3	.7
008 Segeberg-Stormarn-Nord	42.0	46.8	10.6	.7	45.3	44.3	9.7	.7
009 Ostholstein	45.5	46.2	7.6	.7	47.9	43.9	7.4	.8
010 Herzogtum Lauenburg-Stormarn-Süd	43.5	45.8	10.0	.7	46.7	43.1	9.5	.7
011 Lübeck	51.4	40.0	7.8	.8	53.9	37.0	8.2	.9
State Total	46.4	44.1	8.8	.7	48.6	42.0	8.6	.8
Hamburg								
012 Hamburg-Mitte	56.8	33.2	8.4	1.7	59.0	30.6	9.2	1.2
013 Altona	48.9	38.9	10.9	1.4	50.9	35.8	12.3	1.0
014 Eimsbüttel	50.3	36.9	11.2	1.7	52.2	34.6	12.1	1.1
015 Hamburg-Nord I	49.7	37.8	10.9	1.6	50.4	35.9	12.6	1.1
016 Hamburg-Nord II	56.6	32.6	9.4	1.4	57.6	30.8	10.5	1.1
017 Wandsbek	46.3	40.2	12.5	1.1	48.5	36.7	13.9	.9

	Col1	Col2	Col3	Col4	Col5	Col6	Col7	Col8
018 Bergedorf	.9	9.6	31.4	58.0	1.1	9.2	34.2	55.5
019 Harburg	1.1	8.8	29.6	60.5	1.1	8.2	32.0	58.8
State Total	1.0	11.2	33.3	54.4	1.4	10.2	35.9	52.6
Lower Saxony								
020 Emden-Leer	.8	6.9	35.1	57.2	.7	6.3	37.8	55.2
021 Wilhelmshaven	.7	8.7	36.8	53.9	.6	7.7	39.6	52.1
022 Oldenburg	1.0	12.5	36.4	50.1	1.1	12.6	39.7	46.6
023 Delmenhorst-Wesermarsch	.9	9.3	35.6	54.1	.7	10.2	38.2	50.9
024 Cuxhaven	.8	7.8	44.1	47.3	.7	7.6	46.1	45.6
025 Stade	1.1	7.8	47.7	43.4	.8	7.6	48.7	42.9
026 Emsland	.6	6.2	59.8	33.4	.6	4.9	61.7	32.9
027 Cloppenburg	.6	4.7	70.6	24.0	.4	5.0	71.2	23.4
028 Hoya	.9	9.4	45.8	43.9	.7	10.1	47.1	42.1
029 Verden	.8	8.0	44.1	47.1	.7	8.2	46.1	45.0
030 Soltau-Harburg	1.0	9.2	47.8	42.0	.7	9.5	50.1	39.7
031 Lüneburg-Lüchow-Dannenberg	.9	8.3	46.8	43.9	.8	7.7	49.9	41.6
032 Lingen	.6	5.0	60.5	33.9	.4	4.7	62.6	32.3
033 Osnabrück	.6	7.8	45.8	45.9	.6	7.8	48.3	43.3
034 Nienburg	.8	10.3	45.6	43.4	.6	9.7	47.9	41.8
035 Schaumburg	.6	8.4	39.2	51.8	.4	7.6	42.9	49.1
036 Hannover I	.7	10.9	34.8	53.6	.9	9.6	38.3	51.2
037 Hannover II	.7	10.6	33.3	55.4	.9	9.4	37.0	52.8
038 Hannover III	.6	10.6	37.8	51.0	.6	9.5	41.9	48.0
039 Celle	1.0	8.3	45.6	45.2	.8	8.4	49.0	41.9
040 Gifhorn	.7	6.6	44.4	48.3	.5	6.3	47.3	45.9
041 Hameln-Springe	.7	8.7	40.9	49.7	.5	7.9	43.5	48.1
042 Holzminden	.6	7.3	37.4	54.7	.5	6.5	40.2	52.8
043 Hildesheim	.6	7.1	41.3	50.9	.5	6.7	44.7	48.1
044 Salzgitter	.6	6.2	37.4	55.8	.6	5.6	40.7	53.2
045 Braunschweig	.7	10.4	36.2	52.7	.8	9.3	40.1	49.8

DISTRICT VOTE IN BUNDESTAG ELECTIONS, 1972 AND 1976 (continued)

State and District	October 1976				November 1972			
	SPD	CDU/CSU	FDP	Others	SPD	CDU/CSU	FDP	Others
046 Helmstedt-Wolfsburg	46.0	46.6	6.8	.6	48.8	42.9	7.6	.7
047 Goslar-Wolfenbüttel	47.8	44.6	7.1	.6	50.6	40.9	7.9	.6
048 Northeim	51.0	41.8	6.6	.6	53.7	38.1	7.4	.7
049 Göttingen	45.8	44.7	8.6	.9	46.7	42.1	10.5	.7
State Total	45.7	45.7	7.9	.7	48.1	42.7	8.5	.7
Bremen								
050 Bremen-Ost	48.6	36.0	13.7	1.7	52.7	32.7	13.5	1.1
051 Bremen-West	58.4	28.3	11.4	1.9	63.3	25.3	10.0	1.5
052 Bremerhaven-Bremen-Nord	56.5	32.1	10.1	1.3	59.5	29.8	9.5	1.2
State Total	54.0	32.5	11.8	1.6	58.1	29.6	11.1	1.2
North Rhine-Westphalia								
053 Aachen-Stadt	42.0	49.1	8.1	.8	44.1	46.5	8.7	.7
054 Aachen-Land	47.7	46.4	5.2	.6	50.8	43.7	4.8	.8
055 Heinsberg	33.7	60.8	5.0	.6	36.3	58.6	4.4	.7
056 Düren	41.8	52.2	5.5	.5	44.6	49.4	5.4	.6
057 Euskirchen-Erftkreis I	40.7	51.4	7.4	.5	43.5	49.0	6.9	.6
058 Erftkreis II	44.6	44.4	10.5	.6	49.0	39.7	10.7	.6
059 Köln I	51.0	38.1	9.4	1.4	54.0	34.0	11.1	.9
060 Köln II	44.1	43.8	11.1	1.0	46.7	39.3	13.3	.7
061 Köln III	51.3	38.6	9.1	1.0	54.1	34.7	10.5	.8
062 Köln IV	52.1	37.7	9.3	.8	55.8	33.2	10.3	.7

No.	Name								
063	Bonn	33.3	54.5	11.3	.8	35.5	51.8	12.0	.7
064	Rhein-Sieg-Kreis I	34.2	55.5	9.7	.5	38.4	51.9	9.1	.6
065	Oberbergischer Kreis-Rhein-Sieg-Kreis II	40.8	49.5	9.1	.6	45.4	44.8	9.1	.7
066	Rheinisch-Bergischer Kreis	39.6	49.1	10.7	.7	44.0	44.7	10.6	.7
067	Leverkusen-Opladen	47.2	41.7	10.3	.7	51.6	37.3	10.3	.7
068	Remscheid	44.4	45.1	9.7	.8	48.4	41.0	9.6	1.0
069	Wuppertal I	44.6	41.6	12.9	.9	50.5	37.9	10.7	.9
070	Wuppertal II	46.8	40.4	11.9	.9	51.8	36.9	10.3	1.0
071	Solingen	46.3	42.5	10.1	1.1	50.2	37.6	10.9	1.2
072	Düsseldorf-Mettmann I	44.5	44.6	10.2	.7	49.2	39.9	10.1	.8
073	Düsseldorf-Mettmann II	44.8	44.1	10.2	.9	48.9	39.8	10.4	.9
074	Düsseldorf I	40.0	47.8	11.2	1.0	43.0	43.4	12.7	.8
075	Düsseldorf II	50.8	39.6	8.5	1.1	54.2	35.2	9.6	1.1
076	Düsseldorf III	46.7	43.5	8.9	1.0	49.3	39.2	10.5	.9
077	Neuss-Grevenbroich I	38.8	51.3	9.3	.7	42.7	47.7	8.9	.7
078	Rheydt-Grevenbroich II	42.6	49.5	7.4	.6	46.4	45.8	7.2	.6
079	Mönchengladbach	38.5	54.1	6.8	.7	42.9	50.5	5.9	.7
080	Krefeld	45.1	44.9	9.2	.8	48.9	41.0	9.4	.7
081	Kempen-Krefeld	37.9	53.8	7.7	.6	41.5	50.8	7.0	.7
082	Moers	60.4	31.6	7.2	.8	63.7	28.4	7.0	.9
083	Kleve	33.9	60.0	5.6	.4	36.2	58.4	4.9	.5
084	Dinslaken	53.4	38.0	8.0	.6	56.0	35.3	8.1	.6
085	Oberhausen	58.3	34.8	6.2	.7	61.1	32.3	5.9	.7
086	Mülheim	55.6	34.4	9.2	.8	59.1	30.9	9.3	.7
087	Essen I	58.8	34.0	6.3	.9	62.0	31.1	6.0	.8
088	Essen II	65.1	28.9	5.0	.9	67.7	26.3	5.1	.9
089	Essen III	45.3	44.1	9.8	.8	48.3	40.7	10.4	.7
090	Duisburg I	66.2	28.0	5.0	.8	68.7	25.5	5.0	.8
091	Duisburg II	56.5	35.4	7.2	.9	59.8	32.2	7.3	.8
092	Ahaus-Bocholt	29.6	66.2	3.8	.4	31.8	64.0	3.8	.5

DISTRICT VOTE IN BUNDESTAG ELECTIONS, 1972 AND 1976 (continued)

State and District	October 1976				November 1972			
	SPD	CDU/CSU	FDP	Others	SPD	CDU/CSU	FDP	Others
093 Tecklenburg	40.2	51.5	7.8	.5	42.9	49.1	7.5	.5
094 Beckum-Warendorf	39.1	54.2	6.0	.7	41.9	52.2	5.3	.6
095 Münster	37.8	50.6	10.4	1.1	40.9	47.8	10.7	.6
096 Steinfurt-Coesfeld	34.1	60.4	5.1	.4	36.9	58.1	4.6	.4
097 Gelsenkirchen I	63.1	31.0	5.0	1.0	65.3	28.8	4.9	1.0
098 Gelsenkirchen II	63.5	30.4	5.1	1.0	65.6	28.4	5.0	1.0
099 Recklinghausen-Land	52.7	40.7	5.8	.8	55.3	38.0	5.9	.8
100 Recklinghausen-Stadt	55.3	38.4	5.6	.7	57.3	36.0	5.9	.8
101 Bottrop-Gladbeck	61.0	33.0	4.4	1.6	63.3	31.0	4.6	1.1
102 Höxter	27.3	67.9	4.5	.4	29.4	66.4	3.7	.5
103 Bielefeld I	43.9	45.2	10.3	.6	47.9	41.7	9.6	.8
104 Bielefeld II	47.6	41.3	10.2	.9	51.5	38.1	9.7	.8
105 Detmold-Lippe	47.1	41.6	10.6	.7	51.5	37.6	10.1	.8
106 Paderborn-Wiedenbrück	27.2	65.9	6.4	.4	30.7	63.5	5.3	.5
107 Herford	50.3	40.7	8.4	.6	54.3	36.7	8.2	.8
108 Minden	48.3	42.0	9.1	.6	51.2	38.9	9.1	.8
109 Lüdinghausen	46.6	47.5	5.3	.6	49.7	44.7	4.9	.7
110 Wanne-Eickel-Wattenscheid	62.3	31.7	5.1	.9	64.6	29.3	5.2	.9
111 Herne-Castrop-Rauxel	62.0	32.3	4.8	.9	63.8	30.5	4.9	.8
112 Ennepe-Ruhr-Kreis	53.2	37.4	8.6	.8	56.8	33.6	8.7	.9
113 Hagen	51.6	39.5	8.0	.9	55.9	35.3	7.8	.9
114 Dortmund I	54.2	36.2	8.6	1.0	56.7	33.6	8.9	1.1
115 Dortmund II	65.7	28.6	4.7	.9	67.8	26.4	4.9	.9

116	Dortmund III	60.0	32.8	6.1	1.1	62.4	30.4	6.4	.9
117	Bochum	57.9	34.2	6.9	1.0	60.5	31.4	7.2	.9
118	Bochum-Witten	61.9	30.9	6.4	.9	64.1	28.4	6.6	.9
119	Iserlohn	46.9	44.5	7.9	.7	50.9	40.8	7.5	.8
120	Lippstadt-Brilon	35.7	58.2	5.5	.5	39.3	54.9	5.3	.6
121	Olpe-Meschede	29.8	65.5	4.3	.4	32.9	62.5	4.2	.5
122	Arnsberg-Soest	38.4	54.5	6.5	.6	42.1	50.5	6.7	.7
123	Unna	58.3	34.1	6.9	.8	61.4	31.2	6.4	.9
124	Lüdenscheid	48.0	42.2	9.1	.8	52.4	37.4	9.4	.8
125	Siegen-Wittgenstein	45.8	43.5	10.0	.7	49.1	39.1	11.0	.9
	State Total	46.9	44.5	7.8	.8	50.4	41.0	7.8	.8
	Hesse								
126	Waldeck	49.0	42.1	8.2	.8	50.6	39.4	9.0	1.0
127	Kassel	52.9	36.7	9.2	1.2	55.5	32.7	11.0	.9
128	Werra-Meissner	56.9	35.7	6.7	.7	60.5	31.5	7.3	.8
129	Fritzlar	50.0	42.1	7.2	.7	51.5	39.0	8.6	.9
130	Hersfeld	48.8	44.3	6.3	.6	51.4	40.5	7.3	.8
131	Marburg	46.2	45.1	7.0	1.7	47.8	41.6	9.3	1.2
132	Wetzlar	47.8	43.1	8.2	.9	50.2	37.6	11.2	1.1
133	Giessen	46.4	44.5	8.0	1.0	48.9	40.3	9.8	1.1
134	Fulda	34.7	58.5	6.0	.7	38.2	54.2	6.8	.8
135	Hochtaunus	38.9	49.8	10.4	.9	41.7	45.2	12.1	1.0
136	Wetterau	46.5	44.6	8.0	.9	50.2	39.8	8.9	1.1
137	Limburg	39.2	52.6	7.5	.7	41.7	49.6	7.9	.8
138	Wiesbaden	44.3	44.2	10.4	1.1	46.7	39.9	12.3	1.1
139	Hanau	46.0	44.8	8.1	1.1	48.9	40.1	9.8	1.2
140	Frankfurt (Main) I–Main-Taunus	45.0	43.8	10.0	1.2	48.3	38.4	12.1	1.2
141	Frankfurt (Main) II	42.3	44.6	11.5	1.6	45.1	39.5	14.3	1.1
142	Frankfurt (Main) III	44.7	42.9	10.6	1.7	47.8	37.9	13.1	1.2

DISTRICT VOTE IN BUNDESTAG ELECTIONS, 1972 AND 1976 (continued)

State and District	October 1976				November 1972			
	SPD	CDU/CSU	FDP	Others	SPD	CDU/CSU	FDP	Others
143 Gross-Gerau	49.1	41.6	8.3	1.0	52.9	36.4	9.7	1.1
144 Offenbach	45.4	44.0	9.4	1.1	48.9	38.2	12.0	1.0
145 Darmstadt	47.4	41.0	10.2	1.3	49.4	36.6	12.8	1.2
146 Dieburg	45.1	46.4	7.4	1.1	48.5	41.8	8.5	1.2
147 Bergstrasse	44.2	47.8	7.1	.9	46.8	44.2	8.0	1.0
State Total	45.7	44.8	8.5	1.0	48.5	40.3	10.2	1.0
Rhineland-Palatinate								
148 Neuwied	41.7	50.0	7.8	.5	44.4	46.2	8.8	.5
149 Ahrweiler	34.0	60.1	5.4	.5	36.9	57.1	5.5	.5
150 Koblenz	40.3	51.8	7.3	.6	43.1	48.6	7.6	.7
151 Cochem	30.0	60.7	8.6	.7	32.1	57.7	9.3	.9
152 Kreuznach	47.1	41.4	10.6	.8	50.3	38.6	10.0	1.0
153 Bitburg	25.0	68.9	5.4	.6	28.5	65.4	5.4	.7
154 Trier	37.1	56.4	5.8	.7	41.1	52.1	6.0	.8
155 Montabaur	42.8	49.3	7.3	.5	46.0	45.2	8.0	.7
156 Mainz	43.7	45.3	10.1	.8	45.6	41.5	11.9	.9
157 Worms	49.4	41.2	8.3	1.1	51.8	37.1	9.5	1.6
158 Frankenthal	49.9	41.1	7.6	1.5	54.0	36.5	7.8	1.7
159 Ludwigshafen	51.5	41.0	6.7	.9	55.1	36.1	7.7	1.2
160 Neustadt-Speyer	41.7	50.1	7.2	1.1	45.8	45.3	7.6	1.3
161 Kaiserslautern	49.9	41.5	7.2	1.3	52.9	37.3	7.7	2.1
162 Pirmasens	41.0	51.5	6.2	1.3	44.4	47.0	6.9	1.7

163 Landau	37.4	53.4	8.2	1.0	41.0	48.8	8.8	1.3
State Total	41.7	49.9	7.6	.9	44.9	45.9	8.1	1.1
Baden-Württemberg								
164 Stuttgart I	46.7	41.3	11.0	1.0	48.7	37.3	12.9	1.1
165 Stuttgart II	42.1	43.2	13.6	1.1	43.5	39.0	16.4	1.0
166 Stuttgart III	40.5	44.4	14.1	1.0	41.6	40.8	16.7	.9
167 Ludwigsburg	40.5	47.3	11.3	.9	42.5	43.1	13.2	1.2
168 Heilbronn	41.6	47.5	10.1	.8	43.9	42.3	12.8	1.1
169 Leonberg-Vaihingen	39.0	48.3	11.9	.8	41.7	44.4	12.9	1.0
170 Nürtingen	35.0	53.5	10.5	.9	37.1	50.0	11.4	1.4
171 Esslingen	39.3	49.2	10.7	.8	41.6	45.9	11.5	.9
172 Göppingen	39.5	50.2	9.4	.8	43.2	46.4	9.5	.9
173 Ulm	37.3	53.1	8.7	1.0	39.3	50.7	9.1	.9
174 Aalen-Heidenheim	36.9	55.5	6.9	.7	39.2	51.9	8.1	.9
175 Schwäbisch Gmünd-Backnang	36.4	53.8	8.9	1.0	38.8	49.8	10.3	1.1
176 Crailsheim	31.6	57.3	10.0	1.1	32.9	53.2	12.0	2.0
177 Waiblingen	38.7	48.0	12.3	.9	41.9	43.5	13.7	1.0
178 Karlsruhe	40.9	48.3	9.7	1.1	41.8	45.4	11.5	1.2
179 Mannheim I	53.1	38.7	6.7	1.6	56.5	34.4	7.6	1.4
180 Mannheim II	44.4	45.7	8.8	1.0	46.8	41.7	10.3	1.2
181 Heidelberg-Stadt	42.4	47.6	8.6	1.4	43.4	44.4	10.8	1.4
182 Pforzheim-Karlsruhe-Land I	38.0	52.4	8.5	1.1	40.8	49.0	9.1	1.1
183 Bruchsal-Karlsruhe-Land II	36.4	56.9	5.7	1.0	38.6	53.5	6.5	1.4
184 Heidelberg-Land-Sinsheim	37.6	53.5	7.9	1.0	39.9	49.8	9.1	1.2
185 Tauberbischofsheim	30.1	63.1	6.0	.8	31.4	60.9	6.8	1.0
186 Konstanz	34.1	55.6	9.3	.9	37.0	51.6	10.4	1.0
187 Donaueschingen	33.9	57.0	8.1	1.0	36.3	53.4	9.3	1.1
188 Waldshut	32.8	57.9	8.2	1.1	34.4	55.6	9.0	1.1
189 Lörrach-Müllheim	39.3	49.1	10.2	1.3	42.3	45.2	11.1	1.4

DISTRICT VOTE IN BUNDESTAG ELECTIONS, 1972 AND 1976 (continued)

State and District	October 1976				November 1972			
	SPD	CDU/CSU	FDP	Others	SPD	CDU/CSU	FDP	Others
190 Freiburg	38.3	48.4	11.9	1.4	38.9	45.3	14.9	.9
191 Emmendingen-Wolfach	34.5	56.0	8.4	1.1	35.9	54.5	8.5	1.1
192 Offenburg	36.1	55.5	7.5	1.0	37.8	52.7	8.1	1.4
193 Rastatt	32.9	60.2	6.2	.7	34.4	57.6	6.8	1.1
194 Reutlingen	36.0	52.4	10.3	1.2	37.6	49.6	11.5	1.3
195 Calw	33.6	56.3	8.9	1.1	36.9	52.1	9.9	1.1
196 Rottweil	30.6	61.2	7.3	.9	34.2	57.4	7.3	1.1
197 Balingen	28.3	63.6	7.2	.9	30.0	61.2	7.7	1.1
198 Biberach	21.0	73.2	5.2	.7	23.4	71.1	4.8	.7
199 Ravensburg	25.4	66.8	7.0	.8	28.3	64.0	6.9	.8
State Total	36.6	53.3	9.1	1.0	38.9	49.8	10.2	1.1
Bavaria								
200 Altötting	24.5	70.4	4.3	.7	29.0	66.4	3.8	.8
201 Freising	29.3	62.7	7.2	.8	34.7	58.4	6.1	.9
202 Fürstenfeldbruck	30.2	60.5	8.5	.8	36.4	55.4	7.3	.9
203 Ingolstadt	29.4	65.6	4.2	.8	34.2	61.1	3.7	1.0
204 München-Mitte	41.9	46.1	10.5	1.6	48.1	40.7	10.2	1.0
205 München-Nord	43.1	45.2	10.5	1.2	50.6	38.7	9.7	1.0
206 München-Ost	40.1	47.8	10.9	1.2	48.1	40.5	10.4	1.0
207 München-Süd	39.2	47.3	12.3	1.2	46.9	40.5	11.6	.9
208 München-West	38.6	49.4	10.9	1.1	46.2	42.6	10.3	1.0
209 München-Land	28.7	58.5	11.9	.9	36.0	52.4	10.9	.8

210 Rosenheim	1.0	6.1	58.8	34.1	1.0	6.8	63.9	28.4
211 Traunstein	1.0	5.4	63.2	30.4	1.0	6.0	68.2	24.8
212 Weilheim	.8	5.6	61.1	32.4	.8	6.3	66.4	26.5
213 Deggendorf	.8	2.3	68.7	28.1	.8	2.5	72.7	23.9
214 Landshut	1.0	3.7	63.5	31.8	.9	4.4	67.4	27.3
215 Passau	.9	2.5	65.4	31.2	.8	3.3	67.9	28.0
216 Rottal-Inn	.8	2.8	68.9	27.5	.9	3.6	71.9	23.7
217 Straubing	.8	2.9	65.7	30.5	1.0	3.2	69.7	26.1
218 Amberg	1.2	3.8	62.3	32.7	1.0	4.2	66.4	28.4
219 Regensburg	1.2	3.8	60.1	34.9	1.0	4.4	64.8	29.7
220 Schwandorf	.9	2.5	64.1	32.6	1.8	2.4	67.4	28.5
221 Weiden	.9	3.5	58.2	37.4	.8	3.4	62.7	33.1
222 Bamberg	.9	4.0	62.9	32.3	.8	4.4	67.0	27.9
223 Bayreuth	1.3	5.5	50.5	42.7	1.0	5.4	55.6	38.1
224 Coburg	.8	5.3	45.5	48.4	.7	4.9	49.9	44.4
225 Hof	1.0	5.4	42.6	51.1	.9	4.4	46.5	48.2
226 Kulmbach	1.1	4.0	55.3	39.6	.9	3.6	60.3	35.2
227 Ansbach	1.3	7.4	59.7	31.5	.9	6.5	63.2	29.3
228 Erlangen	1.1	8.9	45.9	44.1	1.1	9.0	50.5	39.5
229 Fürth	1.4	7.7	45.7	45.2	1.3	7.0	51.2	40.5
230 Nürnberg-Nord	1.5	9.8	39.8	49.0	1.4	8.5	45.3	44.8
231 Nürnberg-Süd	1.5	8.0	35.1	55.3	1.4	7.2	41.0	50.5
232 Roth	1.2	6.4	54.3	38.1	1.0	5.9	59.4	33.7
233 Aschaffenburg	.9	5.1	53.7	40.3	.7	4.9	58.2	36.2
234 Bad Kissingen	.8	5.1	66.7	27.4	.6	4.8	70.3	24.3
235 Main-Spessart	.8	4.9	60.2	34.2	.7	4.6	63.5	31.2
236 Schweinfurt	1.2	5.5	57.2	36.1	1.1	5.2	61.3	32.4
237 Würzburg	.8	6.7	53.5	39.0	.8	6.6	57.4	35.2
238 Augsburg-Stadt	1.1	6.0	45.9	46.9	1.3	6.4	51.4	41.0
239 Augsburg-Land	1.0	4.4	63.3	31.3	.8	5.1	67.7	26.4
240 Donau-Ries	.9	4.3	64.3	30.5	.7	4.5	68.5	26.2

DISTRICT VOTE IN BUNDESTAG ELECTIONS, 1972 AND 1976 (continued)

State and District	October 1976				November 1972			
	SPD	CDU/CSU	FDP	Others	SPD	CDU/CSU	FDP	Others
241 Neu-Ulm	32.1	60.9	6.1	.9	35.8	57.6	5.7	.9
242 Oberallgäu	28.8	62.9	7.4	.8	34.2	57.8	7.3	.8
243 Unterallgäu	24.1	69.7	5.2	1.0	28.2	65.4	5.2	1.3
State Total	32.8	60.0	6.2	1.0	37.8	55.1	6.1	1.0
Saar								
244 Saarbrücken I	48.1	41.1	9.5	1.3	50.4	37.3	10.5	1.9
245 Saarbrücken II	46.8	46.0	6.1	1.1	47.9	43.5	6.8	1.7
246 Saarlouis	42.9	50.2	6.0	.9	45.0	48.1	5.7	1.3
247 Sankt Wendel	44.0	50.3	4.8	.9	45.8	47.9	5.0	1.3
248 Homburg	48.7	43.4	6.8	1.1	50.4	40.6	7.5	1.6
State Total	46.1	46.2	6.6	1.1	47.9	43.4	7.1	1.6
Total, Federal Republic of Germany	42.6	48.6	7.9	.9	45.8	44.9	8.4	.9

CONTRIBUTORS

DAVID CONRADT is associate professor of political science at the University of Florida. A Fulbright scholar at the University of Constance in 1978–1979, he has written widely on voting behavior and party politics in West Germany. Most recently he has published *The German Polity*.

HEINO KAACK is professor of political science at the Teachers College of Rhineland-Palatinate, Koblenz, and at the University of Bonn, and is the editor of *Parteien-Jahrbuch* [Party yearbook] providing documentation and analysis of the most recent developments of the German party system. He is the author of the authoritative *Geschichte und Struktur des deutschen Parteiensystems* [History and structure of the German party system].

MAX KAASE is professor of political science at the University of Mannheim and director of the Mannheim-based research institute Zentrum für Umfragen, Methoden und Analysen. A frequent visiting scholar in the United States, he has published a number of journal articles on German voting behavior.

WERNER KALTEFLEITER is professor of political science and vice-president of the University of Kiel. He is the editor of the yearbook *Verfassung und Verfassungswirklichkeit* [The living constitution] and the author of the 1977 issue *Vorspiel zum Wechsel* [Prelude to change], an analysis of the 1976 general election.

GERHARD LOEWENBERG is professor of political science at the University of Iowa, where he also serves as director of the Comparative Legislative Research Center. He is the author of *Parliament in the German*

Political System and *Modern Parliaments: Change or Decline?* He is currently working on the role of European parliaments in the management of social conflict.

PAUL NOACK is professor of political science at the Institute of Political Science of the Faculty of Social Sciences at the University of Munich. A former journalist, he is particularly interested in foreign policy questions and has recently published a book on the defeat of the European Defense Community.

RICHARD M. SCAMMON is director of the Elections Research Center in Washington, D.C. He has edited the biennial statistical series, *America Votes,* since 1956 and is the coauthor of *This U.S.A.* and *The Real Majority.*

KLAUS SCHÖNBACH is Akademischer Rat at the University of Münster and former associate of the Zentrum für Umfragen, Methoden und Analysen in Mannheim. His most recent publications include *Trennung von Nachricht und Meinung* [Separation of news and opinion].

KURT SONTHEIMER is professor of political science at the Geschwister-Scholl Institute of the University of Munich. He has written extensively on the political systems of West and East Germany as well as Great Britain. He is the author of the American textbook *The Government and Politics of West Germany.*

RUDOLF WILDENMANN is professor of political science and rector at the University of Mannheim. A television commentator and frequent contributor to newspapers and periodicals on German elections, he has written extensively on the role of the German media and political parties, including the authoritative *Macht und Konsens als Problem der Innen- und Aussenpolitik* [Power and consensus as a problem of domestic and foreign politics].

INDEX

election, *1976*, 66–67, 70–71; intellectuals, 64, 75; leadership, 63–65, 117; media, 186–88, 190; *Ostpolitik*, 37–38, 62; party revitalization, 38n, 39n; public image, *115–17*, 131, *133*, 159; resignation, 63–64, 85, 118, 215; SPD leader, 63–64; Wähler-Initiative, 67; youth, 54

Bremen: age patterns, *1976 FDP, 108*; elections, *1970–76 FDP*, 102–3, 106–7; election, *1976*, 72, 139; elections, state-federal comparisons, *121, 123, 125*; FDP/SPD coalition, 90; SPD, 68

British zone, 9

Bundeshochschulrahmengesetz. See Education, federal university law

Bundesrat: CDU/CSU control, 62–63, 89–91, 105, 109, 164, 180; Polish treaty, 129, 159; state elections, 87; veto power, 87

Bunte, 171

BVP. *See* Bavarian People's party

Capital, 171, 213

Capitalism: Godesberg program, 60; Young Socialists, 61

Carstens, Karl: CDU leader, 113–14, 165; "Freedom instead of/or Socialism," 156; public opinion, *141–42*

Carter, Jimmy, 131, 138

Catholic Center party, 3–4, 6; postwar, 10

Catholics: abortion, 126, 130; BVP, 148; CDU/CSU, 21, 50–51, 114, 140, 143, 148, 151; by region, 140; voting influence, 50–52, *109*

CDU, 6, 30; "Ahlen Program," 157; in Bavaria, 165–66; campaign, *1976*, 131–32, 134, 136, 138–39; CSU conflict, 38, 143–44, 154–56, 163–67; "Day of Europe," 131; elections, *1928–49*, 7; elections, *1946–76*, *18*; elections, state, 118; FDP/SPD coalition, 86–87; FDP state alliance, 110; Mannheim convention, *1975*, 127–28; new middle class, 21; organization, 38–39, 116n; Polish treaty, 159–60; postwar re-emergence, 10–11; public opinion, 43, 115–17, *133*; and UN, 113. *See also* CDU/CSU.

CDU/CSU, 27; abortion, 126; age group support, *55*; Barzel ouster, *57*, 111, 113–14; Bundesrat control, 62–63, 89–91, 109; campaign, *1976*, 37, 48, 100, 186–87; Catholics, 50–51, *53*, 140, 143; constructive vote of no confidence, 111; election, *1976*, 31–32, 48–50, 139–40, 143, 222–24; election, *1976*, forecast *v. outcome*, 223; elections, state, 57–58, 61, 215; elections, state-federal comparison, 112, 120–21; finance, 48; "Freedom instead of/or Socialism," 93, 99, 132, 135, 157, 211; Grand Coalition, 59, 78; IFD affiliation, 206, 210; leadership, *1976*, 38; middle class, 48, 70; "north-south" cleavage, 54n; organization, 40, 80; personality *v.* policy, 157; Polish treaty, 92, 129; polling use, 206, 210; public opinion, *46*, 206, *210*, *217*, *219*, *221*; regional strength, 140, 142–43; rural areas, 72; spiral of silence concept, 40–42; ticket splitting, 33, 35, 104–5; women, 73, 128; youth, 128. *See also* CDU; CSU

Center party (Zentrum), 9, 148

Christian Democratic Union. *See* CDU; CDU/CSU

Christian Social Union. *See* CSU; CDU/CSU

Cities. *See* Urban areas

Coalition. *See* Grand Coalition

Cohen, B.C., 190

Communist party (KPD), 134; East Germany, 16; elections, *1928–1949*, 7; Nazi outlaw, 4; postwar, 10–11; public opinion, 17; working class, 3; youth, 59

Concentration camps, 10, 21

Constitution. *See* Basic Law

Constitutions, state: drafting, 11–12

CSU: age groups in Bavaria, 162–63; Basic Law, 149; Bavarian base, 114, 149; campaign, *1976*, 154–60; CDU conflicts, 38, 143–44, 154–56, 163–67; Center party successor, 6; conservatism, 143, 147–48, 155, 159; elections, *1928–1949*, 7; elections, *1946–76*, *18*; election, *1976*, 160–67; FDP state coalition, 166; "fourth party" threat, 143–44, 154–55, 165, 224; "Freedom instead of/or Socialism," 40, 156–58; membership, 41, 152–54; middle class, 153–54; nationalism, 151; organization, 144–49; Polish treaties, 159–60; public opinion, *115–17*; as regional party, 148–49; rural areas, 114–15, 153; social class, 161–62; women, 162–63; working class, *154*, 158. *See also* CDU/CSU; Strauss

Dahrendorf, Ralf, 9
"Day of Europe," 131
DDP. *See* German Democratic party
DNVP. *See* German National People's party
Dortmund convention, 64–66
DP. *See* German party
Dregger, Alfred: "Freedom instead of/ or Socialism," 156; public opinion, 141–42
DRP. *See* German Right party

Eastern Europe, 44; Brandt, 37–38, 62; East Germany, 9, 16, 63. *See also* Ostpolitik; Soviet Union
Economic reconstruction (WAV), 7
Economy: Brandt-Schmidt policies, 62–64; campaign, *1976*, 64–65, 136–37, 139, 178–79; energy crisis, 63, 84; GNP, 17; recession, *1966–69*, 23. *See also* Industry
Education: employment gap, 136; federal university law, 63; National Democratic party, 23; new middle class, 20–21; university reform, 44, 54, 63; vote determinant, 45, *53*, 55, 81–82
Electoral system: Basic Law, 11–14, 16–17; candidate selection, 31–33, 35–36, 57; mechanics of, 30–31; minimum-vote requirement, 12–16; Parliamentary Council, 12–13; public finance, 25, 47–48, 214, 216; ticket splitting, 4, 33–35, 104–6, 213. *See also* Political parties; *specific party*
EMNID, 205–6, 210, 212, 216
Emsland, 71
Energy crisis. *See* Economy
Eppler, Erhard, 130–31
Erhard, Ludwig, 10, 151, 157
Ertl, Josef, 45, 97
Expellees: All-German Bloc, *18*; industrial growth, 17; political parties, 11. *See also* Refugees

FAZ. *See* *Frankfurter Allgemeine Zeitung*
FDP, 27, 40; age group support, 55; Bavaria, *151*; campaign, *1976*, 95–98, 100–102, 186–87; Catholics, 52, 55; CDU coalition, 84, 86–93, 166, 222; CSU and, 166; elections, *1928–49 comparisons*, 7; *elections, 1946–76, 18*; election, *1976*, 222–23; elections, *federal-state comparisons, 102–3, 112,*

124–25; elections, *state, 84–88, 102–3,* 105–7; finance, 47–48, 100–101; "Freedom instead of/or Socialism," *135*; "Freedom-Progress-Achievement," 98; Freiburg Theses, 83–84; Grand Coalition, 82–83; liberal tradition, 6, 78–80, 94–97, 100–102, 104; Mainz conference, *1975*, 93; membership, 83, 221; middle class, 22–23, 50, 55, 78; opinion polling, 93–95, 206; organization, 80–81, 100–101; *Ostpolitik*, 57; party identification, 45, 108; Polish treaty, 129; public opinion, 44, 78, *133*, *217*, *219*; rural areas, 35; self-sufficiency strategy, 77–83; social classes, 81–82; SPD alignment, 45–46, 48–50, 52, 55, 57–59, 70–71, 82–84, 86–93, 98, 166, 215–16, 222; Strauss dislike, 144; as swing party, 77–78; ticket splitting, 33–35, 46, 104–5; urban areas, 52; women, 96–97, 107; youth, 54–55
Federal Constitutional Court, 16
Filbinger, Hans, 130, 156
Finance. *See* Electoral system, public finance
Flach, Karl-Hermann, 79–80, 84
Ford, Gerald, 138
FR. *See* *Frankfurter Rundschau*
Franconia: CSU strength, 151–53, 161–62; "fourth party" idea, 165. *See also* Bavaria
Frankfurt, 61, 68
Frankfurter Allgemeine Zeitung (FAZ), 172, 209; bias, 173, 176; domestic policy, 178–79; on extremes, 180; "Freedom instead of/or Socialism," 91; on parties, 179; theme coverage, 177, 181, 185–90
Frankfurter Rundschau (FR), 172; bias, 173; "Freedom instead of/or Socialism," 191; on parties, 179; theme coverage, 176–77, 181, 185–88; themes and public opinion, 189–90
Free Democratic party. *See* FDP
"Freedom instead of/or Socialism": Biedenkopf on, 40, 136, 138; CSU use, 156–58; "Day of Europe," 131; Kohl on, 40; media, 134, 177–78, 191; origin, 130, 132, 156; public opinion, 42, 211, 216; SPD response, 68–70, 99, 132; state elections, 40
Freiburg Theses, 83–84
French zone, 11
Friderichs, Hans, 45, 97; public image, 115–17

Lower Saxony, 129; Albrecht election, 91–92; election, *1972, 102–3*; election, *1976*, 72, 105–7; elections, *state*, 58, 85, *102–3*, 118; 139; elections, *state-federal comparison, 102–3, 120, 122, 124*; FDP, 87, 94, 102–3, 105–7, *108*, 110; SPD, 72

Maihofer, Werner, 45, 97
MARPLAN, 203, 212; size, *205*
Matthäus, Ingrid, 96–97
Media: campaign themes, *1976 coverage*, 181–88; campaign themes, *public opinion, 1976*, 188–90; credibility of, 172; and economy, 178–79; "Freedom instead of/or Socialism" slogan, 191; influence of, 170–73; political leaders, 18, 186–88; public opinion, 172–73; role, 213–15; on Strauss, 179; variety, 171–73. *See also specific newspaper*; Television
Mendes, Erich, 78
Middle class: CDU/CSU base, 48, 80; and CSU, 153–54; Grand Coalition, 59; new salaried, 17, 20–23, 26; by region, *141*; SPD/FDP, 48, 55, 61, *109*
Minimum-vote requirement, 12–16. *See also* Electoral system
Modell Deutschland, 65–66, 69
Monarchy, 25
Müller, Joseph, 149–50
Munich: election, *1976*, 160; SPD, 61, 68, 71, 150–51

National Democratic party (NPD), 14, 23, 151
Nationalism, 3–4, 151
National Liberal party, 151
National Opinion Research Center (NORC), 200
National Socialist party (NSDAP), 7; Allied military government, 6; membership, 26; political party effect, 4–9
Neue Revue, 171
Neumann, Erich Peter, 199
Noelle-Neumann, Elisabeth, 199, 201, 206, 220–22; spiral of silence concept, 40–41
NORC. *See* National Opinion Research Center
North Rhine-Westphalia, 58, 144; age groups, *108*; elections, *1970–76 FDP, 102–3*, 106–7; elections, *1972–76 federal*, 71–72, 139; elections, *state*, 58; elections, *state-federal compari-*

son, 122, 123, 125; FDP vote analysis, 93–94; FDP/SPD coalition, 88–89
NPD. *See* National Democratic party
NSDAP. *See* National Socialist party
Nuremberg, 151

Office of the Military Government, United States (OMGUS), 198. *See also* Allied military government
Office of the U.S. High Commissioner for Germany (HICOG), 198
Ollenhauer, Erich, 131
OMGUS. *See* Office of the Military Government, United States
Ostpolitik: Barzel on, 149; Brandt's, 37–38, 62; election, *1972*, 37–38, 49, 57; election, *1976*, 44, 68, 90
"Out of Love for Germany," 132

Palatinate (Bavaria): election, *1976*, 161–62. *See also* Bavaria
Parliamentary Council. *See* Electoral system
Party Finance Law, *1967*, 48
Poland: German treaty, 92, 129, 159–60
Political parties: Allied military government, 4, 6, 9–17; consolidation, *1928–76*, 6, *8*; finance, 25, 47–49, 80–81, 100–101, 214, 216; fragmentation, early, 4; legal rights, 25–26; origins, 2–3; membership, 26–27, 38, 140; minimum-vote requirement effect, 13–16; new middle class, 17, 20–23; Noelle-Neumann, 40–42; "north-south" cleavage, *54n*; opinion research, *204*; public opinion, 25–27, 40–42, *217, 219*; regional/special interest, 4, 7, 11, 148–49; stability, 27, 55–56. *See also* Electoral system; *specific party*
Polling. *See* Public opinion
Press and Information Agency, 206–7
Proportional representation. *See* Electoral system, Basic Law
Protestants: and CSU, 151; party preference, *1972–76, 51–53*; SPD, 55
Public opinion: Cologne election study, *1961*, 200–201; conservatism, *1976*, 128; FDP, *1976*, 78, 93–96; "Freedom instead of/or Socialism," 42, 135; party polling use, 39, 204–6; party system, 23–26, 46–47, *115–17*, 216–17, *219, 221*; platforms v. politicians, *1976*, 188–90; polling access, 203, 207–8; polling costs, 214; polling controversy, 195–97, 208–13; polling de-

Stern, Der, 47, 171; polling use, 214, 218–19

Stoltenberg, Gerhard, 134; biography, 126; "Freedom instead of/or Socialism," 130, 132; public image, 114–17, 133, 141–42

Strauss, Franz Josef, 72, 88, 129; biography, 149–50; CDU/CSU conflict, 38, 40, 126, 143–44, 164–67; conservatism, 149–50; election, *1976,* 44, 66–67, 155, 158; FDP coalition, 91; fourth party threat, 154–55; "Freedom instead of/or Socialism," 68–69, 130, 156–57; media, *1976,* 179–80; *Ostpolitik,* 57; public image, *115–17,* 133, 140–42; Sonthofen speech, 118–19, 130; Spiegel affair, 149; TV debate, *1976,* 47, 70, 99, 138

Stücklen, Richard, 156

Süddeutsche Zeitung (SZ), 191; bias, 172–73, 180; campaign themes, *coverage,* 176–79, 181, 185–88; campaign themes, *public opinion,* 189–91; "Freedom instead of/or Socialism," 178, 191; political leaders, 179–80, 183

Swabia: and CSU, 151, *153;* election, *1976,* 161–62; fourth party idea, 165

Tandler, Gerold, 156, 158–60

Television: CDU use, 134; credibility of, 170; CSU use, 159; debate, *1976,* 99, 104, 138; networks, 169–70; public opinion, 170

Thatcher, Margaret, 131

Ticket splitting: elections, *1957–76,* 33–35; election, *1972,* 104–6; election, 44; in Empire, 4. *See also* Electoral system; Second ballot

Time Public Relations, 95

Trade unions: election, *1976,* 68, 72, 138; regional strength, *144;* SPD, 68

Unemployment, 63–64, 91, 130; campaign, *1976,* 136–37; energy crisis, 84; youth, 136. *See also* Economy

United Nations, 113

United States Information Agency (USIA), 198

Universities. *See* Education

Upper class, 141

Urban areas: CDU/CSU, 55; SPD, 60; voting patterns, *1970–76,* 50–53, *109*

USIA. *See* United States Information Agency

Vogel, Hans-Jochen, 151, 160

von Hayek, Friedrich, 61, 156

von Stackelberg, Karl-Georg, 210

"Vote freedom!" 132

Wähler-Initiative, 67

WAV. *See* Economic reconstruction

Weber, Max, 113

Wehner, Herbert, 63–64, *115–17*

Weimar Republic, 9, 21, 54, 56, 148; leadership, 10–11; minimum-vote requirement, 12, 16; party system, 26–27; proportional representation, 4, 12, 14; public opinion, 24–25; social class, 20

Welt, Die: bias, 172–73; campaign themes, *coverage,* 176–77, 181, 185–88; campaign themes, *public opinion,* 189–91; "Freedom instead of/or Socialism," 177–78; on political leaders, 179–80

West Berlin. *See* Berlin

Wickert Institutes, 211; size, *205*

Wildenmann, Rudolf, 171, 213

Wirtschaftswoche, 47

Women, 37; CDU, *1976* campaign, 73, 128, 132; elections, *1972–76,* 110, 162–63; election, *1976,* 72–73, 107; FDP, *1976* campaign, 96–97; suffrage, 72

"Work for Germany," 156

Working class: and CSU, 154, 158; by region, *141;* SPD, 60–61; voting patterns, 3, 20–22, *109*

Yom-Kippur War, 63

Young Socialists (Jusos): campaign, *1976,* 42–43, 66; Brandt influence, 59–60, 64; Godesberg program, 60; ideology, 38n–39n, 60–61

Youth: CDU, 128; election, *1972,* 26; election, *1976,* 55, 72–74, 137; SPD support, 59–60; unemployment, 54, 136–37

ZDF. *See* Zweites Deutsches Fernsehen

Zeit, Die, 47, 172

Zentralarchiv, 202–3

Zentrum. *See* Center party

Zimmermann, Fritz, 165–66

Zweites Deutsches Fernsehen (ZDF, Second German Television Network), 170, 203; political polling, 220–21

AEI's *At the Polls* Series

In addition to this volume, the following titles have been published by the American Enterprise Institute as part of the *At the Polls* Series, a collection of studies dealing with national elections in selected democratic countries.

India at the Polls: The Parliamentary Elections of 1977, Myron Weiner (150 pp., $3.75)

Ireland at the Polls: The Dáil Elections of 1977, Howard R. Penniman, ed. (199 pp., $4.75)

Italy at the Polls: The Parliamentary Elections of 1976, Howard R. Penniman, ed. (386 pp., $5.75)

Scandinavia at the Polls: Recent Political Trends in Denmark, Norway, and Sweden, Karl H. Cerny, ed. (304 pp., $5.75)

Australia at the Polls: The National Elections of 1975, Howard R. Penniman, ed. (373 pp., $5)

Japan at the Polls: The House of Councillors Election of 1974, Michael K. Blaker, ed. (157 pp., $3)

Canada at the Polls: The General Elections of 1974, Howard R. Penniman, ed. (310 pp., $4.50)

France at the Polls: The Presidential Election of 1974, Howard R. Penniman, ed. (324 pp., $4.50)

Britain at the Polls: The Parliamentary Elections of February 1974, Howard R. Penniman, ed. (256 pp., $3)

This series also includes *Britain Says Yes: The 1975 Referendum on the Common Market* by Anthony King (153 pp., $3.75).

Studies are forthcoming on 1977 elections in Israel, Greece, Australia, and Spain and 1978 elections in Colombia, France, and New Zealand.

DATE DUE